Self Creation
Psychoanalytic Therapy and the Art of the Possible

SELF CREATION
PSYCHOANALYTIC THERAPY AND THE
ART OF THE POSSIBLE

FRANK SUMMERS

THE ANALYTIC PRESS

2005   Hillsdale, NJ   London

The following materials are printed with the permission
of their publishers:

Earlier versions of the text appeared in the following
publications:
Ch. 2 - 2003, *Contemporary Psychoanalysis*, 39(1), 335–353.
Ch. 3 - 2000, *Psychoanalytic Psychology*, 17(3), 547–565.
Ch. 4 - 2001, *Psychoanalytic Psychology*, 18(4), 635–655.
Ch. 8 - 2002 is partially drawn from *Comparative Treatments
of Depression*, New York: Springer, pp. 112–143.

Published by
The Analytic Press, Inc., Publishers
    Editorial Offices:
    101 West Street
    Hillsdale, NJ 07642

www.analyticpress.com

Designed and typeset by Laserset, Cary, NC

Library of Congress Cataloging-in-Publication Data

Self creation : psychoanalytic therapy and the art of the possible /
Frank Summers
        p.   cm.
        Includes bibliographical references and index.
        ISBN 0-88163-396-8
        1.

    RC

                                        2005

Printed in the United States of America

10 9 8 7 6 5 4 3 2 1

To Alan, who created himself

CONTENTS

ACKNOWLEDGMENTS

I wish to thank Tricia Mulvihill and Eleanor Starke Kobrin for the outstanding effort they put into the copyediting of this manuscript. I owe a special debt of gratitude to Dr. Paul Stepansky for both the extraordinary time and energy he invested in this project and the exceptional quality of his editing. His assiduous labor was beyond the call of duty, and I am lucky, indeed, to have him as a colleague and friend.

PREFACE

C ontemporary psychoanalytic theory offers a wide variety
of tenable ways to understand the dynamics of problems
people confront in their daily lives. Nonetheless, our
understanding of and ability to change pathological patterns lag
behind our comprehension of them. The problem of how to
translate insight into behavioral change has plagued psychoanalytic
thought and therapy from the inception of the field. It seems
likely that this quandary exists because our attention to grasping
dynamics was for a great while thought to be sufficient to achieve
therapeutic goals. Whatever the specific reason, it is clear that
the attention of psychoanalytic theory has been excessively
weighted toward gaining insight into patients' problems at the
expense of understanding how insight may be translated into
behavioral change. The effects of this gap in clinical theory are
seen in the consulting room on a daily basis. Often patients feel
they understand a problem but do not know how to solve it.
With disquieting frequency, when a patient asks, "I understand
that, but what do I do about it?" the clinician does not have a
good answer. In the clinical case conferences that I conduct, it is
common for the presenting therapist to feel that a problem is
understood, yet both members of the therapeutic dyad are
stymied in their efforts to alter an entrenched pattern.

This book is not a journey into the world of psychoanalytic
theory, and my subject is not psychodynamics. Despite the
plethora of theories purporting to explain the origins and
structure of psychological problems, we have precious little
knowledge of how to make those theories effective in the conduct
of daily life. For that reason, this work is dedicated to translating

insight into the creation of new ways of being and relating. The reader should not expect to find a contribution to the psychoanalytic theory of development, pathology, or understanding achieved in the clinical process. I *do* hope to have added to our understanding of the therapeutic action of psychoanalytic therapy. The book begins at the point at which issues are understood, but the desired changes have not come about. In each of the cases discussed, you will find that the psychodynamics, rather than being a topic of discussion, are only summarized to provide the necessary background for extended deliberations on therapeutic action. In these pages I hope to have contributed to clinicians' ability to understand how insight can be used to effect fundamental changes in personality structure.

A note about my use of the words "therapist," "psychoanalytic therapist," and "psychoanalyst" is in order. Because this work is about psychoanalytic therapy, I use "therapist" as shorthand for "psychoanalytic therapist." In this work, "psychoanalytic therapy" is the broadest term for psychoanalytic treatment, encompassing both psychoanalysis and what is conventionally referred to as psychoanalytic psychotherapy. I regard the ideas offered here as applicable to both forms of psychoanalytic therapy. Therefore, I have included cases seen in both psychoanalysis and psychoanalytic psychotherapy.

PART ONE

A Psychoanalytic Theory
of Self Creation

1

POTENTIAL SPACE IN PSYCHOANALYTIC THERAPY

"I know that, Doctor, but it doesn't change anything!" These words, or similar ones, are the dreaded but all-too-frequently-heard expressions of patient frustration with the inability to translate understanding into sought-after shifts in behavior. Freud's (1914) response to this problem was his concept of "working through," the repetition of the insight until gradually the desired changes come about over time. However, because Freud never developed this concept beyond repeated insight with time (Mitchell, 1997), it did not become an additional clinical strategy. Consequently, Freud's concept of working through was little more than an acknowledgment that therapeutic effect requires time and repetition of interpretations. What Freud could never successfully explain was why time and repetition were necessary. Having no clinical strategy with which to address the problem, Freud (1937) ultimately became pessimistic regarding the movement from insight to fundamental therapeutic change. He ascribed the intransigence of symptoms to such unyielding factors as the death instinct, the conservative nature of the ego, and the adhesiveness of the libido. Since Freud's time, the gap between understanding and change has been widely recognized as a therapeutic problem and has been addressed from a broad array of theoretical viewpoints.

At the point in the therapeutic process when a patient is unable to extricate himself from the old patterns despite many hours of hard, insightful therapeutic work, both members of the therapeutic dyad become very frustrated and sometimes

3

concerned that the treatment is failing. Complicating and frustrating the change process is the fact that attempts to overcome stubborn configurations tend to reenact the very pattern the analytic couple is trying to change (e.g., Levenson, 1991; Stolorow, et al., 1987; Mitchell, 1988, 1997). For example, if the patient is competitive, he is likely to experience the analyst's interpretations as an effort to attain an advantage that must be combated. This reaction is then interpreted, the patient again feels on the short end of the competitive stick, and the analytic dyad becomes consumed in a repetitive cycle from which there is no apparent escape. Expecting interpretations to be mutative, both patient and analyst can become discouraged and disillusioned when awareness does not alter long-standing patterns. The frustration of the analytic couple at this point issues from the circle of continually revisiting the pitfalls of the patient's patterns and their developmental origins while failing to alter them by means of this awareness.

Despite Freud's almost cynical end-of-life posture, the classical viewpoint has tended to support Freud in attributing the difficulty to the patient's resistance or intellectualization, leading to a clinical strategy of continued interpretation to undo the resistance. From this perspective, the solution tends to emphasize heavily repeated interpretation (e.g., Fenichel, 1938; Greenson, 1965; Ekstein, 1966). Some classical theorists underscore the importance of infantile fixations and the reconstruction of early trauma (e.g., Novey, 1962; Stewart, 1963). Others see mourning early objects as central (Glenn, 1984). Agreeing with Freud that time and repeated interpretation are the key change factors, none of these authors sees any reason to depart significantly from the interpretive stance.

Ego psychologists have maintained a steadfast adherence to interpretation while offering clinical suggestions for shifting the content of what is understood. Strachey (1934), in his famous paper on therapeutic action, concluded that reduction of superego anxiety was the touchstone of analytic change. Others have proclaimed that attention to ego mechanisms and defenses achieves greater patient responsiveness than does a complete focus on drives and their vicissitudes; other neoclassicists have advocated more emphasis on the here-and-now transference than they find in Freud's clinical approach (e.g., A. Freud, 1936; Hartmann, 1939). Contemporary structural theory holds that therapeutic action is best facilitated by analysis of presenting ego mechanisms (e.g., Busch, 1995). In brief, classical ego psychology, as represented, for example, by Strachey (1934), the newer ego psychology championed by Gray (1990), Busch (1995), and others, and even Gill's (1981) emphasis on the here-and-now transference, are all based on the principle that patients will be able to make the necessary therapeutic movement if they receive properly timed and theoretically appropriate interpretation. This trend has been epitomized by Brenner (1987), who seeing no special phase of "working through," regards the patient's failure to change as just one more resistance to be overcome with repeated interpretation. Nonetheless, Brenner does acknowledge that analysis takes a long time and that the lengthy duration of the process cannot be explained.

Despite the insistence by Brenner and others in the classical tradition that the gap between insight and change is a resistance that requires only continued interpretation, there is good reason to question the usefulness of attributing a therapeutic stalemate to the patient's "resistance." As Freud and subsequent generations of psychoanalytic clinicians have discovered, time and repetition do not necessarily render an interpretation more effective. Patients who do experience insight at a deeply affective level frequently have difficulty translating the understanding into behavioral change. One can find an abundance of evidence for this phenomenon in the analytic literature. Many of the early cases of hysteria, such as Anna O (Breuer and Freud, 1895) and Dora (Freud, 1905), had affective insight into the source of their symptoms without being able to free themselves from them. Indeed, even Freud's later cases, such as the Rat Man (Freud, 1909) and Wolf Man (Freud, 1917), do not demonstrate that repeated interpretation results in symptom reduction. Given the stubbornness of symptoms despite repeated interpretation within the transference, many classically oriented analysts have found the need to go beyond interpretation to make effective use of insight (e.g., Gedo, 1979; Valenstein, 1983; Burland, 1997).

Beyond the classical tradition, one finds in contemporary case material a common theme of the analyst using techniques in addition to interpretation because insight did not achieve sufficient therapeutic benefit. The quandary of the contemporary analyst is well illustrated in a case described by Carlo Strenger (1998). In vivid and exquisite detail, Strenger tells the story of Daphne, who came for help due to somatic complaints, compulsive rituals, and excessive anxiety that was straining her family to the breaking point. Initially Daphne seemed to respond well to Strenger's interpretations. After about four months of treatment, he commented that she had lived a life under the threat of doom. This insight had remarkable effect; soon thereafter Daphne ceased her frequent visits to the emergency room and relinquished an excessive preoccupation that her children were in danger.

However, as happens all too frequently in such cases, the analysis was far from over. It turned out that Daphne was leading an empty life in which she was stalemated by feelings of inadequacy and self-hatred. The analytic pair understood deeply the origins of these feelings, but Daphne could not shake herself from them. After years of apparent impasse, Strenger decided to take a risk by abandoning his interpretive posture and telling Daphne his experience with her insistence on maintaining a sense of failure and self-hatred. Strenger's clinical strategy not being at issue here, the importance of this case for the present purpose is that it illustrates so well the quandary of contemporary analysts. I regard Strenger's stalemated experience with Daphne as representative of what frequently happens when analyst and patient work well together. Some change is made, but the lifelong patterns are stubborn, and, because understanding has only a limited impact on them, the analyst often resorts to extra-interpretive clinical strategies. Furthermore, as previously mentioned, efforts to change the patient's configurations become absorbed into those same patterns in the transference-countertransference interactions. The preponderance of evidence suggests that such therapeutic stalemates reflect not the patient's "resistance," but the limitations of interpretation to move the patient beyond historical patterns.

THEORIES OF PSYCHOANALYTIC TECHNIQUE

The failure of interpretation by itself to change recalcitrant pathological patterns has led many analysts to amend, rework, or even jettison the classical theory of technique, a trend that has spawned a variety of clinical innovations. Theorists who have departed more radically than ego psychologists from the traditional model fall into two broad categories. One camp sees the problem of classical technique in the content of what is being interpreted. Kleinians, in opposition to ego psychologists, tend to see the limitations of the ego-psychological approach in both the interpretive focus on libidinal wishes and overattention to defenses (e.g., Segal, 1981). Theorists of this persuasion contend that analytic change is best facilitated by addressing early, primitive, especially aggressively dominated fantasies and see little mutative impact in interpreting ego defenses against this unconscious material. Lacanians also believe the problem in the ego-psychological model lies in its focus on ego mechanisms as opposed to direct interpretation of the unconscious (Lacan, 1953). Analysts from both these schools agree with ego psychologists that therapeutic action lies in correct and well-timed interpretations of the unconscious; their argument with the classical model rests on the content of what is being interpreted.

Theorists of the second group do not believe that modifications in interpretive content or style will provide the movement needed to change longstanding patterns. Kohut (1971, 1977), finding that affective understanding did not release many patients from pathological patterns, initially attempted to amend classical theory but ultimately concluded that a new paradigm was needed. Eventually, his clinical experience led him to the view that, even when interpretation worked, the mutative effect was due not to making the unconscious conscious but to the new relationship it formed (Kohut, 1984). His abundant and rich case material is replete with descriptions of patients who were little affected by making the unconscious conscious.

Many of Kohut's most devoted collaborators have extended his paradigm to the point of questioning even more deeply the mutative effect of interpretation. Bacal and Newman (1990) have declared that the analyst promotes change by performing selfobject functions, a viewpoint that led them to question the role of interpretation in facilitating therapeutic change. Bacal (1985, 1998a, b) now believes that an analyst's optimal responsiveness is the key variable in therapeutic change. His case material illustrates the pivotal importance of analytic responsiveness to the patient (Bacal, 1998a, b). Stolorow and his colleagues (1987; Stolorow and Atwood, 1992) also view selfobject functions as crucial to therapeutic action but emphasize the contextual dependency of the process. For other self psychologists, the crux of therapeutic action is the depth of intimacy achieved between patient and analyst (Shane, Shane, and Gales, 1997).

Winnicott (1965) and the British Middle School theorists have reported many cases in which affective understanding had minimal impact while the containing and holding functions of the analyst during the patient's regression to dependence achieved powerful and lasting therapeutic change (e.g., Winnicott, 1954; Balint, 1968; Guntrip, 1969; Khan, 1974). Relational analysis sees the emotional impact of the analyst as the most critical mutative factor (e.g., Aron, 1996; Mitchell, 1997). The relational perspective, along with certain branches of self psychology, breaks decisively from classical theory in the key role given to the affective connection between analyst and patient, an emphasis so important that the efficacy of interpretation is cast into doubt by some theorists of these persuasions. Clinicians in this category believe that the problem of the recalcitrance of stubborn patterns to interpretation is resolved not by changing the content of interpretation but by shifting clinical strategy away from interpretation to the analytic relationship. Stern and his colleagues (1997) also contend that in addition to interpretation the therapeutic relationship is crucial for change, but in a different sense from other relational theorists. The Stern group holds that intersubjective moments occur between patient and analyst that lead to "implicit relational knowledge," an experience that can reorganize the psyche.

All the therapeutic strategies mentioned here—technical emphasis on the defenses, changes in interpretive content, and shifts to emphasis on the analytic relationship—are directed to the analyst's offerings, with the result that the patient is viewed as a recipient of analytic intervention. Although contemporary psychoanalytic approaches conceptualize the analytic process in ways decisively different from the classical perspective, they share, often implicitly, the classical assumption that the patient changes by absorbing the analyst's offerings, even if the nature of those provisions is characterized differently from its conceptualization in traditional theory. The distinctions among theoretical viewpoints lie in the nature of what the analyst provides, but none includes a conceptual place for the patient's role in therapeutic action, as though the patient simply imbided the right experience, whether that be interpretive content, emotional experience, or analytic functions, the sought-for mutative change would occur.

It may seem surprising to depict the relational viewpoint as casting the patient in a passive role given the emphasis on mutuality of both participants in the construction of transference–countertransference patterns from this perspective (e.g., Aron, 1996; Hoffman, 1998). While this accent on co-construction may seem to conceptualize the patient as an active participant in the process, this concept was meant to underline the *analyst's* participation in the *patient's* transference patterns. The patient's construction of the transference relationship is a time-honored analytic principle and not at issue here. To the extent that relationalists emphasize negotiation between patient and analyst in the construction of a new relationship, the relational perspective is an important advance toward viewing the patient as a participant in therapeutic action (e.g., Pizer, 1998; Slavin and Kriegman, 1998). The negotiation that is emphasized from the relational perspective, however, means only that the subjectivities and interests of both parties are involved; it does not imply that new meaning is being created. The analytic pair may negotiate a relationship that meets the needs of both participants without the patient's creating a new way of being. Therefore, a clinical strategy emphasizing dyadic interaction and negotiation is in as much danger of not providing the psychological space for the patient to become an agent in his own transformation as any other clinical strategy. Furthermore, from the relational viewpoint, while both parties participate in the relationship, it is the analyst's impact on the patient that tends to be given credit for the new relationship and its therapeutic benefit (e.g., Mitchell, 1997). In this way, the relational viewpoint shares the assumption of most contemporary analytic schools that the crux of therapeutic action lies in what the analyst does. Such approaches tend implicitly to cast the patient in a passive posture.

Some interpersonal theorists have suggested that the problem of working-through insight can be effectively approached by integrating cognitive-behavioral techniques into analytic therapy (e.g., Wachtel, 1982, 1986, 1993; Frank, 1993). These theorists may seem to represent an exception to the focus on the therapist's activity as they advocate the inclusion of "action techniques" into the therapeutic armamentarium. These methods, however, are introduced by the therapist for the patient's experimentation. Although the patient is encouraged to attempt new behavior, he is doing so at the therapist's exhortation. As in any behavioral strategy, the patient's behavior is not self-initiated; he is performing an activity designed by the therapist. Consequently, the patient is not psychologically active in the sense of finding and creating his own new ways of being and relating. No matter how well intentioned and carefully designed, behavioral techniques subject the patient to following a script written by the therapist. In more exclusively psychodynamic approaches, including the most traditional interpretive posture, the patient must absorb analytic offerings, but at least his behavior is left to him. In the psychoanalytic sense of activity as autonomously motivated behavior (Rapaport, 1953), the patient is put in a psychologically more passive position than is true of even the most conservative analytic theories. Thus, the technical recommendation for resolving working through by including "action techniques" in the therapeutic strategy not only provides no role for the patient's self-initiated behavior, but also actively constricts the patient's ability to create ways to utilize insight.

ACTION, CREATION, AND EMOTIONAL GROWTH

There are several reasons to doubt that passive absorption is an effective means of therapeutic change. The minimization of the creative role of the patient in much psychoanalytic theory conflicts with the shift in the goal of analysis from the resolution of intrapsychic conflict to self-realization, the growth of the self. This change is the recognition, from many theoretical viewpoints, that awareness of previously unconscious motives alone is often insufficient to achieve analytic aims. The corresponding implication of this new goal is that the analyst's role includes assistance in the development of new patterns. It is difficult to imagine how a patient can create new modes of being and relating by absorbing the analyst's contributions, whether those offerings take the form of interpretation, new functions, or the emotional impact of the relationship. If self-development is the goal of the analytic process, the therapeutic action of psychoanalysis must include room for the patient to create new ways of being and relating.

That activity and creation are central to emotional growth is demonstrated convincingly by developmental research as well as advances in learning theory. Investigations of the mother–child dyad from a variety of developmental research traditions indicate that the child requires not only affective attunement, but also the space to experience his own affective states and participation in relieving distressing emotions. The opportunity for self-regulation is as critical as caretaker regulation. Beebe and Lachmann (1998, 2002) found that the most secure babies were not those whose mothers were most closely in tune with their affective states, but rather those infants that fall in the midrange of affective and vocal matching with their mothers. They concluded that infants need both mutual regulation and the opportunity for self-regulation, an opportunity impeded by overattunement. Similarly, Bowlby (1988) and Ainsworth et al. (1978), in their studies of attachment, found that securely attached infants had mothers who were emotionally available and made a push toward autonomy. Even more poignantly, Demos (1992), observing children from a different theoretical perspective, found that a child's sense of agency is best promoted not by the parent who relieves stress by providing immediate comfort, but by the parent who allows the child to experience distress and helps to resolve it in a way that makes the infant feel like a coparticipant in the relief of tension. Demos's findings led her to the view that there appears to be "an optimal zone of affective experience that allows the infant enough psychological space to feel an internal need, to become an active participant in trying to address the need" (p. 220). Observations of children and parents indicate that children do not replicate their parents' behavior but *react to* parental input (Beebe, Jaffe, and Lachmann, 1992; Demos, 1988, 1992). That is, children do not receive meaning from parental ministrations, but rather create meaning from the relationship. Although only the briefest summary of the developmental evidence can be related here, it is safe to conclude that these findings, from a variety of traditions, indicate that the opportunity for active self-creation is necessary for the growth of the self.

Recent advances in learning theory have recognized the importance of procedural as well as declarative-semantic learning (Damasio, 1989; Reiser, 1990; Zola-Morgan and Squire, 1990; Levin, 1991). Procedural learning is "knowing how," learning by doing, and this knowledge cannot typically be translated into symbolic terms. Declarative-semantic learning is "knowing that" and is the way history or mathematical formulae are learned; its content can be represented symbolically. It is now recognized that much learning occurs through action and nonverbal interaction (Reiser, 1990; Evans, 1998). For example, bicycle riding is learned by doing and the "memory" consists of knowing how to do it, rather than statements that can be recalled. Once the skill is acquired, it will be remembered and can be called forth and used when necessary, but it cannot be reduced to symbolic expression. Of most significance for the present context is that procedural learning takes place in the activity of the learner. This fact amends the role of the teacher from the largely didactic one required for declarative-semantic learning to the provision of opportunity and guidance for the student's activity. The success of the bicycle instruction will depend largely on the teacher's ability to facilitate the learner's riding activity.

The model of procedural learning fits best the acquisition of interpersonal skills. A child learns how to relate to the parent in the process of parent–child interactions well before the child is able to put such learning into words. The parent provides the opportunity for the child to interact, and, while engaging the interaction, the child learns the rules of social relating. The importance of procedural learning in knowledge acquisition and its significance in child development demonstrates the importance of action, of learning by doing, in emotional growth.

Furthermore, there is substantial evidence from the adult development literature that adults, at least until middle age and often beyond, continue to have "growth expansion motives," that is, the need to expand creatively their interests and capacities in both the social and vocational arenas (Buhler, 1951; Kuhlen, 1964). Indeed, this literature suggests that the need for generativity, the creative urge to contribute to society, is greatest in the middle adult years of life (Erikson, 1963; Kuhlen, 1964; Frenkel-Brunswick, 1963). These findings indicate that the desire and need to make a creative mark, to develop one's own interests and make a unique contribution, increases at least into middle age, and, in healthy persons, remains until the end of life. Of equal importance is the finding that personality change can occur at any stage of the life cycle. The developmental obstacles and crises that cause some adults to stagnate lead other people in the direction of positive change, expansion of life, and growth, given a properly conducive environment (Neugarten, 1968). The data from adult development indicate that people who have the most success adjusting to the tasks of middle age show emotional flexibility: the capacity to shift investment among people and activities. Such persons expand their experience to a wider variety of people and more complex relationships than was true in their earlier years. Successful adult development requires "new learning—not only of specific new cathexes, but of a generalized set toward making new cathexes" (Peck, 1968, p. 90). As a consequence, learning in adulthood is as unlikely to occur through passive absorption of information as is childhood learning. The data indicate that adults learn and change most effectively when they are actively involved in adopting new strategies and techniques. These results from adult development research, along with the data from learning theory, call into question how much therapeutic change can be effected by a patient's observing but not actively contributing.

In the analytic process, taking in something from the analyst inevitably raises the question of whether the content of the internalization fits the patient's experience or is a mimetic reproduction of the analyst's conveyances. This question is critical for therapeutic action because any change that does not correspond to the patient's experience can only be compliance, a further alienation from the self, rather than a contributor to its development. Authenticity, then, in the sense of correspondence with experience, is necessary for meaningful analytic change. This problem is no less applicable to the internalization of functions or the emotional impact of the analytic relationship. Executing new functions, even if psychological and reflective, that do not emanate from the patient's experience will only be mechanistic repetition of strategies gleaned from others. If the patient models the analyst without the corresponding personal experience, these new behaviors, even if they seem self-reflective and analytically reasonable, lack therapeutic benefit. Similarly, if the analyst's emotional effect on the patient does not resonate with the patient's preexisting disposition that can be elaborated into new ways of being, such influence will bury the patient's authenticity, rather than facilitate it. It is safe to conclude that any concept of therapeutic action in which the patient does not actively contribute on the basis of authentic personal experience is in danger of becoming a relationship of compliance (however well disguised), rather than a creation of new self-structure.

In brief, learning theory, developmental research, and advances in psychoanalytic theory all point to the conclusion that emotional growth requires creative action, a fact that suggests the central importance of potential space in the therapeutic process.

None of this implies that interpretation should be jettisoned as a useless relic of the past. Because, to be meaningful, newly created ways of being and relating must issue from expanded awareness, the depth exploration provided by the interpretive process is necessary for the emergence of alternatives to defensively motivated patterns. The analyst's offered understanding, most poignantly in the transference, highlights the patient's motivations for adopting long-held patterns and the ensuing untoward consequences. Interpretations of the patient's defenses and established configurations enable awareness that shifts the relationship from blind enactment to consciousness of inter-actional patterns. This awareness, while it does not necessarily impel the sought-after analytic movement, connects the patient to deeper motivations and affective potential than could be reached within the context of the defenses. Moreover, the more the patient understands his ways of relating to the analyst, the less satisfied he is with the old ways of being, a dissatisfaction that intensifies the desire to relinquish them. Consequently, the interpretation of patterns, by expanding consciousness of the self, makes their continuance less satisfying and motivates their abandonment. In brief, efforts to manage one's ways of relating without understanding the motivations behind them cannot emanate from a deep appreciation for experience and, consequently, can result only in the continued burial of important aspects of the self. Depth understanding is required for meaningful change, but insight alone is often insufficiently mutative because it does not provide alternatives to the established patterns. Understanding is necessary but insufficient to achieve meaningful changes in the organization of the psyche.

POTENTIAL SPACE AND THE
PSYCHOTHERAPEUTIC PROCESS

In previous work I suggested that understanding is useful for gaining access to the depth of the patient's psyche but in itself does not typically lead to the creation of alternative ways of being (Summers, 1999). Consequently, I concluded that the creation of self can be achieved through a dual process of interpretation and the use of the psychotherapeutic relationship for the creation of new ways of being and relating. In addition to interpretation, the analytic process must provide the opportunity for the creation of new patterns to replace those targeted by analytic investigation. The analytic space, from this viewpoint, includes not only room for interpretation, but also a space for the patient's creation (Summers, 2001). Potential space then becomes central to the analytic process. Winnicott's (1971) concept of the analytic setting as potential space was meant to provide room in the relationship for the patient to create a new object relationship, a phenomenon Winnicott called the analytic object. Such a technical stance requires attention to and nurturance of the patient's need for a spontaneous gesture. The interpretive aspect of the process being assumed here as a necessary feature of therapeutic change, our focus is on the next stage of the process, or what happens after interpretation reaches to a deep level of understanding. My aim now is to extend the model delineated in my previous book (Summer, 1999) by showing how the psychoanalytic therapist can create and then use potential space in the therapeutic setting for the creation of self. It is my contention that Winnicott's concept of potential space provides psychoanalytic therapy with a way of addressing the vexing problem of translating insight into new ways of being and relating.

When Winnicott (1951) introduced the notion of transitional phenomena into psychoanalytic theory, he conceptualized a third area of experience, an intermediate level between "objective reality" and "absolute fantasy." He regarded transitional phenomena as originating in the phase of infancy in which the child first recognizes the self–other distinction but is unable to accept the mother's externality. In this phase, the child exists in a paradoxical world in which she can treat an object as though it were a part of the self, even though she knows it is not. Winnicott regarded this realm as the area of illusion between the omnipotent fantasy life of early infancy and the later acceptance of objective reality. Although the infant, if all goes well, will gradually relinquish the transitional object and make the shift to reality, the transitional realm of experience remains a capacity throughout life. Areas of experience that require some degree of illusion, such as aesthetics, religion, creative work, and "imaginative living," all owe their origins to the transitional-object phase of infancy and depend on the intermediate level of experiencing that began in that stage.

It was only later in his career that Winnicott (1971) applied the concept of transitional phenomena explicitly to the therapeutic process by regarding psychoanalytic therapy as taking place in the "overlap of two subjectivities." Prior to this idea, analytic space was conceptualized as exclusively for the patient's material, the analyst's interpretations, and the patient's response to those insights. By introducing the transitional arena into the psychotherapeutic process, Winnicott shifted decisively the concept of therapeutic action by including an area for the patient's creation. In this way, a new purpose was added to the understanding of the patient: the creation of self. Although, in Winnicott's view, all such space originated with transitional experience, he did not apply the concept only to patients presumed to suffer from arrests traced back to that developmental phase. He regarded transitional space, which he now also called potential space, as any undefined area to which a variety of meanings might be given, thus loosening its original connection to a particular developmental period. In this way, potential space became the necessary condition for the creation of new aspects of the self. In keeping with this shift in the concept of the psychoanalytic process, the term potential space is used here rather than transitional space in order to stay free of developmental connotation.

For Winnicott, potential space in the therapeutic process referred to the opportunity for the patient's creativity within the therapeutic dyad. The therapist's subjectivity operates as a "limiting membrane," a constraint on the patient's subjectivity; and when the two overlap an intermediate realm emerges that contains a set of givens within which a variety of different meanings can be bestowed. The "formlessness" that Winnicott regarded as the definitive feature of potential space refers to the maximal openness the therapist can tolerate so that the relationship can be created according to the patient's needs within the givens of the therapist and the setting. Potential space in the therapeutic process, then, is an interpersonal space limited by who the therapist is and what he can tolerate, but otherwise open for the patient to create its form and meaning. Winnicott ultimately concluded that this intermediate realm defines the psychotherapeutic setting.

As potential space is designed to provide optimum opportunity for the creation of new aspects of the self, minimization of structure is crucial because the less structure, the more room available for creation. Nonetheless, the boundary is as important as the ambiguity because potential space, derived developmentally from transitional space, exists within a relationship constrained by the limits of the other. This boundary distinguishes potential space from fantasy, just as its openness differentiates potential space from reality. Fantasy, like a dream, has no boundary in reality; existing in unbounded space, it can be created wholly by the psyche. At the other end of the spectrum lies tightly structured, hierarchical organizations, such as the military, that have predetermined meaning, leaving little room for creativity. In contrast to both fantasy and authoritarian settings, potential space is designed to maximize creative opportunity in the real world. Any situation open for the introduction of meaning, such as the artist's canvas, contains potential space; but, within an interpersonal relationship, the purpose of potential space is self-creation. The key feature, then, is the intent. The difference between potential space and other relationships lies in the former's purpose of providing space for self-creation.

Because potential space is defined by the very fact that it has no determined meaning, any meaning it is to have exists only as potential and, therefore, lies in the future. Potential space has a not-yet-formed quality; its meaning is to be created. Because the potential of the space can be seen only in projection toward future possible meanings, the future is an essential component of potential space. This expansion of analytic temporality is one of the features that marks potential space as decisively different from interpretive space.

Pursuing self-creation requires that the therapist restrain many of her needs and desires in order to sustain the openness required for creating new meaning. Clearly, there are limitations to the therapist's ability to sustain formlessness, but the intent must be to establish an openness by diminishing the degree to which her needs influence the analytic space. Having a unique obligation to make the space as available for generating individual meaning as possible, the psychoanalytic therapist does not respond to the patient's needs as do the parties to any other relationship. The intent of the space being to open the relationship for the patient's creativity, the therapist's responsibility is to be aware of and attempt to contain any desire to influence the space out of personal need. Rather than responding as she would in other contexts, the therapist "holds" the situation until the patient can make use of it (Winnicott, 1956, 1960; Slochower, 1996). This "holding" is an application of the intent to design a space for the patient's creation.

The analytic boundary will inevitably limit the extent to which the patient can use the space to create new meaning. It is not possible, nor even desirable, for the therapist to keep her subjectivity completely out of the process. The therapist's subjectivity is the membrane that limits the therapeutic space and forces recognition of the analyst as a separate subjectivity (Summers, 1996). The therapist's subjectivity, therefore, becomes the boundary within which potential space is formed. That the therapist's subjectivity is inextricably embedded in the analytic process does not mean, however, that the therapist has license to include his subjective experiences in the analytic engagement in whatever way he might wish. Potential space demands that the therapist remain focused on providing maximal opportunity for the patient's creation of meaning.

Some of Winnicott's closest collaborators, such as Masud Khan (1971), have extended the application of potential space to the therapeutic endeavor. Khan saw the analytic arena as a play space in which the patient must be given the opportunity for creative expression both inside and outside the consulting room (Hopkins, 1998). According to this theorist, the analyst's task is to provide this opportunity, even if it means offering directives. More recently, a growing number of analytic theorists have adopted the concept that the analytic process is at least in part a potential space for the patient to elaborate arrested aspects of the self. Bollas (1989) has pointed out that the true self does not possess a preformed meaning but is a potential that can be discovered only through object usage. From this viewpoint, the process must not only offer understanding to arrive at the unformed inherited potential, but also provide a space in which those meanings can be elaborated. With a different emphasis from Khan, the aim of Bollas's (1993) approach is to provide the freest play possible for the unconscious. Similarly, Modell (1991) views the aim of psychoanalytic therapy as maximizing creativity, a goal that is achieved by the patient's playful use of the therapeutic space.

Recently, some analytic theorists without explicitly close theoretical or personal ties to Winnicott have proposed that the patient's activity is a key component of therapeutic change. More and more writers from the classical tradition have concluded, on the basis of their clinical work, that something more than understanding is required to effect significant analytic change. These clinicians tend to see interpretation as an endless repetition with questionable results unless emended with another intervention. Valenstein (1983), for example, has proposed that insight often requires chance-taking action by the analysand that must be encouraged by the analyst. Insight is assimilated, according to this view, by taking action, trying new behavior that promotes ego autonomy. Burland (1997) also contends that insight is insufficient because the affects brought to consciousness must be worked through by the patient. He suggests, therefore, that more attention be given to what the analysand must do to move from insight to new behavior. Sedler (1983) also sees working through as primarily the task of the patient. These theorists represent a growing trend in classical thinking about working through that departs from the technical recommendations of traditional ego psychologists, such as Brenner. The crucial differences are that such writers as Burland, Valenstein, and Sedler believe analytic change can be effected only if the patient adds something to the analyst's interpretation.

An increasing number of psychoanalytic commentators outside the ego-psychological tradition are beginning to see the importance of including the patient's creation of self as part of the therapeutic process. Without explicit mention of Winnicott, Stern (1997) arrives at a conclusion remarkably similar to that of the English analyst: the goal of analysis is not to make the unconscious conscious but to articulate previously unformulated experience. From her dialectical perspective, Benjamin (1995) believes conflict resolution lies in the patient's ability to tolerate conflict between opposing positions. If this goal is to be achieved, the patient must have new ways of experiencing the analytic relationship, and the analyst's task is to provide the opportunity for such experiences. According to Benjamin, the analytic goal is not so much the provision of insight as the creation of a transitional space that provides the opportunity to experience others and the world in more complex ways. Similarly, Sanville (1991) sees the analytic relationship as a safe environment in which the patient can "construct intermediate space, and . . . intermediate time" (p. 67). The goal of creating new aspects of the self is to be achieved only within a play space in which the patient is free to create "new versions of the self" (p. 67). Strenger (1998) does not emphasize play space as much as these other authors but, in conjunction with them, sees the goal of analytic therapy to lie in the creation of individuality, a process that requires assembling various aspects of the self in new, creative ways.

None of these psychoanalytic theorists disputes the value of interpretation, but they all believe that in addition to insight, a process of self building must occur that requires new experiences in addition to the absorption of understanding. Therefore, the analytic space in which such experiences can take place must be provided. I have suggested that the interpretive process is necessary to penetrate the patient's defenses in order to arrive at psychic depth but in itself rarely issues in the replacement of the old self with new ways of being and relating (Summers, 1999). Consequently, I described therapeutic action as a dual process consisting of an interpretive phase that operates as a propaedeutic for the building of a new self. In this dual model of therapeutic action, the old self is transcended only as new ways of being and relating are created in the second phase.

The trend in this type of theorizing is to move the model of psychoanalytic technique toward an ever-greater recognition of the importance of potential space in the psychoanalytic process. Although the theorists discussed have all provided convincing illustrations of the need for a theory of clinical technique that can guide clinicians in facilitating new ways of being and relating, we do not yet have a well-elaborated theory that serves this function. As we have seen, learning theory and the developmental evidence strongly suggest that creative activity is crucial to any theory of change, and recent thinking about therapeutic action has pointed the analytic process in the direction of including the creation of new aspects of the self. The purpose of this book is to advance this developing trend by offering a concept of therapeutic action that conceptualizes potential space as an inherent part of the process and shows the profound and far-reaching implications for clinical technique that result from so doing. We will see the various ways in which the therapeutic field is changed when this type of space is established and the alterations in technical stance that follow from each of them.

In potential space, the nature of the therapeutic relationship and the roles of the participants are decisively expanded in order to foster the patient's creation of new ways of being and relating. Once a psychological configuration is understood, the therapist suspends interpretation as well as any other techniques or interventions for the purpose of facilitating the creation of new meaning by the patient. In other words, the space is given over to the free play of the patient's imagination. Whatever associations, memories, or sensations now appear are viewed not as a source of understanding the patient's current patterns, but as incipient indications of the shape a new self might assume. In potential space, then, the analytic material is regarded from the perspective of its possibilities for the patient's creation of new patterns rather than understanding the old ways of being and relating. An important component of this function is the analyst's ability to see the patient's material not just for what it says about the patient's past and present, but for its potential, its possibilities for new creation.

In this way, the future dimension takes on a central importance it did not have when the therapist's task was largely confined to understanding. Furthermore, the therapist must not only open the space for the creation of new possibilities, but also have a vision, some sense of the potential that can be realized by the patient in the therapeutic space (Loewald, 1960). The analytic therapist has the responsibility to facilitate ways the patient can use insight for the creation of new aspects of the self. For his part, the analysand's role is no longer limited to providing material for the analyst's interpretations and absorbing them. An actor in the psychoanalytic drama, the patient uses the therapist's provisions to forge new components of the self. The introduction of potential space into the analytic process, then, implies a new model of clinical technique, a model in which the analyst, with an eye on the future, aims to find and facilitate the realization of the patient's potential, and the latter uses the space to create new meaning and new ways of being.

We may conclude that once potential space is introduced into the analytic process, the therapeutic relationship is fundamentally transformed. When the analytic process shifts to the need for creation, the therapeutic relationship shifts from an interpretive modality to potential space. Both the patient's and analyst's roles are restructured: the patient is a creator, and the analyst, a facilitator. The field is no longer filled with the patient's material that must be understood but is open for yet-to-be-determined meaning. At this point, the future takes on new prominence. Let us now turn to exploration of this decisive change in temporality that takes place in potential space.

2

The Future as Intrinsic to the Psychoanalytic Process

Historically, psychoanalysis has addressed time primarily from the perspective of the past. Such a temporal focus was perhaps inevitable given that the psychoanalytic theory of pathogenesis has always emphasized early experience, whether the childhood roots of pathology are conceived as actual events or early fantasy life. There is no reason to question the idea that the patient's early experience is a crucial dimension of the analytic enterprise. However, a temporal orientation concentrated almost exclusively on the past has limited both the analyst's understanding of the patient and the ability of the analyst to help the patient transcend the dilemmas of present life. As we have seen, the creation of new ways of being and relating requires the use of potential space in the analytic process, a space that is organized not around the past, but around the future. As this space is defined by what it may yet become, it follows that when the analytic process reaches the point at which potential space is opened for creation of new aspects of the self, the analytic space must be reorganized around the future.

The most notable exception in the classical literature to the temporal focus on the past is the theoretical work of Hans Loewald. Using ego-psychological language, Loewald (1962) pointed out that the expectations, demands, and prohibitions that become organized into the superego determine the psyche's relationship to the future. From Loewald's viewpoint, the concept of the superego brings the future into the psychological organization. In a later contribution, Loewald (1972) showed

25

that the objective measure of time as a linearity consisting of past-present-future is not adequate for psychoanalysis because time is experienced as an interaction of the three temporal modes. However, despite his recognition that motives can be either forced from the past or attracted by the future, Loewald continued the psychoanalytic lineage of looking at the future primarily as affected by the past while minimizing the influence of the future on the experience of past and present. In this way, Loewald, despite his dissatisfaction with the concept of linear time, was unable to break completely from it.

More recently, Cooper (2000) has made hope, the expectancy of a better future, a central component of the psychoanalytic process. For Cooper, psychoanalysis is a kind of logic of hope in which the patient's defenses and symptoms express not only a conservancy of the past but also a hoped-for different future. Endemic to the process, in Cooper's view, is the patient's difficulty in bearing hope while attempting to keep it alive, however unconsciously. Cooper's work is an important advance, for he demonstrates that the future is embedded in the very fabric of the analytic process. Implicit, but not explicitly articulated, in Cooper's concept of psychoanalytic therapy is a shift in the nature of unconscious mental phenomena. In Cooper's logic of hope, desire, or a wish rendered unconscious, is an arrested effort to make a different future. In this way, the unconscious is not just an attempt to preserve the past but also an effort to hold out hope for a better future.

As the patient's problems emanate from the constrictions of early life, a central goal of the analytic process is to create new possibilities or, more accurately, to help the patient realize occluded possibilities. The analytic space, then, becomes defined by goals, projections into the future that require a reconfiguration of the patient's sense of temporality. Typically, the analysand cannot conceive of new possibilities; she does not have a belief in a different future. In a very real way, then, there is no sense of future because the horizon of the patient's life is an endless present. Without a sense of futurity, the patient has little hope of overcoming the limitations of the childhood self. In this way, the inability to conceptualize a different future is a major obstacle to analytic progress, a barrier as great as unresolved past conflicts. If this obstacle is to be removed, the patient must envision a different future, a future with new ways of being and relating. Without such a vision, the patient remains stuck in old patterns. Viewing the analytic process in this way, the current psychic organization is no longer understood solely in terms of its past or present relationships. The present moment gains its meaning in the trajectory toward the future, and the past gains new meaning in the context of the experience of future and present.

This type of contemporary analytic theorizing contains an implicit movement away from linear time. We are now beginning to see that if we apply the analytic focus on the subjective experience to time, the future becomes a prominent part of our grasp of the patient's world. The mind, then, is not a spatialized line of causation but a projected narrative in which each component gains meaning according to its fit in the narrative. Our ability to see the psyche in this way permits us to see that present and past achieve their full meaning within the context of their fit into a projected future. In this way, one can see that in the use of potential space, the future is placed at the heart of the psychoanalytic process.

This shift in analytic theory is pregnant with implications for the way the analyst conceptualizes the patient's experience and especially for the way the analytic process is conducted. We may now build on this emerging theoretical development by showing both the intrinsic nature of the future in all psychic experience and, most important, the decisive clinical implications that follow from abandoning linear temporality in favor of a central focus on the future. Linear time applies to the natural world in which past events result in present ways of experiencing. But the experiencing subject does not live in a linear temporal world: the future embeds the present with its meaning. This difference has been well defined in philosophical terms by Bergson (1910) and more recently by Bruner (1986), who has shown that viewing the unconscious as a missed possibility implies a narrative concept of mental process. As Bruner has pointed out, there are two ways of investigating human experience. From the point of view of science, the researcher seeks an invariant world that is subject to testability over different situations. By contrast, the human condition consists of the construction of worlds, narratives that cannot be tested but can be understood or misunderstood. The humanist, in contrast to the scientist, investigates these worlds to see how phenomena within them make sense. Bruner shows that the human world is a narrative continually projected toward the future. It is this shift to the narrative world that is implied when the future is grasped as central to experience.

The narrative view of the psyche has gradually gained currency in some contemporary theorizing. More than a quarter-century ago, Schafer (1976), in his call for an action language, suggested that analytic parlance ought to describe motivation as an intending subject moved to action to achieve goals. Subsequently, Schafer (1983) spelled out the implications of this view for the concept of self: the self is a narrative, a story or group of stories organized according to underlying intention. At about the same time, Spence (1982) advanced the view that psychoanalysis is about the construction of a narrative that must fit together a variety of life experiences. This view of the self as a narrative makes intentionality central to mental functioning and the analytic process, and this shift puts the future into the heart of the analytic enterprise.

The primary role of the future in the analytic relationship, then, implies more than a change in the analytic process. It also denotes a concept of mind as an ever-expanding flow toward the future within which present and past gain meaning. Such a concept of mental organization requires a conceptual foundation different from the naturalistic attitude on which Freud attempted to ground psychoanalysis. Here the findings of phenomenological philosophy can help us clarify a concept of mind that sustains the use of potential space in psychoanalytic therapy.

THE PHILOSOPHICAL BASIS OF TEMPORALITY

Philosophical understanding of time sees the future as inherent in all experience of present and past. As first established by

Husserl (1904) in his lectures on internal time consciousness, extended by Bergson (1910), and later elaborated by Heidegger (1926) and Schutz (1932), temporality, the experience of time, does not follow the linear model of objective time as past-present-future. Time is experienced as projected, thrown toward the future, and, as we move toward our future, we encounter the past. As the past meets us in our project, we live in the present. Each present moment is embedded within some future project, a conception of life's trajectory, and gains its meaning only in that context. Thus, the present cannot be experienced outside its context as a moment in the future project. When two people are talking on the street, the meaning of that encounter is determined by the intentions of both parties. The meaning of their conversation is decisively different if one person is trying to sell the other a product, hand him a coupon or beg for money, or if the two are friends meeting after a long absence. This phenomenological grasp of the temporal experience shows that linear time is an abstraction, a spatial concept of time that does not fit lived temporal experience in which the future is inherent in all action.

Both Husserl (1904) and Bergson (1910) found that the meaning of experience is given in the fulfillment of intention. Schutz (1932) built on Husserl's concept to show that the meaning of any act is defined by the projected goal in which the present moment is embedded. There is no "objective" event to which meaning is attached. Rather, Schultz demonstrated that meaning lies in the projected intention of the actor. Action is directed toward the foreseen goal. In this way, Schutz distinguished between action and behavior: action takes place in the future perfect tense—we act toward a goal as "having been done." Action is meaningful precisely because it aims to realize a projected goal, whereas behavior is not necessarily meaningful.

Ordinary-language philosophers, from their analysis of how language is used and organizes experience, have similarly concluded that intentionality is built into our experience of the world. J. L. Austin (1962) began this movement by demonstrating that all linguistic expression is *performative*: it does something.

Austin showed there is no distinction between language that *states* and language that *does*. All linguistic usage carries an intent to *do* something to someone. Two decades later, Searle (1983) argued that, because intentionality is built into language, the mind is inherently intentional. Searle argued convincingly that all experience contains intentional states as part of its content. The meaning of experience is given by the intent. The cause of human action cannot be separated from the experience; the intention is built into the experience.

These philosophical findings show that any concept of mental functioning must begin with the experience of the future as an inherent part of any present experience. They also suggest that the mind is in essence narrational, a temporal flow projected into a future in which the present gains its meaning. Thus, the future is not simply one temporal modality but an inherent component of experience that gives meaning to psychological events. We are now in a position to see how this understanding of temporality applies to current psychoanalytic theory.

Psychoanalytic Theory

The philosophical understanding of time conforms to much contemporary psychoanalytic theory. Object relations, as represented by Winnicott and elaborated by Khan, Bollas, Green, Modell, and others, as well as self psychology and even some elements of contemporary neo-Kleinian theory, whatever differences they might otherwise have, are united in their reconceptualization of development as the growth of the self and psychopathology as some form of arrest in that process (Summers, 1994). The concept of developmental arrest means that what had been in the process of developing was restrained in some way; that is, the sense of a future was occluded. If the undeveloped aspect of the psyche is a developmental arrest, as is now being attested to by much of contemporary theory, then the unconscious is not confined to thoughts and feelings of the past, but includes the as-yet-not-happened future. Unconscious mental phenomena include undeveloped potential, movement to the future that has been blocked or delayed.

The theoretical movement shifting the conceptualization of development to the self-organization, and unconscious mental phenomena and psychopathology to a blockage in the developmental process, brings the forward trajectory into the heart of psychoanalytic theory (e.g., Summers, 1999). In Bollas's (1989) terms, the articulation of the self is the fulfillment of one's destiny. When important potential components of the self remain unrealized, the path of life is not one's destiny, but fate, an imposition from without. This aspect of unconscious mental phenomena consists not of finished entities, such as thoughts or wishes, but of potential, the not-yet-realized aspects of the psyche. We might say that the unconscious as potential consists of unrealized destiny.

Arrested aspects of the self will seek disguised expression in the form of symptoms (Summers, 1999). Each pathological outcome consists not only of the traumatic experience of the past, but also of the future potential that has not been realized. Therefore, the developmental-arrest model makes the experience of the future central to the understanding of unconscious mental phenomena and symptomatic outbreak. The future does not just enter the analytic arena at the level of the superego, constricting and limiting desire, as Loewald thought; the future inheres in desire itself or, more broadly, in all meaningful motivation.

Contemporary developmental research supports the view that the future is embedded in the psyche from the inception of life. Close observation indicates that from her earliest days the infant comes to expect responses from the caretaker and reacts negatively to failed anticipation (e.g., Beebe et al., 1992). Additionally, the infant performs certain behaviors, such as sucking on its own, for no purpose other than to do it herself; such behavior has no apparent "because motive" but, rather, is done "in order to" acquire the ability to perform the activity (Tomkins, 1978). Goal-directed action seems to be built into the human psyche virtually from birth. In summary, philosophical findings, current psychoanalytic theory, and developmental research all converge to show that the future is inherent in psychological experience rather than entering at a particular point of psychological organization, as Loewald thought.

TEMPORALITY AND THE CLINICAL PROCESS

It follows that the analyst who looks at time in only a linear fashion, in which the past affects the present and future, adopts a simplistic and limited view of temporality that does not fit the lived experience of time. Because the present moment is embedded in and gains meaning only in the projected future, or future-perfect tense, understanding the patient's present requires that the analyst grasp the patient's experience of the future and how the present moment fits into it. The emptiness, passivity, and complacency we see in so many patients reflects their loss of future, an inability to live in the future-perfect tense, and this empty future issues in the bleakness of their present lives. Because the present and past gain meaning via their relationship to the projected future, or the future-perfect tense, when the future looks dim the present becomes empty, and the past, constricting. In the context of a bright-looking future, the present shines and the past is viewed as potentially useful, as a way to transform the present. To be sure, we can all look at the past and find reasons why the future looks so barren and the present empty, but it is equally true that the void in the future leads to an empty present and a sense of imprisonment in the past.

There are also clinical reasons to abandon strict adherence to linear time. As we have seen, the historical analytic emphasis on understanding the past has had limited therapeutic benefit. The difficulty of effecting long-term change by understanding the roots of these configurations in the past, recognized by analysts of many persuasions, long ago led to an emphasis on the here-and-now transference. Freud's (1912) famous statement that no one can be hanged in effigy was meant to put clinical emphasis on the resolution of the neurosis in the transference. Nonetheless, Freud's (1937) pessimism in his last writings regarding the possibility of effecting longstanding change suggests that this shift did not lead to satisfactory results. Gill (1981, 1994), expressing his own displeasure with traditional technique, concluded that the inadequacy of analytic results could be attributed to insufficient emphasis on the here-and-now transference. However, Gill was less persuasive in explaining why interpretation that was ineffective when directed to the past roots of behavior would be appreciably more effective when focused on enhanced awareness of present patterns. The assumption seemed to be that giving words to behavior in the here-and-now analytic interaction would issue in the alteration of patterns. However, analytic experience has not really supported this idea. Gill's case examples do not show a strong connection between here-and-now transference interpretations and character change.

Furthermore, as discussed in the previous chapter, transference interpretations tend to be gathered into previously existing patterns. So, while the therapist may view understanding the past as a road to a better future, the patient sees the past as a confirmation of hopelessness; we might even say that the patient uses the past to seal the fate of future repetition. To borrow a phrase from Fairbairn (1958), the patient "closes the circle" of her object relationships. One can, of course, interpret this closed circle, but that interpretation is as easily encircled in the repetitive pattern as any other. This is why, toward the end of his life, Fairbairn gave up the belief that interpretation alone could free the patient from recurring patterns and concluded that the analyst must put a "breach" in this closed circle by becoming a new object, a "beneficent, parental figure."

We may now apply to this problem our concept of pathology as developmental arrest. If the patient's historical patterns are a product of the obstruction of the developmental process, the repetition of these configurations reflects the failure of certain aspects of the self to become realized. The growing child is limited to the patterns of interaction permissible in the early environment even if such modes of being are divorced from the patient's authentic experience. Not knowing she is capable of any other way of being, if the patient contemplates the future at all, it is as a bleak repetition of current patterns, a sense of fate that keeps her repeating the past no matter how well it might be understood. In a very real way, the patient does not have a sense of future but only an endless repetition of the past. We might call this a "fate neurosis," a belief that the pain of current life is the fate of the entire life, and when the past is observed it looks like the cause of one's fate.

The vexing clinical problem of how to extract the analytic couple from the closed circle of object relationships, a process aptly termed the "bootstrapping problem" by Mitchell (1997), has been the stimulus for many theoretical and clinical alternatives to classical theory, such as self psychology, object relations, and relational theory. I suggest that to overcome this difficulty we must go beyond shifting theoretical orientation and reconceptualizing the clinical process to reconsidering temporal modalities. For too long psychoanalytic theory and technique have been constrained by a linear concept of time that has led us to look at our interventions, of whatever type, almost exclusively in terms of past and present. That temporal modalities gain meaning only within the context of the future suggests that psychoanalysis has been missing perhaps the most crucial temporal dimension of therapeutic action. This omission is particularly striking when one considers that our aim is to achieve growth, a process that looks to the future. We must consider the very real possibility that the patient's experience of the future may be blocking growth as much as or perhaps even more than the effects of the past. If this is so, the unconscious that consists of truncated future possibilities must be made conscious and brought to fruition in new ways of being and relating.

When repeated interpretation of the transference is not alterative, the resulting clinical impasse may be a result of the patient's inability to contemplate or implement a different future. The aspect of the unconscious that consists of unrealized future possibilities tends to be left out of repeated transference interpretations, with the consequence that the process does not help the patient create alternatives to the pathological patterns. At this point the therapeutic relationship must be transformed from an interpretive field to potential space so that the patient can use the relationship to create new ways of being and relating. Because such creations require an image of the forward trajectory of the patient's life, the therapist must see the importance of the future in the psychological organization.

Consider the case of Max, who suffered from severely inhibited aggression. Entering therapy because he felt he was underutilizing his potential, Max was passive and compliant and feared risk-taking. As is common in such cases, analytic investigation uncovered intense anxieties to aggressive expression, primary among these being his fear of damaging others and of being abandoned. The origins of this anxiety lay with a fragile mother who quickly and easily fell into tearful despair when others were angry at her or even disagreed with her. Max frequently heard his volatile father verbally attack his mother, who sobbed uncontrollably in response. Furthermore, whenever Max or either of his brothers was vocal in opposing her desires or opinions, her sense of injury was apparent, and she quickly became anxious and defensive. To avoid such wounds, Max's mother tended to acquiesce to her sons' desires and had great difficulty saying no to their requests. Enraged at this compliance, her husband, adding to the woman's woes, frequently criticized her for being "soft" on the children. Max was frightened to see his mother so easily hurt and felt guilty watching her devalued by his father. In response to the conflict between his parents, Max tried to help his mother feel better by acceding to her desires. Eventually, he learned to succumb to her opinions and wishes, however misguided he felt they were, to avoid hurting her and feeling guilty about her plight. Although angry at both his father for his mistreatment of his mother and at his mother for her weakness, he repressed his anger out of fear of provoking his father and hurting his mother.

This inhibition became manifest in the transference as Max agreed with my comments even when he clearly had doubts. His characteristic response to an interpretation he did not find helpful was to search for something in my remarks with which he could find some degree of agreement. Even though at times he had to stretch, he preferred to emphasize an aspect of my comments with which he could concur rather than admit that my remark did not feel right. I pointed out his apparent anxiety about disagreeing with me, and we were able to connect it with his fear of his mother's fragility. Despite this important analytic work,

Max continued to disavow all potential disagreements with me and aggressive communications to others in his life. While he understood his anxiety about expressing aggression in the therapeutic relationship, this awareness did enable him to change his behavior. To the contrary, he submitted to my interpretation of the inhibition, thus repeating the lifelong pattern rather than altering it.

What is often missed in such therapeutic stalemates is that the patient sees no alternative. No matter how well the pattern is understood, the patient continues to return to the default position for lack of an alternative. Having inhibited all potential aggressive expression, Max did not see how to bring aggression into any relationship, including the therapeutic dyad, and he did not believe any relationship with an aggressive component could be sustained. He saw no possibility of a future in which aggression played a role and consequently felt stuck in a frozen present.

A way out of such a clinical stalemate can begin with a shift in the patient's sense of the future. If the patient is able to envision the possibility of utilizing aggression in present relationships she can unfreeze the present. If the patient is to create a sense of futurity, the therapist must take an active role in the establishment of this new temporal modality, but, as we know, to suggest that the future could be different is pointless. The patient does not believe optimistic prognostications and often regards the clinician who makes them as Pollyannaish at best or, at worst, as so self-absorbed as to be unable to understand the patient's experience. Therein lies the analytic dilemma: because the patient is unable to see a future, the analyst must help in the creation of a future, but the patient is mired in the deadening past and will not accept another view. This predicament is one way of conceptualizing the problem of therapeutic action.

For the therapist's belief in a different future to resonate with the patient, there must be an unarticulated, latent sense of futurity in the patient. Because only possibilities that preexist in the patient will be meaningful, what the therapist finds must already be in the patient, in however nascent a form. On the other hand, fully formed experience is not going to lead to something new. In between experience that is "not yet" and "the already formed" lies the potential space in which new ways of being and relating based on authentic experience can be created. The resolution of the dilemma of therapeutic action, as we have described it, lies in the ability of the therapist to perceive the patient's latent potential and assist its articulation. When previously dormant potential begins to be realized, a new view of the future is initiated.

To return to Max, this principle means that I had to find some dormant potential for aggression. Although his motivation for coming to therapy was to achieve more professionally, I glimpsed his aggression in his marital relationship. On occasion he had mentioned that his wife, who worked only part-time, did few household chores; and when he came home from a long day at work, he often found the house in a disheveled state despite his spouse's having been home for most of the day. Finding a disproportionate burden of the household organization falling on his shoulders, he expressed to me a vague sense of annoyance. I pointed out that he felt the household situation was unfair given the long hours he worked in comparison with his wife. He acknowledged this fact but said he did not think anything "could be done about it." I replied that his disturbance about the situation implied that he wanted it to be different. Max said, "Of course, I would *like* it to be different, but I don't see how." Undaunted by his pessimism, I asked him how he thought the relationship ought to be. Although Max was originally reluctant to engage in such a discussion, with my encouragement he was eventually able to describe the kind of relationship he had hoped for when he married. He depicted his vision of a mutual relationship in which both contributed equally, including the household tasks, and as he said this his anger swelled at his wife for not holding up her end. I interpreted that he had a conviction of how he felt his marriage should be, but he had been suppressing this vision. We then struggled with Max's suppressed hope that his marriage would fit his expectations, his pessimism regarding any possibility of changing the way it had been, and his anger at its current state along with his ambivalent hope it would be different. Max noted that the more we talked about how he wished the relationship to be, the angrier he became. As I pointed out the anger at his wife and encouraged its expression, Max felt I was pushing him, and I highlighted his growing anger at me. When he demurred, I said that he did not believe our relationship could sustain his anger, and I guessed that he had a different vision of how the therapeutic dyad could evolve. Max said that he wanted to be free to express himself, including his disagreements and negative reactions to comments of mine. This discussion allowed me to pursue his reactions to interpretations he found unhelpful, and he began to convey his authentic responses to my comments, including his unhappiness with interventions that seemed to miss the mark.

This shift in our relationship initiated a new freedom in Max's ability to use his aggression in both his relationship with his wife and his career, the most obvious points at which he saw the damaging effects of his inhibition. As Max talked openly about his future, he admitted to considerable ambition, including the desire to start his own company. After intensive discussion of his timidity and long-suppressed desire to be an entrepreneur, Max eventually launched his own business venture, an act of entrepreneurship of which he never had thought himself capable. Also, his marital relationship underwent a decisive upheaval that ultimately resulted in a far more equal, but more overtly contentious and conflictual, relationship than it had ever been.

The life-altering changes Max created began with his contemplation of a different future in his marital relationship, but the decisive factor may not have been so much the vision of a different marriage as the ability and willingness to envision a future of any type. All our understanding of his timidity bore no fruit until he had a sense of futurity. The occasion for this shift in the trajectory of his life was the marriage, but it seemed that seeing a future in that situation spurred a new sense of futurity in all areas of his life. The ability to consider an aggressive form of relating to me not only issued in the direct expression of negative reactions in our relationship, but also strengthened his sense of conviction that he could find more authentic ways of relating to others, including his wife.

The appearance of the newly experienced future was prepared for by the interpretive process but came to fruition as the potential space was employed for the articulation of latent potential. The stalemate of understanding without change, or "resistance" in classical terms, was overcome by deploying potential space for the creation of a new future. The trajectory that came to contain the hope of new possibilities stimulated new ways of being and relating that gave new meaning to the present and led out of the therapeutic impasse. We saw this process when Max's ability to project himself into the future-perfect tense resulted in a new-found aggression with me. We can see from Max's therapeutic journey that to utilize this concept of therapeutic action, the therapist must give the future a central role in the meaning of the present. Furthermore, the future must be articulated from a latent potential preexisting in the patient. The therapist bears the burden of finding the unexpressed potential and encouraging its expression so that what is understood can be used to change the present. I will now demonstrate how this concept of therapeutic action works via the detailed discussion of the therapeutic process with a patient who had no sense of futurity.

CLINICAL ILLUSTRATION

Helen, a 26-year-old engaged woman working as a domestic, came for help because she found herself in the midst of the same type of depressive episode from which a previous therapist helped her extricate herself in adolescence. From a middle class family, Helen left college after one year because she had been depressed and preferred to stay with her therapist with whom she had begun treatment during her summer break. Helen reported a history of neglect and rejection. She was a big, awkward girl whom her mother seemed to view as an embarrassment, continually criticized her, and yet seemed to feel Helen was a threatening, dangerous figure whose potential explosiveness could erupt at any time. Although her older sister's college education was paid for by the parents, Helen was told she was "on her own" when she reached 18 years of age. Her father, chronically depressed and uncommunicative, was absorbed in his career, paid little attention to the family, and was obsessively preoccupied with status. Helen's view of her father was represented by a dream she had early in the analysis in which her father was dressed in a thespian costume, admiring himself in the mirror. He was given to volatile rage outbursts with minimal provocation. For example, one day he felt that Helen held her fork "the wrong way" at dinner, flew into a rage, verbally abused her, and left the dinner table. Her sister, being feminine and coquettish, was her mother's favorite, and she bought her clothes and other feminine accessories. By contrast, Helen favored a counterculture lifestyle, wore unusual clothing, and loved reading. Virtually every aspect of Helen's behavior was a source of criticism from her mother.

In high school, Helen became depressed after her mother, for reasons that were never made clear, forced her to break up with the only boyfriend she had. Helen did not recover until she entered psychotherapy some years later. At that time, Helen began working as a domestic, employment she held for the next five years instead of returning to college; she developed a social life and met her fiancé. She ended her psychotherapy feeling that it had helped her a great deal, but in the year since its termination she experienced increasing difficulty functioning and found herself depressed, although she did not see any reason why she should feel that way.

Helen was in a long, difficult analysis, only one aspect of which is discussed here. In the course of the analysis, it became clear that she expected little from her life and did not think in terms of the future in any respect. Without goals toward which she was striving either in the long-term or in day-to-day living, she never initiated social plans, although she rarely declined an offer. When her previous therapist suggested that she did not have to return to college, she thought, "Why not?" She had never expected college to lead to anything; she only knew that the prestigious liberal arts college she attended fit her father's need for status. At the time she entered psychotherapy, Helen was living a barren existence with few personal possessions and little furniture; she slept on a mattress on the floor. Not believing she could effect any changes in her environment, if something broke, instead of having it fixed, she went without it. When a light bulb went out, she lived without the light. Only when her apartment was almost completely dim did she consider getting new light bulbs.

We understood this lack of expectation for herself and her life as an introjection of both parents' attitudes toward her. Since her mother saw her as a problem to be survived or avoided, Helen did not regard herself as someone who deserved comfort or for whom any environmental changes should occur. Her father considered her an embarrassment (except when she satisfied his need for prestige, as by attending a prestigious college), and she treated herself the same way. Feeling that she did not know how to act socially, she often felt self-conscious in large gatherings. The two activities she enjoyed were listening to music, which she did mostly when she cleaned houses, and reading, which she did in almost all her spare moments.

Frequently I commented to Helen that I was struck by her lack of a future. Being a bright, sensitive person, Helen immediately understood the implication that her life did not have to be this way, but she was nonplussed by it. She knew what I meant because she realized that others strive to fulfill goals they deem important, but she felt that living for goals, having a purpose, or even fitting in socially was "for other people." This was true of her work, also; she liked being a domestic because she could put on the radio and get lost in the music, as though she was not even conscious of what she was doing. I told Helen that the reason I raised the issue of her lack of expectations for herself was that she was depressed, and I was searching for the reasons. Had she ever considered that her life without goals meant that her life lacked meaning, and that without meaning depression might result? No, she had not thought of that. Believing that the only motivation she would ever have was survival, as long as she got through each day, she felt she was doing the best she could. I said that her attitude fit with a self-definition that had been a necessary adaptation earlier in her life but now left her with a bleak view of her life's horizon. This attitude issued from her chronic depression.

Our understanding of her survival mentality as an internalization of her mother's attitude had little mutative impact. Suppression of desire led to an emptiness that could be understood as her mother inside her, but also resulted from an inability to contemplate a future. Without goals her life was empty of meaning, and she called this emptiness "depression." If it could be said that Helen was highly repressed, this repression was directed against anything that pointed toward the future. Any desire beyond daily survival was far from her consciousness.

Helen's maternal introject was a replication of her mother's view of her life as unimportant; Helen thought of that as the definitive word on her sense of self and her expectations. Having her mother inside her was not a problem to be overcome, in her view, but a sealed fate, a stable condition that she regarded as proof of her hopelessness. All of this was held with equal finality in the transference: my job was to help her survive as her previous therapist had. Unable to contemplate living beyond mere maintenance, Helen did not think that I thought her capable of more: goals beyond subsistence were for "other patients." Helen thought I regarded her as a pathetic "charity" case who could not be cured like "real" patients and presumed that I expected to do no more than assist her to survive with her disability, like a patient with a permanent physical deformity. Helen knew that by adopting this attitude she was repeating her mother's view of her, but this understanding did little to alter her expectations of herself or her conviction that I agreed with them. Although she readily agreed with my interpretation that her attitude toward the analysis repeated the maternal relationship, Helen felt helpless to change her bedrock belief that her role in life was to endure. My further comments that by failing to project herself into a future she was, in fact, carrying out her mother's injunction to live out a meaningless life without any sense of achievement or satisfaction, but it had no impact on her inability to see possibilities nor budge her frozen sense of temporality.

Many times she feared that I would become intolerant of her continual expressions of sorrow, pain, and emptiness. In fact, it was often difficult to tolerate her seemingly endless self-hatred and negative interpretations of all that occurred in her life including the analytic process. Helen often expressed surprise that I had not evicted her from therapy, and there were times when I felt that I might be foolish to continue such a repetitive, apparently stalemated process. Had I acted on my sense of hopelessness, however, I would have reenacted the cycle of futility that began for her in the maternal relationship and was now embedded in the very fiber of her self. I identified that pessimism as a potential collusion with the powerful draw of her maternal introject that saw her as undeserving and hopeless. Determined not to allow the maternal introject to consume the analytic field as it dominated her, I refused the temptation to participate in her lifelong pattern of consigning herself to a marginal existence. Throughout the treatment, I continued to regard my moments of pessimism as my experience of her most pernicious dynamic, the power of her negative maternal introject.

While Helen saw her life as frozen, I did not see her survival mentality as a static state, but as an adaptive construction required to endure a traumatic childhood that was the only world she knew. Her despair implied that she was despairing *over something* that she was not getting from life. Therefore, I viewed her discouragement as an indication that she had a buried longing for much more from life, even if she did not consciously expect to get it. I operated on the principle that a life in the future-perfect tense was potentially within her, and it was my job to find indications of it and nurture them. In this way, I sensed potential in her that she did not perceive.

Despite my view of her latent capabilities, for a sustained period the analysis seemed to be at an impasse as our insights into her sense of emptiness led to little therapeutic movement. We were both disappointed that this apparently meaningful interpretive work seemed to be bearing so little fruit. Without a projected future, Helen was stuck in an endless present with no apparent way to break free from it. To Helen, whatever she liked passed through her life as a fleeting moment in the present; it did not exist in the future-perfect tense. Missing for Helen was a sense of futurity, a trajectory for her life. Despite the fact that we repeatedly understood the origins of her survival mentality in the past, this attitude did not change because such insight did not help her project a future as part of her self. Our understanding, no matter how accurate, could not be effective because grasping the historical roots of her maternal introject of hopelessness did not build hope; the understanding of her frozen present did not create a future. Moreover, without belief in the future, Helen had no alternative to the maternal introject.

Therefore, I shifted my clinical strategy from interpretation of past and present to a focus on finding disavowed indications of a potential future. The underlying principle of this therapeutic stance was that Helen needed to find a future within which her present could become meaningful before she could use her understanding of past and present. I, therefore, reversed the temporality of my interpretive stance by searching for the latent potential in her for the development of a future. At this point, I asked her, "If you were not focused on survival, what then?" Initially perplexed by this question, she eventually was able to recognize that she would then feel lost. "I would not know what to do. It's like I wouldn't be anywhere." I told her that contemplating this possibility put us in a void, and I wanted to hear what came up. She said that what she most loved was reading. "Of course, if I had the opportunity, I would love to pursue literature." When I noted that I had never before heard her mention this interest (although I had noticed she read a great deal), she said that she had never articulated this desire even to herself and was surprised to find herself bringing it up. In the act of saying "of course" she wanted to pursue literature, Helen discovered a potential ambition that had always been there, but she had never before allowed herself to formulate it into a possibility. Even though she loved to read and did it incessantly, she had never given thought to pursuing it. In fact, the concept of "pursuing an interest" felt alien to her. As we discussed the fact that she did not register anything as a desire or interest to be followed, she was struck with the thought that she had never thought of reading as an activity that could be developed. In fact, she had never thought of reading as an interest but, like everything else that happened in her life, as simply something she did, as though it happened to her.

My indicating to Helen that she had a passion for reading that she had never registered as an interest to be pursued allowed her to entertain the idea that literature could play a role in her life beyond a way to pass time. Initially, Helen felt a combination of excitement about the possibility of following a lifelong passion and fear of allowing herself a forlorn hope by falling prey to an illusion. I said it was clear she was excited by the possibility of having any future at all, especially one that included literature, because any goal implied that she mattered, but she could not fit such a thought into her sense of self. To avoid the anxiety of projecting herself into the future, she avoided a sense of futurity and stayed frozen in an endless present of survival points with little sense of achievement or satisfaction.

Surprised at my emphasis on her love of reading, Helen said that she had never regarded the development of an authentic interest to be in her province. I said that reading was not the only activity that she found enriching, and I mentioned that she listened to music while doing her work because she had a love for blues, jazz, and other musical forms. Furthermore, she expressed intermittent complaints about societal injustices and much of her reading was about the plight of the underprivileged, especially people of color. Initially, Helen was jarred that I had recognized these thoughts and interests; again, she had not conceptualized any of them as attributes of who she was until I underscored them. Nonetheless, with my encouragement, she was able to discuss her convictions about societal inequalities and her enjoyment of music and dancing. In our discussion, I did not need to bring to her attention the fact that she had never made the effort to nurture any of these interests in a planned way; she made the point herself and connected this attitude with her passion for literature. It had never before occurred to her that enjoyment of these endeavors could be developed so that they could play a significant role in her life. As a result of this awareness, it became clear to Helen that her attitude of endless present moments did not just apply to long-term life goals, but to her daily existence. For example, Helen had never thought of going to hear live music. If the music she liked happened to be on the radio, she heard it; if not, she gave no thought to seeking it out.

At this point, I highlighted the connection between the lack of teleology in her life and her depression. Living without goals, I emphasized, made her life purposeless, and depression is the name we give to this sense of futility. I suggested that precisely because she had never thought of her interests as desires that could direct her life she was enslaved in an endless present that had no meaning and left her feeling empty. I commented that what she called "depression" was tantamount to a life of reactive living.

These discussions introduced the concept of the future-perfect tense to Helen, an idea she found intriguing. At this point she began to give serious thought to finding an organized way to study literature and began to initiate her own entertainment. She went to listen to live music, attended clubs, and went dancing. Concretizing her passion for the study of fiction, Helen returned to college to immerse herself in the study of English literature.

This process shows the importance of the analyst's recognition of the patient's unrealized potential. I saw in Helen the possibility for a future in her love of literature before she did. However, it is equally important that I did not spin this story out of whole cloth. I wove it from what I saw: her ample intelligence, insightfulness, interest in the human process, and avid reading habits. Helen was able to use my appreciation of her potential to fashion her first thoughts of the future, and as she did so she began to have a sense of her life as projected toward the future. That I engaged her world of endless struggle in the present meant that she did not see my vision of her potentially positive future as a Pollyannaish fantasy. She knew that my view of her potential was derived not from a denial of her despair and hopelessness, but from a full engagement of them. This willingness to respond to my belief that she was capable of a different future was not won easily. It required my living through years of painful, agonizing depressive episodes. She tested my resolve with various expressions of anger, both direct and passive, as well as repeated feelings of hopelessness that she urged me to accept but later acknowledged relief that I did not. My seeing her subsistence approach to life in this way and willingness to engage her despair gave me credibility when I saw something beyond the immediacy of her experience. She was able to give credence to my sense of her potential to develop her interests only because she knew that I saw the necessity of her survival mentality. I understood why she could see no future, and yet I saw the potential in her to move beyond subsistence to futurity. This experience of my work with Helen is typical of patients without a sense of futurity: the therapist needs to grasp their hopelessness before a belief in something more can be engaged.

Thus, a new analytic space was constructed out of my interaction with Helen, a potential space in which she could project herself into the future. Helen used the analytic space not only to understand, but also to construct a playground for experimenting with new ways of being (Sanville, 1991). Helen did this in many ways, one of which was her willingness to "play" with seeing herself in the future. Could she really pursue her academic interest in literature? Could she find a way to use it to build a professional life? The answers were less important than the queries because asking the questions implied that she possessed a future. By stimulating a sense of futurity in Helen, I was simultaneously recognizing her potential. Without such an experience of time, there cannot be a trajectory for one's life, and there is no sense of latent capabilities that can be used for the creation of new ways of being and relating. I had ample indications for Helen's life of her attraction to certain activities and that could be built into formulated desires. By responding to my recognition of this potential, Helen built a sense of futurity that made "potential" a meaningful concept for her.

There was no transformation of her depression until she began to have a glimpse of herself in the future-perfect tense. When she started to project her interests as formulated desires, she saw that there was more to her than the endless struggle for survival. In having a trajectory toward the future, Helen felt that she could have an influence, that the future could be different. Once she began to live in the future-perfect tense, her life decisively changed. In the large sense, she made a plan to return to college and eventually graduated with a degree in English literature. On a daily level, Helen organized a social life to ensure experiencing activities and events she enjoyed, and she joined organizations that had goals in concert with her value system.

With a sense of future, she could experience the possibility of alternatives to her mother's denigrating attitude. Now as we discussed the origins of her maternal introject, Helen felt that she had an alternative stance from which to experience it. Rather than an inevitability, her maternal introject felt like one among many possibilities and an especially painful one that arose from her life circumstances. Experienced in this way, the present was no longer an endless series of disconnected points but moments that fit into life projects. As Helen began to live in the future-perfect tense, she felt a striving that led her to see the maternal introject as an enemy of the potential self she could become rather than a representation of a sealed fate. This loosened grip of the negative introject, in turn, stimulated a more positive cast to her sense of futurity as she could begin to appreciate her skills and talents. When that happened, she began to feel for the first time that her life had meaning.

My recognition of Helen's passion for reading and understanding social injustice led to her eventual recognition that she longed for intellectual stimulation and academic pursuits and to contemplate how she might pursue these interests. Ultimately, she made the decision to return to school and put herself through undergraduate and later graduate school, taking a master's degree in literature. However, the academic arena was not the only venue of change. Helen's desire awakened in many areas of her life: vocational, social, sexual, interpersonal. For example, as she developed a belief in her future, she left domestic work and became a waitress at increasingly prosperous restaurants to support her education. After completing her graduate work, she entered the professional world where today she enjoys considerable success. As she moved forward with her life, she realized that her husband, whose life was ruled by inertia, represented the stagnation of her former existence and, after attempting to arouse some ambition in him for many years, eventually divorced him. Helen also began to engage in the cultural life of her community and enjoyed it a great deal.

Many other changes emerged from Helen's newly created life, but the details need not concern us here. The essential point for our purpose is that once Helen saw herself as living beyond the present with a future that had meaning to her, she not only developed her interests, skills, and talents, but pursued their fulfillment. Her sense of futurity stimulated the realization of a variety of formerly latent capabilities even without specific analytic discussion. In fact, many of these changes were either discussed only in passing or not at all in therapy. Once Helen used the future, her life assumed a momentum of finding and creating new ways of being. These changes indicated that the maternal introject was superseded by the new development of a self with a future. From a clinical viewpoint, the crucial fact is that Helen was able to adopt her new pursuits only after the future had become part of the analytic space.

CONCLUSION

As Loewald (1972) enjoined us many years ago, the linear view of time can severely limit the analyst's ability to free patients from repetitive patterns, as was shown in this case by the recalcitrance of Helen's maternal introject to interpretations of past and present. The construction of a future made possible the use of insights about the past and present that, in themselves, added to Helen's ability to build a future for herself. Could we have cut to the chase and created this sense of future without awareness of the past and present patterns? It is unlikely because any suggestion of a different future without understanding the roots of her patterns was interpreted by her as a superficial, unfounded, Pollyannaish fantasy. The conviction of her fatedness had to be grasped as a response to her family environment before she could even consider the possibility that there were other ways of experiencing her life. Helen had to see that her sense of helplessness was not somehow built into her endowment, but was rather a construction from her past, before she could take seriously any genuine pursuits. Only the understanding of her sense of fate as a response to a deadening upbringing allowed her to consider that her life could have an outcome other than the one emanating from her bleak assumptions. These desires became conscious only after the potential of other experience was created in the analytic space by understanding the past and its repetition in the transference.

It is this grappling with the past and the transference that distinguishes psychoanalytic treatment from a purely existential approach that emphasizes only the creation of meaning. Frankl (1984) has advocated a form of existential psychotherapy the purpose of which is to provide the patient with a sense of meaning. While this theory overlaps with the technique advocated here, there is a fundamental and decisive difference because Frankl's "logotherapy" gives little place to understand either the patient's history or the transference, both of which are germane to the current clinical strategy. By dismissing these dimensions, Frankl loses the depth of experience that has always been the hallmark of psychoanalytic therapy. Without such exploration, any view of the future is likely to be superficial and unlikely to have staying power. Most importantly, only the plumbing of affective depths can achieve the sense of authenticity necessary to combat childhood patterns. The technical strategy advocated here integrates these uniquely analytic dimensions with the importance of creating a future trajectory.

While understanding was necessary for Helen to project an authentically felt future, it is equally true that insights into Helen's hopelessness and helplessness did not alleviate the persistence of her depression until she experienced herself as possessing a future, a person for whom goals mattered. This new experience, so long dormant within her, recast the past as the suffocation of a potentially authentic self, rather than a sealed fate. Helen's creation of a future, then, gave new meaning to her past. This revision, or retranscription, of the past, in turn, helped free her to make further changes in her life until her self was reorganized with a future and a new present and past.

Understanding makes possible the creation of authentic meaning, and the creation of a future sheds light on the past and present. We might say there is a dialectical movement between understanding past and present, on one hand, and the trajectory of meaning toward the future, on the other. This dialectical process is missed by a purely existential clinical technique. Helen's therapeutic movement shows the importance for the analytic process of a fluid concept of temporality that includes the mutual influence of the three temporal modes, any of which may be prominent at a given phase of the analysis. The mobilization of a belief in a realizable future is at least as much an analytic task as the understanding of the past and present. And as we saw with Helen, just as insights help with the ability to project a future, the latter capacity makes possible new understandings of present and past.

We have seen that the development of a realizable future requires the therapist have a vision of the patient's capacities that goes beyond the immediacy of the patient's experience. In this way, the analytic therapist's vision of the patient's potential is central to the action of psychoanalytic therapy, and we now turn to this aspect of the process.

3

THE THERAPIST'S VISION
OF THE PATIENT

We have seen the importance of potential space in therapeutic action and the shift in the concept of temporality to which it leads. As we observed in the case of Helen, when the analytic field becomes potential space, the therapist needs to view the field from the perspective of the future-perfect tense, defining the space by what it *may be*. Such a concept implies that the therapist possesses a vision of the patient's potential, a sense of where the patient may be able to go. Although perspectives on therapeutic action differ among theoretical schools, any therapist who aims to nurture undeveloped potential must ponder a vision of who the patient can become. From the classical perspective, mental excavation uncovers discrete mental events, variously labeled affects, wishes, or drives. From the viewpoint of self realization, analysis uncovers not only previously unconscious affects but also potential ways of being and relating. The patient is not only understood as a present personality with past antecedents, but also envisioned as a future self who realizes currently dormant potential. In this way, the sense of futurity is inextricably linked to the therapist's vision of the patient.

Once the future dimension enters psychoanalytic thought the therapist's vision, implied in the aim of self realization, becomes a crucial part of the process. There is, then, a split in psychoanalytic theory between (1) theorists of the actual who tend to understand the present in terms of the past, thus presuming the analytic goal to be the assumption of a niche in preexisting categories; and (2) theorists of both the actual and the possible, who include in their view of analysis a way of opening new modes of self-expression, thus adding the dimension of the future to the analytic craft and potentially creating new categories for the realization of self.

One must distinguish two types of analytic vision. Shifting the analytic goal to self-realization requires a vision of persons and the possibilities that inhere in the human condition. This conceptualization of who people can be is to be distinguished from the particular vision relevant to each individual patient that emerges in the psychoanalytic dialogue. The pioneer in appreciating the importance of the therapist's vision of the patient in the psychoanalytic process is Hans Loewald.

LOEWALD

Loewald (1960) viewed the patient–therapist relationship as analogous to the parent–child dyad. He put it this way, "The parent is in an empathic relationship of understanding the child's particular stage in development, yet ahead in his vision of the child's future and mediating this vision to the child in his dealing with him" (pp. 25–26). Using a metaphor from Freud, Loewald likened the analytic process to sculpting in which the therapist whittles away until the figure comes into being. According to Loewald, the therapist, like the sculptor, "must have . . . an image of that which needs to be brought into its own" (p. 21). The patient provides the rudiments of this image through self-revelation, but the therapist creates a form from these elements. Loewald's concept gives a kind of Platonic cast to the analytic craft: the therapist cannot help the patient without an idea of who she can be.

Maternal empathy, in Loewald's view, is an appreciation of the child's stage of development, but from the beginning of life the child has his own inherent movement beyond the present. Here we may add to Loewald's reflections on the mother–child dyad Winnicott's (1960) concept of the spontaneous gesture that moves the child to new experience, toward the acquisition of new knowledge, mastery, and exploration of the world. The mother's empathy includes appreciation for both who the child is and who the child may become. The mother is "behind" in following the child's spontaneity by meeting it with a response of her own. If the mother's reaction fails to connect with the child's gesture, there is a danger of divorcing the child from his experience and molding him to a preformed idea. So, the maternal response both engages the child's spontaneity and adds a vision that the mother constructs from it, an addition to which the child must respond.

The parent's vision is mediated through identification, and the child ultimately adopts a view of himself that incorporates the parent's vision of his future. According to Loewald, the therapist's vision of the patient's future creates an object relationship in which the therapist both follows and is ahead of the patient. If the therapist gets "too far ahead," he runs the danger of molding the patient to an imposed image; but without a vision of the patient's future, he cannot help the patient realize possibilities of which he may not be aware. Just as the parent's responses to the child must cohere with the child's experience, the therapist's vision of the patient must fit, and the criterion for the aptness of this fit is the coherence of the patient's affective responses. The patient, like the child, does not see other possibilities; the therapist's holding a different future for the patient creates the conditions for new ways of being.

How the therapist molds this vision depends to some degree on his view of human possibilities. For Freud (1915), people seek a tensionless state of pleasure that can be achieved only momentarily before tension builds anew. Unable to reach the enduring tensionless state we seek, people are condemned to unhappiness in Freud's (1895) view. But, theorists of the possible look for the ways to transcend the limits of such antinomies. In my view, the analytic theorist who can best help us here is Jessica Benjamin.

BENJAMIN'S ANALYTIC VISION

Benjamin (1995, 1997) points out that central to the weakness of traditional analytic theorizing about gender is oedipal complementarity, a theory that interferes with the realization of potential by restricting gender possibilities. The boy who can identify only with his father, and the girl only with her mother, are restricted to narrow ways of being. The woman who was not allowed a preoedipal identification with the rapprochement father shifts from identificatory love to idealized love and tends to form idealized, masochistically tinged attachments to men in a futile effort to achieve the power and desire thought to reside in the male. The man who cannot identify with his mother has little containing function and is consigned to empty phallic activity in which he can only discharge into the object as a defense against his limited capacity to contain. Unable to own affect and desire, each is crippled in the development of subjectivity and is unable to experience the other as a separate subjectivity. Both the man's empty activity and the woman's masochistic idealization are defenses against lack of full subjectivity, a deficit that includes the incapacity to attain full sensual enjoyment. Without the opportunity to identify with both the masculine and feminine, active and passive, the critical step to ownership of one's own states, and therefore appreciation of the other's subjectivity, cannot be taken. In Benjamin's view, oedipal complementarity as an ideal forces analysis to arrest rather than promote psychological growth, or to limit rather than expand human possibility. By moving analytic theory beyond oedipal complementarity, Benjamin has provided an analytic vision of human possibility far more optimistic than Breuer and Freud's (1895) resignation to common unhappiness.

Benjamin has created a psychoanalytic theory of the possible in which authorship of one's life requires the containment and transcendence of opposing tension states. Exclusive reliance on one pole of any antinomy impedes the ability to possess the full range of psychological states. Neither activity nor passivity alone can achieve ownership; the capacity for both is needed for the development of full subjectivity. Benjamin's work articulates a psychoanalytic concept of ownership by seeing beyond the antinomies within which Freud presumed the human condition to lie and thereby provides the therapist with an expanded, optimistic vision of human possibility in which she can view the patient's material.

INTERPRETATION

The inclusion of the therapist's vision as central to the process adds a dimension to the function of interpretation. When the therapist illuminates an aspect of the patient's behavior he is not only pointing out what the patient feels or is afraid to feel but also suggesting the existence of alternatives. For example, if the patient laughs while complaining of the therapist's limited availability, the therapist points out that the patient is covering his anger with the laugh, possibly intimating a reason for the anxiety around direct aggressive expression. The patient is invited to try a new experience: feeling and communicating anger. The pregnant implication is that this aggressive expression is a possible way of relating for the patient; that is, the therapist has a vision of the patient that includes the use of aggressive responses. If, however, the therapist believes the patient is capable of certain forms of self-expression. To continue with our example, often therapists believe that the patient's aggression is so potentially dangerous that attention should not be called to it, she will do supportive psychotherapy in which the aggression is not brought to consciousness. Such a therapist does not have a vision of the patient that includes ways of being aggressive, and the result is an unwillingness to interpret the patient's suppressed aggression. The assumption of every interpretation is that the patient has the potential to do otherwise.

Each interpretation includes both the illumination of a previously walled-off aspect of the patient's behavior and an implication of what might be different, an implied vision of how the patient might relate to others or the world. This look to the future is my understanding of what Kohut (1982) meant by the "forward edge of development." A series of interpretations suggests a composite of who the patient might become. As Loewald (1960) suggested, without such a vision, the therapist cannot help the patient realize new possibilities. However, as is well known from clinical practice, a patient does not simply adopt new ways of being because the therapist suggests they are latent. Quite the contrary, as I illustrate later in the case of Zelda, despite the need and desire to break out of pathological patterns, the analysand tends to remain wedded to the old ways of being and relating, often at great cost. This underside of the ambivalence is conceptualized in classical terms as resistance. As I have indicated elsewhere, sustaining the old patterns provides a sense of self that is jeopardized by their relinquishment (Summers, 1993, 1997). As we saw in chapter 2, the recalcitrance of pathological patterns constitutes a defense against a different future so that the patient's sense of time is frozen, and the future is nonexistent. She either does not see other possibilities or, if she does, cannot believe in their concrete implementation. By subjecting the patient's current patterns to in-depth exploration, the therapist is not just interpreting the present and past but also suggesting the existence of alternatives—the possibility, that is, of a different future.

The therapist's vision is a counterforce to the patient's sense of temporal stagnation. This is why Loewald (1960) believed that the analytic process was not possible without the therapist's vision of possibilities the patient does not see. Here we have a different way of understanding the time-honored concept of the analytic alliance: the therapist is allied with the patient's latent possibilities. The analysis is fought on the battleground of the therapist's vision, which is derived from indications of the patient's buried self and the patient's refusal to explore a different future. The analysand's defenses oppose the realization of latent possibilities, the stifling of which created the very frustration and symptoms the analysis is attempting to change. A central component of the analysis is the recognition and continual working through of the patient's defenses against the realization of possibilities contained in the analyst's vision of the patient.

Loewald hinted that, by emphasizing the therapist's vision, he was pointing the way to a different emphasis in therapeutic action. He stressed the importance of appreciating the patient for who he is so as to bring his potential to fruition, a critical therapeutic stance he regarded as the spiritual side of the analytic process. Loewald's conceptualization of this spiritual aspect underscores the critical distinction between topographic shifts and the emergence of new ways of being and relating. Loewald did not, however, draw out the implications of this sketch to forge a new technical strategy. In his view, the mutative power of the therapist's vision lies in the patient's identification with it. This emphasis on identification presents a major problem in his theorizing as it conflicts with his idea of the therapist as the sculptor, whittling away until the patient's form emerges. If the therapist's vision is based on the evolution of the analysand's material, the patient will experience the vision as an authentic reflection of a self in *status nascendu*. This emergence of the self in the process of analytic inquiry renders unnecessary identification with the therapist's vision. If we carry to its logical conclusion Loewald's contention that the therapist's vision is formed from the patient's material, the therapeutic action lies not in identification but in the dialectical interplay between the therapist's vision and the patient's spontaneous gesture. The result of this process is the emergence of the true self.

As Loewald pointed out, the therapist's fear of molding the patient to a preformed image prevents the conceptualization of the therapist's vision and the future dimension as key components of the analytic process. Although the fear of imposing one's prejudices on the patient is an understandable concern, it can be avoided if the therapist forms and reforms this vision in accordance with the emergence of the analysand's material. As defenses are interpreted and subside in the course of the analysis, the image of the patient's future must be constructed from indications the patient provides. It is this dimension of the therapist being "behind" the patient that mitigates against the intrusion of the therapist's preconceptions. Furthermore, as Loewald showed, the therapist cannot help the patient realize new possibilities without a vision of the future. Given the inevitability of the future dimension, more harm can be done by the therapist's suppressing her image of the future than by recognizing it and consciously formulating it in response to the evolution of the patient's material.

To therapists who might question the possibility of distinguishing the true from the false self, consider that all psychoanalysis and psychoanalytic therapy is predicated on just such a distinction. Every defense interpretation is based on precisely the ability to differentiate affects regarded as belonging to the patient's experience from anxiety-motivated protective strategies. Anyone who conducts psychoanalytic therapy operates on the same premise that underlies the distinction between the true and false self. The difference between the true self–false self distinction, on one hand, and the defense/affect interpretation, on the other, lies in the difference between ways of being and discrete mental events, not in the judgment of differentiating affective experience from self-protective strategies.

Jonathan Lear (1998) has perceptively pointed out that psychoanalysis is not a form of esoteric knowledge but a special kind of mental activity characterized by in-depth self-reflection. While I agree with Lear that psychoanalysis is defined by process rather than content, any conceptualization of analysis as a reflective process would be incomplete without including the fact that investigation of the self is guided by the therapist's vision of the patient which, in turn, grows out of the patient's affective expression. Furthermore, the reflection that is the hallmark of psychoanalysis reaches gold when the patient is able to create new meaning, a process made possible by interpretation but not tantamount to the interpretive exercise. Reflection alone does not define analysis because understanding by itself frequently falls short of achieving the analytic goal of self realization. The special activity that is psychoanalysis comprises not only understanding the self that is, but also the use of the spontaneous gesture to create possibilities that have not yet been. In the dialectic between the therapist's vision and the patient's spontaneous gesture, the latter is a creative expression that forces a re-vision on the therapist who uses this new image to foster new possibilities, possibilities that include the patient's spontaneous creations leading the therapeutic journey in new, unforeseen directions.

CLINICAL ILLUSTRATION WITHOUT THE
THERAPIST'S VISION: ANNA O

One way to see the clinical value of conceptualizing the therapist's vision of the patient is to look at a case in which such a concept is missing or ignored by the therapist. There is no better example of this omission than the very first analytic case, Bertha Pappenheim, or Anna O. Breuer's treatment affords such a clear illustration of the effects of ignoring the therapist's vision that the case is worth reviewing in some detail.

As is well known, in July of 1880, Bertha Pappenheim, a gifted 21-year-old woman, while nursing her ill father, became ill with a persistent cough, weakness, and anorexia (Breuer and Freud, 1895). After being forbidden to care for her father, she deteriorated even further. She took to her bed and developed hysterical blindness, muteness, and paralysis while alternating between "clear" states in which she seemed rational and "naughty" states in which she was irritable, angry, and agitated. Breuer found her in autohypnotic states during which she muttered in an apparently incomprehensible manner.

It is now known that Breuer was impressed by more than the young woman's illness. He recognized the powerful intellect, eloquence, and imagination that had been "undernourished" by the severely limited educational opportunities available to her (Hirschmuller, 1989). Struck by her fluency in five languages and her astounding memory for detail, Breuer immediately saw that he was in the presence of a prodigious intellect. But Breuer took note of more than her considerable intelligence: he admired her tenacity, critical thinking, independent judgment, compassion, and good nature. Breuer was convinced that her capacity to help people would serve her well in life and "should be exercised at the earliest" after the termination of treatment (Breuer and Freud, 1895, p. 21).

The family was training Bertha to carry on the Orthodox Jewish tradition by becoming a homemaker. Her father was puritanical and severely restrictive, insisting that his daughter follow the lifestyle dictated by his religious beliefs; and her mother was hypochondriacal and preoccupied with the loss of two daughters to tuberculosis. Breuer observed that Bertha "sought compensation in passionate fondness for her father, who spoiled her and reveled in her highly developed gifts of poetry and fantasy" (quoted in Hirschmuller, 1989, p. 276). In Breuer's unpublished case history, he noted that his patient was in total disagreement with her father's religious views even as she tried so hard to please him and ultimately devoted herself to him. She went through the motions of learning to become an Orthodox housewife while she withdrew into private fantasy to escape the tedium of her life. Nobody in her family noticed that she had withdrawn from the world of her external behavior; they seemed unaware that, in a very real sense, she was "not there."

When Breuer echoed Bertha's "mutterings," she talked to him about what bothered her, described her states, symptoms, and hallucinations and embarked on chains of associations that led her to the beginnings of her symptoms. After sessions she invariably felt better and functioned well until the next day, when the cycle repeated itself. Although she began to recover, when her father died, her symptoms worsened, and Breuer admitted her to a private sanitarium where he was able to visit her only once every three days. Another cycle ensued: she did best on the day after Breuer's visits, was distractable on the second day, and by the third day had deteriorated markedly.

When her condition improved sufficiently for her return to Vienna, Breuer began to visit her two or three times a day. During these hypnosis sessions, he took her back to the period of the first phase of the illness, and she insisted on reliving the events in exact reverse order to arrive at the psychic trauma of each symptom. According to Breuer's (1895) published report, each such symptom disappeared after the retelling, although he acknowledged that some symptoms disappeared spontaneously and others were not removed until later. We know from the unpublished record that the treatment did not achieve the complete result Breuer had indicated; in fact, Bertha Pappenheim spent three months after termination in a Swiss sanitarium and was hospitalized on three subsequent occasions over the next four years (Hirschmueller, 1989).

After the last of these hospitalizations and about five years after her treatment with Breuer ended, Bertha Pappenheim, then 29, moved to Frankfurt with her mother, a move that was a critical turning point in her life (Tolpin, 1993). Bertha became a part of the social circle of her mother's family; the Goldschmidts were wealthy German Jews, cultured and sophisticated. These relatives, who accepted Bertha and appreciated her intellect and wit, exposed her to their strong values and social purpose, especially the German feminist movement and social welfare. For the rest of her life, Bertha Pappenheim devoted herself to fighting for the rights and needs of Jewish refugees from Eastern Europe, orphans, homeless teenage girls, pregnant teens, and unmarried women. She founded a home for delinquent and pregnant teens over the opposition of Orthodox rabbis. For refugees, she helped establish programs to meet educational, vocational, and social needs. She became an outspoken feminist, deploying her extraordinary intellectual and linguistic talents to the study of the history of Jewish ghetto women and translating the works of former Jewish feminists. She also wrote essays on the subjugation of Jewish women, outwardly expressing her convictions in clear opposition to her parents' beliefs. There is no indication of any symptom return from the time of her move to Frankfurt.

The evidence points to the conclusion that Breuer's "talking cure" helped considerably but did not lead to the total and lasting cure that Breuer had hoped for and was implied in his published case report. Bertha Pappenheim's recovery was not complete until at least five years after her treatment with Breuer had ended. She found purpose and meaning in her life only after she formed bonds with the Goldschmidts, who helped her relinquish her compliance, give voice to her convictions, and exercise her talents.

It is striking that this realization of her potential included not only her opposition to Orthodox Judaism and her outspoken advocacy of women's rights, but also the very character traits that Breuer had identified in 1880 when he first saw her. During the last 40 years of her life, Bertha Pappenheim deployed in the performance of extraordinary acts of social justice, the natural compassion and kindness Breuer had so quickly identified. Her obstinacy and critical judgment, two traits also recognized by Breuer, formed the basis of her feminism and opposition to the orthodoxy in which she had been brought up. Her life became meaningful and fulfilled not at the time of her termination from Breuer, but when, in the context of relationships that nurtured her potential, she was able to bring to fruition her talents and dormant personality traits. This exercise of her potential was not separable from her movement to health; it was the very essence of overcoming her neurotic misery. Her social work was the realization of her natural compassion and capacity to help others, a need Breuer recognized but could not help her meet. Her scholarly studies of Jewish feminists and translations of their works and essays employed the exceptional intellectual capacity that had been stifled by her family and given expression in her early life only in the pallid substitute of private fantasy.

Breuer recognized and took seriously Anna's "mutterings" as an effort to communicate. His recognition of who she was and his ability to see the meaning in her communications accounts for Anna O's coming alive in his presence and her subsequent return to her symptomatic and dysfunctional condition after he left. To Breuer's credit, he deplored the upbringing that had stifled the development of her impressive potential. Recognizing how unfulfilled she was, he saw that her outward compliance prevented her from giving voice to her beliefs and potential and that her "private theater" and devotion to her father were compensation for an empty life. Furthermore, unlike her father, Breuer grasped the importance of her being able to use her talents for social good.

However, because Breuer believed the treatment was only about getting affects "unstuck" by reliving the roots of their strangulation, he did not regard her unrealized potential as a target of the treatment. Although Breuer seemed to bring Bertha out of her arrested state, these improvements were only temporary as his limited concept of the treatment did not include a vision of Bertha's potential. It is plausible to conclude that this omission was a major factor in her continued illness when he terminated with her. The incomplete nature of Breuer's treatment can be attributed, at least in part, to the fact that, although he saw her need to utilize her potential, he separated that need from the therapeutic process. Breuer *had* a vision of Bertha's future, but rather than regarding it as part of the treatment, he believed that the exercise of her gifts could wait until after the treatment ended. Consequently, she had no opportunity to realize her potential during the time she saw Breuer. The physician's failure to include his vision of Bertha as a potentially productive intellect and compassionate advocate for the unfortunate limited his ability to help her transcend the confines of her repressive upbringing. While Breuer relieved Bertha's suffering a great deal by giving audience to her previously repressed affects and dissatisfaction, he ultimately could not help her become free to utilize her talents and suppressed personality dispositions. Had he regarded his vision of Anna's future and the nurturing of her potential as part of the treatment, he might have helped her create new ways of being and relating to replace the constrictions of her past.

It was left to the Goldschmidts to facilitate the realization of her personality traits, intellectual potential, values, and convictions. While Breuer grasped this potential, the Goldschmidts helped her to realize it. These relatives helped Anna bring to fruition the potential Breuer recognized but had been unable to effect. To her family she was invisible, Breuer saw who she was under her surface compliance, and the Goldschmidts helped her become that person. In a very real sense, the Goldschmidts completed the therapeutic process begun by Breuer.

A CONTEMPORARY CASE WITH THE ANALYST'S VISION

Now let us compare Breuer's treatment of Bertha Pappenheim with a bit of the psychotherapeutic process of a contemporary case in which the therapist's vision of the patient was integrated into the therapeutic endeavor. Zelda, a case discussed elsewhere in detail (Summers, 1999), entered therapy for help with long-term depression and a severe binge-eating disorder. By her own admission, her mother had never bonded with her, and playing a passive role in the family, submitted to her husband's volatile, destructive temper outbursts. These explosions had intimidated Zelda and her two siblings to the point that the family lived in fear of them. Manifestly beautiful, Zelda had always been regarded by her family and herself as "the pretty one" who lacked intellectual capacity. Playing this role with exquisite skill, she was charming and flirtatious, easily attracting the attentions of men. The duplicity she felt in assuming this external posture evoked self-hatred, an attitude she never expected to change. Despite viewing her social adaptation as a false and even offensive presentation, she felt trapped in it. Although Zelda regarded her flirtatiousness as fraudulent and the admiration she won from it unreal, it was her primary way of relating to others.

Zelda felt overwhelmed by life tasks and allowed her husband to assume all household responsibilities, financial and otherwise. Never voicing her own desires, Zelda assumed she was helpless to control her fate. Although she hated her job, she felt it was the best she could do; miserable in her marriage, she felt hopelessly dependent on her husband. Indeed, Zelda seemed not to question her helplessness and did not expect to be able to make any significant changes in her life. She came for help because she was depressed and bulimic but saw no connection between those symptoms and her fraudulence, self-hatred, and helplessness.

Most striking about her presentation was the virtual absence of volition. Nothing she did or said ever seemed to emanate from desires of her own. In Winnicott's terms, there was no spontaneous gesture. As Zelda lived according to the cues of others, her actions were all *re*-actions, anxiety-driven protective strategies. Furthermore, Zelda had never questioned her obliviousness to her own affective states and assumed her therapy would be as other-oriented as the rest of her life. Without ambition or goals, Zelda voiced few desires, had little awareness of her affects, and seldom overtly opposed others' ideas; she would agree on the surface no matter what her affective reaction may have been.

Sensing the value I placed on understanding, Zelda quickly agreed with my interpretations, a strategy designed to convince me of her self-inquisitiveness. When I noted that she appeared to value my comments only to please me, she said that she had manipulated and conned her previous therapists and expected to do the same with me. In response to my comment that she seemed unwilling to assert her own viewpoint, Zelda acknowledged her need to do so but voiced the belief that such assertiveness was "butch." This admission illuminated her equation of femininity with helplessness. Here Benjamin's vision of transcending antinomies was most helpful. Because Zelda had a deep conviction that agency is masculine, she believed she had to choose between her feminine identity and the pursuit of her desires. I set my sights on helping Zelda become author of her life by transcending this antinomy.

We understood her need to charm and please others as the way she learned to avoid her father's hair-trigger temper, to which the rest of the family had been subjected. Despite this awareness, Zelda continued to feel that noncompliance was too threatening to risk. Notwithstanding her disavowal of ambition and desire, Zelda remarked that there had to be some meaning in having binged almost in front of her parents' eyes as an adolescent. Later, when she defined herself as the "pretty one" who had been socially popular while feeling empty inside, I suggested that her bingeing was a protest against being imprisoned in an identity she found devaluing and false. Unable to contain tears at being recognized, Zelda felt that a plea from deep inside her had finally been heard. Most meaningful to her was the realization that I saw her bingeing as a reflection of her buried desire to be more than her looks, a meaning she had not been able to articulate to herself.

My remark was an interpretation, but it conveyed more than defense against affect; it reflected a vision of Zelda as desiring something beyond her shallow life of pleasing others and implied that alternatives were possible. For a period of time after my recognition of her bingeing as a plea from her buried self, Zelda felt like crying almost every time she entered my waiting room for an appointment. Tears provided the outlet for the feeling that another person saw potential within her for an enriched life and ownership of that life was not inconceivable. Entertaining such a notion was so novel and fantastical to her that she could respond only with an emotional flood.

My conviction that the fulfillment of goals was not only possible but potentially gratifying to her came not from a blind optimism but from indications contained in her behavior. Her symptoms indicated a sense of emptiness for which she attacked herself mercilessly, yet, with even the slightest prompting, she showed abundant intellectual and emotional curiosity regarding herself and others. I was convinced that I was in the presence of a woman with untapped intellect starved for mental stimulation, a woman convinced of her inability to achieve goals but seething with rage at her imprisonment in a life without authorship. From the behavior she showed me I constructed an image of her as capable and desirous of exercising intellect and ambition without any loss of femininity. Guided by Benjamin's (1997) vision of transcending oedipal complementarity, I was "ahead" of Zelda in recognizing her as craving intellectual stimulation and possessing a stifled ambition for achievement.

Zelda's response to this interpretive theme was that she had construed her identity as "the pretty one" to mean she was stupid. When we understood her lack of intellectual confidence as a reflection of her parents' need to dismiss her as "the pretty one" whose only value lay in her physical attractiveness to men, she concluded that therapy "supported my intelligence." In this way, the interpretation of her socially agreeable veneer as a defense was not only an illumination of her anxiety in recognizing her affective states and sense of vulnerability, but also the furnishing of a certain kind of holding, the provision of an environment in which her intellectual capacity and interests were seen and valued simultaneously with awareness of her vulnerability and motivations. She felt "held" not because I gave empty reassurance but because, by seeing possibilities beneath her limiting self-definition, my vision embraced very real capabilities, such as her intellectual talent. Thus, when we reached beyond her defenses, I did not see only a "defect" or deficiency as Zelda expected but new possibilities that included a capacity for intellectual discourse and the desire to achieve.

IIere we can see a technical implication of thematizing the therapist's vision of the patient. Inclusion of the therapist's image of the analysand's potential in the interpretive process balances the patient's anxiety and vulnerability with unrealized potential. This addition to the interpretation minimizes the dilemma therapists frequently face of either injuring the patient or becoming overly cautious to avoid doing harm. The patient is more able to accept feelings of inadequacy if, at the same time, he sees that these painful affects are connected to undeveloped capacities.

As Zelda began to entertain the possibility of creating new ways of being from long-dormant potential, her dissatisfaction at never having used her intellect nor pursued ambitions began to emerge. She complained bitterly that her brother had been expected to go to medical school, while she had assumed the world of academia was beyond her. Despite evincing abundant curiosity about the body, health, the mind, and their relation to emotions, she had never considered the possibility of pursuing any of these interests. Now, however, she connected her chronic depression and bulimia with what she referred to as "the starvation of my intellect." In the midst of this discussion, Zelda unleashed a spate of rage at her parents for their devaluation of her that she recognized as the root of her eating disorder. The desire to use her capacities and the emerging frustration at their arrestation may be regarded as a spontaneous gesture, the appearance of desire previously buried beneath her anxiety and helplessness.

In the course of the recognition that her charming, socially acceptable veneer was a defense against her feelings of inadequacy and emptiness, Zelda began to display direct indications of her aggression. Angry at me for attacking her social adaptation without comforting her, she felt that I was not properly taking care of her by abandoning her at the end of each hour, leaving her alone with her pain. While I had hoped to see some expression of her buried aggression, I was taken aback by the virulence of her rageful outpouring. Feeling unfairly accused, I was tempted to either defend myself or interpret her rage as a reaction to injury. Nonetheless, I decided that what Zelda needed most was a welcoming of long overdue aggression, the deployment of which would be necessary if she were to assert herself and pursue ambition. I responded by commenting that her apparent unfailing agreement with my interpretations must have hidden an angry reaction that she was unable to articulate at the time. Zelda was shocked to find her criticism taken seriously; but, having no belief that aggressive feelings could become a meaningful part of the therapeutic dialogue, she was convinced that her aggressive outburst had irreparably disturbed our bond. However, I noted that she was now developing the ability to communicate long-buried aggressive feelings. I believe that this appreciation for the patient is what Loewald (1960) was referring to when he emphasized the spiritual side of the psychoanalytic process.

My posture was that this expression of anger toward me created a new dimension in our relationship: the use of aggression to assert some control and influence in how I related to her. My acceptance of her aggression and welcoming of it as part of the therapeutic dialogue, a process referred to by Bollas (1987) as "celebrating the analysand," facilitated the inclusion of her aggressivity within the previously aggression-inhibited therapeutic relationship. A significant dimension to this incorporation of aggressivity into her personality organization was that it did not come at the cost of enjoying femininity and receiving the attentions of men. Rather, Zelda was able to regard herself as possessing both "masculine" and "feminine" traits, neither threatening the other. In the full force of her anger, Zelda did not feel "butch." This transcendence of the antinomy demonstrates the crucial role of the analyst 's nurturing the patient's dormant side.

I saw her aggressive explosion as the emergence of long-dormant potential, the transformation of which could facilitate the realization of buried ambition. That her aggression surfaced initially in such intense form is to be expected given her history of compliance and does not diminish the fact that her explosive outpourings constituted a spontaneous gesture. Of course, this is not to say that all aggressive explosions by patients should be welcomed as the emergence of the true self. The celebratory response to Zelda's aggression was a therapeutic posture guided by an understanding of her inhibitions and a vision of her buried desire to become ambitious. That her aggression had been suppressed made her explosion a positive development: the appearance of the potential to use her anger to assert her volition. Clearly, this was an especially significant step for Zelda, given her inability to experience a sense of agency. I regarded her aggressive outbursts as the initiation of a sense of agency, an assertion of her desire that opposed what I was doing. My vision of her potential use of aggression led me to welcome it as a move forward.

After Zelda saw that her forceful expressions of affect disturbed neither our relationship nor her femininity, she was able to use them when necessary for the purpose of exercising her capacities and achieving ambitions. At that point Zelda began to consider new career paths and intellectual interests. Eventually she began graduate school in a field that had always interested her but that she had never pursued because she believed that the considerable discipline and study it demanded was beyond her.

I have presented only snippets from a long and complex analytic treatment to illustrate the importance of the therapist's vision in helping a patient realize new possibilities. The ownership Zelda was eventually able to achieve emerged as she transcended her simplistic categories of masculine–feminine and active–passive. Although Benjamin's (1997) vision provided guidelines for Zelda's possibilities in general terms, the image of who Zelda could become was constructed from elements of her personality emerging in the analytic process. Most important, this vision was continually reformed in accordance with Zelda's spontaneous shifts in the psychoanalytic field.

This concept of treatment is in clear contrast to Breuer's (1895) clinical strategy with Bertha Pappenheim. As we have seen, Breuer had a vision of his talented young patient as utilizing her intellectual talent and natural compassion. However, because he did not regard this image as relevant to his therapeutic work he neither nurtured her frustrated talents nor helped her to achieve her ambitions. Even as Breuer's work with Bertha revealed her rich inner life, he was not able to see more than strangulated affects beneath her defenses. This exclusive focus blinded him to her stifled longings to utilize her starved intellect, compassion, and ambition. And it is this restricted concept of treatment to which we may attribute much of the limitations of his therapeutic efforts.

HELEN, AGAIN

Let us now return to Helen. As we saw in the previous chapter, much like Zelda, she had no sense of a future. Although far more intellectual in her interests than Zelda, Helen had given no thought to formulating those interests into organized ambition; neither woman lived in the futureperfect tense. As with Zelda, the crux of the therapeutic action for Helen lay in the evolution of the ability to project herself into the future. Recall that Helen was able to adopt such a trajectory only after I recognized her passion for literature as having the potential to take on form, to become a future project. Helen's association to her love of literature was a spontaneous gesture to which she gave no meaning. Experiencing this passion as no more than a form of immediate gratification, she had never regarded reading as an interest that could be developed in any way. Helen read like she did everything else: in an endless present. It was incumbent on me to see the possibility that her interest in literature could become more than a pastime. I saw her passion as a kind of "calling," that is, as a critically important part of who she was and what her life could become. The development of this interest, therefore, whether or not it would have vocational implications, would be an essential part of her self definition. I formulated a vision of her as someone for whom the understanding and use of literature was central to her core self. It was my image of Helen built from her talent and passion for literature that began her journey toward the inclusion of literary pursuits as a life ambition.

As we saw in the previous chapter, in this process Helen experienced herself in the future-perfect tense for the first time in her life. My recognition of her love of literature was the beginning vision she required to begin to regard herself as possessing a future.

CONCLUSION

As we saw in our discussions of the therapeutic process with both Zelda and Helen, if the future is to enter the patient's world, the therapist must have a vision of the patient as possessing interests and talents that can be formulated into a projected future. The therapist's vision is necessary for the future to take form in the patient's mind, and the sense of future is essential to the self. Nonetheless, it would be an unfortunate oversimplification of the process to say that self formation is set in motion by the therapist's vision. It must be remembered that the therapist's vision is constructed from raw materials provided by the patient's behavior, interests, talents, and passions. The therapist must build an image of who the patient might become that is not yet seen by the patient but, nonetheless, must fit the depth of the patient's experience if self development is to be authentic.

Authorship of the self, then, requires that the therapist formulate a vision that can be used by the patient. This image will necessarily be modified by subsequent clinical material as the evolution of the analytic process moves the therapy in new and unforeseen directions. Neither Helen nor Zelda was able to see that her interests were not simply pleasures of the moment but potential elements of the self. Helen's interest in literature and Zelda's in health, nutrition, and the body were virtually unnoticed by these women until seen by the therapist. What we have seen in this chapter is the importance of the therapist's vision for the formation of disparate interests, desires, and talents into a self with goals that can guide the patient's life.

Thus the development of futurity and the therapist's vision are interlinked processes, both necessary for the realization of the patient's self. The vision that stimulates the fulfillment of inborn capacities results in a self living in all temporal modalities with a trajectory toward a fulfillable future. This new self is created in the therapeutic process, and we are now ready to look more closely at how patient and therapist interact to bring this about.

4

THERAPEUTIC ACTION AS THE CREATION OF MEANING

When repeated interpretations of the analytic interaction catalyze little movement, patient and analyst may think they are back at the start, but in fact they are not in the same place as their early encounters. The patient, now aware of the meaning of her habitual ways of relating, is not satisfied to continue them. Awareness of the circularity moves the analytic dyad into a relationship in which the old patterns are unacceptable, but no new configurations have emerged. As the patient now questions his reliance on historical transference patterns, the analytic relationship loses its previously defined form and leaves an ambiguous space where there was once a pattern of relating.

As we saw in chapter 1, the establishment of newly authentic aspects of the self requires that the concept of working through either be abandoned or, at a minimum, decisively altered so that the patient can make her own contributions to the therapist's offerings. Learning best takes place by doing, and the process of learning by doing dictates that clinical strategy goes beyond the concept of working through to a view of therapeutic action that embraces the patient's role in creating new patterns. Therefore, to understand therapeutic action, it is important to grasp the basic elements of the creative process.

Repeatedly working on a problem in a seemingly fruitless manner until a sudden change occurs has been found to be typical of both scientific and artistic creativity (Csikszentmihalyi, 1996). A comprehensive understanding of creative production, according to Csikszentmihalyi, includes access to and mastery of a domain, the identification of a problem within the domain, a great deal of hard work on the problem, a period of incubation, a sudden flash of insight in which the problem is seen in a novel way, and finally a great deal of work evaluating and elaborating the insight. Emphasized in this process is the persistent confrontation of a problem without result until a sudden change seems to suggest a fresh approach (Csikszentmihalyi, 1996).

This description of the creative process can be fruitfully applied to psychoanalytic therapy. The therapist's insights make sense to the patient only within the context of understanding her history and dynamics, a groundwork analogous to the mastery of the domain that has been identified as necessary for creative activity. Within the horizon of understanding the patient's life, an individual trait or dynamic will come into focus. This problem will then be the target of analytic investigation, and the dynamic in question then becomes highlighted for solution within the domain.

The failure of interpretation to have immediate impact typically results in a repetition of the proffered insights in the hope of eventually overcoming the patient's historical patterns. As these characterological configurations tend to be stubbornly recalcitrant, the problem becomes how to employ insight to make personal changes. Csikszentmihalyi's studies of creative people show the importance of the seemingly futile, frustrating labor that acts as a preparatory phase for the emergence of creative solutions. In psychoanalytic therapy, the hard and seemingly unproductive battle to overcome stubborn traits and dynamics constitutes the "persistent confrontation" of a problem that Csikszentamihalyi identifies as the necessary propaedeutic to the flash of insight in the creative process. The attempt to translate understanding into new psychological patterns often incubates unconsciously until a sudden association suggests a new approach. If the breakthrough association is to become part of the self, it must be elaborated in subsequent analytic work. The continued articulation of the nascent new direction in the therapeutic process is tantamount to the elucidation of creative insight identified as a key component of scientific innovation.

For the analytic procedure to catalyze self-creation, the time-honored notion of working through must be replaced by the principle that the value of the insight is a function of the way the patient both interprets and makes use of it to fashion a new way of being. The patient's way of understanding the analyst's insight may not be identical to the meaning the analyst gave it. This difference may be one of emphasis or it may be more fundamentally substantive; the patient may even see something in the analyst's intervention that the analyst did not see herself. In some instances, the patient's interpretation of the analyst's comments may bear only a minimal resemblance to the original intention. Whatever the degree of difference in the patient's construction, she will respond to the therapist's understanding according to her preexisting psychological organization, a response which may leave the interpretation intact or modify it in any number of ways. Furthermore, the way the patient uses the insight is a contribution that comes from the patient, a contribution that in Winnicott's (1960) sense "meets" the interpretation. The translation from insight to building new aspects of the self is a piece of creative work that can only be accomplished by the patient. Thus, both the patient's interpretation of the analyst's offerings and the use the analysand ultimately makes of it constitute a creative response to analytic insight.

If a new self is to be created from latent potential, the use to which the insight is put must be of the patient's creation. Nonetheless, as we saw in chapter 1, psychoanalytic theories of technique tend to emphasize the therapist's activity in the change process while reserving a primarily incorporative role for the patient. Placing the patient's innovation at the heart of therapeutic action contrasts with the notion of internalization and its counterpart working through, concepts that provide little room for the patient's creative use of insight. The latter concepts treat therapeutic action as a product of the patient's absorption of the analyst's understanding. By contrast, the current view sees the essence of therapeutic action to lie in the patient's way of processing and using the analyst's understanding.

SOCRATES IN THE CONSULTING ROOM

The function of interpretation in therapeutic action has an analogue in the search for knowledge that takes place in a Platonic dialogue (Hamilton and Cairns, 1961). When Socrates inquires of some poor nonreflective soul as to the nature of some term the latter has used, the object of Socratic inquiry typically makes several attempts to define a word he commonly uses only to find each stab at a definition demolished by Socrates's questions. After it becomes clear Socrates's partner cannot define the concept, the pair may appear to be back at the start, but in fact a new beginning occurs just at the point of frustration with the attempted definitions. At that juncture, Socrates usually asks a question that opens a new arena, and the dialogue is launched. However, the question would not have had the same effect at the start of the dialogue because the interlocutor was sure of his beliefs. Socratic inquiry, which appeared to be getting nowhere, in fact served the invaluable purpose of shaking the partner's unwarranted confidence in his knowledge—the removal of hubris essential for growth—and thereby opened up new possibilities. (It is noteworthy that in Plato's (n.d.) dialogue, *The Meno*, the slave, having no stake in believing he has knowledge, requires no such preparation to learn.)

Psychoanalysis would do well to heed Plato's distinction between the start and the beginning. As Socratic questioning humbled the partner's hubris, it displayed the unexamined assumptions on which he had built his beliefs and, in a very real sense, began the journey toward new knowledge. Analogously, the therapist's interpretations of the patient's presenting modes of being and relating illuminate the defensive nature of those patterns, thus making the analysand aware of the limits of his self-knowledge. Socrates's questioning of assumed truths is analogous to the analyst's defense interpretations often presented in question form, such as, "Did you experience something just there that you avoided?" And just as with Socrates's partner in dialogue, the understanding of defenses often appears to be leading only to frustration as the patient sees her defenses gradually erode but seems unable to find alternative modes of self expression. It is this humbling process of recognizing that "maybe I do not know myself as well as I thought I did" that can produce an openness to new experience in a manner similar to the receptiveness of Socrates's dialogic partner. Far from being pointless and stalemating, analytic understanding of presenting patterns, even if it does not lead to discernible change, can serve the critical function of putting the patient in the position of readiness to experience something new, to consider new ways of being and relating. We might say that the interpretive process has a propaedeutic function.

To be sure, the psychoanalytic process cannot be equated with a Platonic dialogue. There are decisive differences in both method and aim. Plato used dialogue for a purely intellectual purpose. The psychoanalytic process, of course, has a different aim: emotional understanding and the transformation of the psychological organization. The analogy with the Platonic dialogue should not be misconstrued to mean that the analyst questions in Socrates's didactic manner. The analyst's questions, like Socratic queries, are designed to promote the patient's self-awareness, but unlike Socrates's questions, analytic inquiry aims to achieve emotional engagement with previously unseen parts of the self. Rather than being an aggressive intellectual exercise to demonstrate the other's ignorance, the analytic method is a way of enhancing awareness of emotional life. The analogy I see between the Platonic dialogue and the analytic process lies in the preparatory function of both Socratic questioning and defense interpretation. These processes operate by reducing self-certainty and thereby create an ambiguity that can be utilized for a new beginning. Socratic questioning and defense interpretation till the soil for the planting of new seeds.

An example of how a seemingly fruitless defense interpretation shifts the therapeutic field can be seen in the case of Leo, a very bright and decisive 35-year-old investment banker.

He came to therapy for help with marital problems that he feared might be insurmountable. The couple had tried marital counseling to no avail, and the marital therapist, Leo's wife, and Leo all concluded that both members of the marital pair needed individual help to learn to live in a relationship. In the first interview, Leo made clear that he had assumed throughout most of his life that he would never marry, but he felt that the woman who became his wife was so attractive, talented, and special that he changed his mind. In Leo's account of the relationship, after the couple was married, his wife revealed an "agenda" for them that included the purchase of an expensive house and cars and the execution of seemingly endless household tasks. While Leo was not opposed to his wife's goals, he felt his patience was being tried by his spouse's unrelenting demands and insensitivity to their effect on him. Pressured to carry out his chores and errands without delay, he believed that his wife's agenda was her top, perhaps her only, priority and that he had become an instrument for its fulfillment. Furthermore, he complained that his wife's effort to dominate also extended to leisure-time activity; in his view, she tried to limit his time with his friends, and when he did see them, she was vigilant about his whereabouts, what he was doing without her, and the time of his arrival home. If the group included a woman, Leo's wife typically barraged him with a litany of questions that he interpreted as her lack of trust in him. She had very little social life apart from him and sought none, despite Leo's encouragement that she pursue social contacts.

The most significant and traumatic incident of Leo's childhood was being sexually abused by a male neighbor. The most painful aspect of the event, however, was not the abuse itself, but his father's refusal to intervene when Leo told him of the assault. Leo never forgave his father for failing to protect or help him in any way. This passivity in the face of Leo's trauma was a decisive moment in his life as his hatred and disdain for his father never abated. At the time of his entry into psychotherapy, he had not spoken to the older man in many years and refused all contact with him.

Small in stature, Leo had been bullied by bigger boys throughout much of his childhood despite his considerable athletic talent. He was an exceptional student but joined the military out of high school, an event that began his determined effort to become physically strong and capable. He went through a rigorous training program and successfully completed many dangerous, clandestine missions. After his discharge from the service, he continued a strict exercise and weightlifting regime that resulted in considerable physical strength despite his size. Nonetheless, Leo continued to regard himself as not only weak physically but emotionally "soft" in the sense of being solicitous and accommodating to others. Leo was frequently shocked to find that his coworkers were intimidated by his behavior, regarding him as abrupt, harsh, and potentially explosive. The idea that others were frightened of him was so unfathomable to Leo that he could not absorb the information and did not believe it.

As he recounted the marital situation with considerable consternation, Leo's attitude was stark, harsh, and filled with sarcasm almost to the point of coldness as he denounced his wife's "agenda" as stupid, irrational, and controlling. When I observed that his attitude seemed to suggest anger at his wife, he did not deny the affect but was reluctant to admit it. In response to my comment that he seemed hesitant to avow anger, he grudgingly conceded that he was often angry at his spouse, but he hated to admit the feeling. Similarly, he easily acknowledged contempt for his father, with whom he had ended all contact, but was disinclined to verbalize angry feelings despite his scorn for the older man. Affects such as derision were easily accessible to him, but not anger. Whenever I suggested that his contemptuous attitude implied anger, he reluctantly assented, as though I had discovered a secret he had been hiding.

When I noted Leo's difficulty admitting angry feelings, he said that he knew his anger was dangerous, and he believed himself capable of killing. He based this belief on two pivotal incidents. When he was in high school, a male student insulted his sister, and Leo responded by beating up the other boy. In the second incident, a drunken patron in a bar provoked him into a fight. Leo grabbed the man by the hair and slammed his head on a table. In both instances, he wanted to kill the other person. Since those two occurrences, Leo had tried to avoid confrontations whenever possible because he feared he might succeed. He recounted many incidents with coworkers in which he believed the other person to be stupid, incompetent, irrational, or manipulative. When he felt others were trying to blame him for their errors, he found ways to exact revenge, and no one ever seemed to outmaneuver him. His attitude was that by avenging any wrong done to him, he was avoiding becoming angry and doing damage that he would later regret.

Early in the psychotherapy, Leo focused on his hatred of his father and what he regarded as his wife's irrational demands. Feeling that he had to get away from his spouse and her unrelenting demands, Leo frequently felt like fleeing the relationship and, at times, physically removed himself from the house for brief periods. Leo wanted to believe in a direct relationship between his wife's and his coworkers' behavior and his response, whether it be withdrawal in the case of his wife or an active effort at revenge toward his coworkers. Nonetheless, whenever I observed the anger implied in his behavior, he did not fail to admit it was there, although he felt that escape was a preferable response to any threat to freedom.

My clinical strategy was two pronged. First, I interpreted the anger in events in which he felt like escaping, such as from his wife's injunctions, or was disdainful, as he was toward his father. I successfully questioned the immediacy of his connection between his wife's behavior and his own; although he concurred with these interpretations of his anger, he continued to look to escape, and the therapy appeared to be stalemated. Second, I understood his inability to translate this recognition of his anger into life situations as his equating anger with destructiveness. Again, he realized the truth of these interpretations but could not use the insights to bring his anger into problematic situations. Whenever his wife became aggressive about imposing an agenda of tasks on him, he either fantasied escape or removed himself from the situation rather than become overtly angry at her. I questioned the persistence of this behavior despite acknowledgment of his negative feelings. Leo knew that he preferred to escape rather than directly resist situations he found aversive because he feared the power of his aggression, but he was puzzled that he was unable to make use of this understanding. Becoming perplexed, Leo wondered about his reactions to distressing situations, but self-inquiry was not equivalent to finding an answer. It bothered him to not be able to provide an explanation for his behavior.

Given the failure of interpretations of anger to modify Leo's behavior, it would have been tempting to conclude that no progress had been made. However, to do so would have been to miss a subtle but crucial therapeutic distinction. Whereas until this point he had assumed a direct connection between his feeling of suffocation and withdrawal, he now questioned this assumption. No longer confident that he understood his actions, Leo wanted to know why escape seemed like such a natural and even inevitable response. Relinquishing his illusory self-certainty, Leo recognized the ambiguity in his own behavior and the holes in his logic. This stimulation of an inquiry into something he had never before questioned began a shift in the therapeutic space. Correlatively, the therapeutic relationship changed from my efforts to stimulate reflection in Leo to his self-reflection on previously unexamined behavior.

The key therapeutic step of Leo's willingness to probe his immediate reactions is analogous to Socrates's interlocutor's recognition that he did not know what he thought he knew. When Meno found out through Socrates's questioning that he did not know what virtue was, a necessary step was taken in his education as he became open to new ideas on the subject, a process that culminated in his gaining knowledge of virtue (Hamilton and Cairns, 1961). When Leo went through an analogous process in which he finally saw that his assumptions did not make sense of his behavior, he began to wonder what might lie between his feeling of suffocation and the desire to withdraw. The result of this self-inquisitiveness was initially the recognition of his anger and eventually its inclusion in events that would typically have led to withdrawal or disdain.

In the midst of this self-questioning, I asked Leo to associate to his wife's intrusiveness. He responded with a series of thoughts and feelings having to do with his rage at being sodomized and the humiliation he suffered at the hands of children who teased and belittled him for his small stature. As he spoke, his anger and shame intensified quickly until he had to restrain himself from punching the couch. Here was the anger, I said, at the neighbor who had abused him, at his father's passivity, and at his wife for suffocating him. The intensity of his rage at his spouse, which was now almost uncontrollable, was linked to these early figures in his life and the abuse he suffered. At this point it was clear to Leo that what he had regarded as automatic behavioral reactions were, in fact, mediated by potent affects. When he allowed himself space between his wife's behavior and his reaction, he found an outpouring of intense negative feeling, much of which made him anxious. The connection Leo now saw between his spouse's intrusiveness and his withdrawal was not the result of an intellectual understanding but of the discovery of the affective links to his behavior. When I commented that he seemed to feel that his wife abused him, he responded that freedom was most important to him because he needed to know that he could "escape," and he connected this association to the sexual abuse.

He then admitted to a variety of hateful and even murderous fantasies toward his father and his wife, all of which scared him. It occurred to Leo that he had ceased all contact with his father to avoid acting on the rage he was experiencing at that moment in therapy. The connection between his wife and his father puzzled him because his father's sin was passivity and his wife's, intrusiveness. However, when we meditated on his rage at the older man, we were able to see how the two figures had become associated in his mind. He found his father's weakness in failing to respond to the abuse to be humiliating. The link between the two figures was the sense of shame he felt in both relationships.

Nonetheless, the awareness of his murderous, hateful feelings and humiliation was distressing to this intellectual young man. He blamed me for the new image he was constructing of himself. His focus now shifting to my persistent inquiry into his behavior, he found my relentless inquisitiveness to be intrusive. Feeling that I was as tenacious as his wife in pursuing him, even if our goals were different, he wanted to flee the therapy to get away from what he regarded as my unswerving inquisition. I asked him to pause rather than leave or withdraw, to notice how he felt about my probing into his motives. When he did so, he immediately sensed a mounting anger along with the anxiety that he would explode uncontrollably if he felt his emotion in full force. Although he was initially reluctant to articulate his rage, over a period of months he was able to verbalize the potent negative affects. Each time he unleashed an angry invective at me for intruding on his privacy, he anticipated that I would end the treatment. It seemed self-evident to Leo that because he had been honest with me about his unhappiness with some of my behavior, our association would draw to a quick close. He expected that I would tell him that, if he was so dissatisfied with my conduct of the therapy, he ought to seek help elsewhere. In every such instance, Leo was surprised at my willingness not only to continue to see him but also to engage his anger and explore its roots. I noted that he had remained interested in pursuing our relationship despite his strong objections to my clinical strategy. Although he was initially puzzled by this comment, I clarified my point by observing that his anger at me did not prevent him from pursuing a relationship with me. I went on to say that although his negative feelings damaged neither his positive feelings nor our relationship, he expected these consequences from my side of the relationship. In the context of this discussion, Leo expressed surprise and relief that we were able to have this conversation despite the anger that had become an aspect of the therapeutic dialogue. As he did so, Leo saw that his anger at me, no matter how powerful it became, did not damage our ability to talk to each other. It was this experience of vocalizing his anger at me without the anticipated consequences that ultimately resulted in a marked reduction of his anxiety in aggressive expressions.

The continuation and engagement of the relationship was a new experience for Leo. After he expressed dissatisfaction with my behavior, our discussions of his anger at his wife and father, the unresolved feelings around his sexual abuse, and many other issues, represented a new way of relating. As he became forthright about his anger at me and found that these negative feelings were a part of our relationship, Leo no longer felt that anger was a destructive force. Seeing that I continued to be available to him despite his anger, Leo was able to explore the roots of his aggressive responses. His anger at me was rooted in his feeling that my persistent questioning was intrusive and therefore shaming, an effort to expose his "weakness." He saw that his anger was his protective reaction to the threat of shame, the danger of exposing a feeling of defectiveness. In this way, anger had taken on a new meaning for Leo: rather than an intent to destroy the other, anger was a way of fighting back, an effort to protect against vulnerability. Viewed from this perspective, anger now took on a less negative, potentially even constructive intonation.

This shift in what anger meant to Leo made possible the examination of his affective responses to his wife in the moment of their occurrence. If he remained with his wife when she persisted in her demands, his anger intensified; Leo was now able to identify a quickly growing anxiety. Similarly, instead of bypassing his hatred of his father's weakness, he paused on it and realized the depth of anger he harbored. Beyond these situations, he was able to apply his conscious experience of anger to a variety of situations and thereby channel its expression to self chosen ends. If he felt treated unjustly or threatened, Leo unleashed a quick, acerbic response that halted the objectionable behavior. By his own account, Leo attributed the freedom of his negative expressions to the shift in the meaning of anger from an intent to injure to a useful means of self-protection. When Leo left therapy some years later, satisfied with the experience and his marriage, he referred back to this alteration in the meaning anger held for him as the most significant step in the therapeutic process.

Leo's therapy illustrates the way seemingly fruitless defense interpretations can become nutrients in the transformation of the therapeutic space. Although Leo could not respond for a long period of time to interpretations of his anger or any strong affect, he was able to see that his own way of viewing his psyche did not hold up to scrutiny, and it was this recognition that shifted the therapeutic field by changing his attitude to a self-reflective questioning. This opening of a new space in Leo's heretofore closed system of relating made possible the awareness of anger when it was pointed out to him in the therapeutic process. The growing consciousness of anger resulted eventually in Leo's ability to experience and contain anger within the therapeutic relationship. The latter, in turn, eventuated in the creation of a new meaning for anger. This series of therapeutic steps demonstrates that the presumably circular, futile interpretive process was, in fact, the first step in the opening of the therapeutic space for the creation of new meaning.

TRANSFERENCE AND POTENTIAL SPACE

The essential discovery of transference was that unresolved affects from childhood find a new target later in life resulting in adult relationships that bear the mark of earlier caretaking bonds (Freud, 1912). In Freud's view, because the same affect can be directed to different objects, transference preserves selfsame affectivity in the experience of different objects. From the earliest days of psychoanalysis, transference has been recognized not only as a powerful process that explains many pathological phenomena as well as the dynamics of the analytic relationship but also as the most effective weapon in the battle against the patient's pathology (Breuer and Freud, 1895; Freud, 1912, 1914). Freud discovered that the tendency to transfer the experience of early relationships to adulthood is especially characteristic of the analytic relationship, not due to the nature of the relationship but as a product of neurosis. For example, the Rat Man transferred the fear of his father onto Freud (1909), and Dora did the same with her sexual feelings for her father (Freud, 1905). Because the target of the patient's early life dramas is directed to the person of the analyst, the battle to overcome the patient's neurosis can be waged in the battleground of the analytic relationship. In this way, Freud regarded transference as the analyst's most effective weapon in the conduct of his war again the neurosis.

Since Freud's conceptualization of the process, different ways of viewing the transference have arisen in conjunction with the emergence of various psychoanalytic schools of thought. For example, in the Kleinian view, the analytic patient repeats the relationship to the breast (Klein, 1952). From the viewpoint of Kleinian influenced object relations theory, it is the early child–parent pattern that is repeated, either directly with the patient in the role of child and the analyst as the parent, or in reversed form in which the therapist is cast in the role of child, and the patient becomes the parent (e.g., Racker, 1960; Kernberg, 1988). According to self-psychological theory, the therapeutic process mobilizes unmet childhood needs resulting in a treatment relationship in which the patient repeats early childhood longings and the therapist is seen as the parent who was needed to fulfill selfobject functions (Kohut, 1971, 1984). In any of these conceptions, transference is seen as the retention of the same experience across different objects. Thus, while these more recent ideas reconceptualize the content of transference, they maintain its essential nature as a repetition of an early relationship. The purpose of transference being repetition, in any of its forms it preserves the nature of early experience.

By distributing old feelings to new objects, this repetition fits potentially new experience into old categories. Thus, there is an active effort on the patient's part to repeat past experience even if contemporary events appear to be different. Transference is a repetition the patient *insists* on despite conflicting evidence, and the patient even recruits experiences to sustain this mode of experiencing (Spezzano, 1993). For example, if the patient is narcissistically vulnerable, the therapist's efforts to understand are experienced as humiliations. If the patient is envious, he will envy the therapist's knowledge. If the patient uses hostile defenses, he will use the therapist's interpretations as reasons to attack the therapist. The therapist's efforts, no matter how well intentioned, are recruited in the service of repeating preexisting patterns.

In saying that transference maintains the same affect with a different object, we have emphasized the conservative nature of this process. Might it not also be said that the distribution of old affect to a new object indicates that transference is a creative process? It is this idea that has led some theorists to regard the transference as the creation of meaning, rather than its conservation. Perhaps the most articulate advocate of this position is Chodorow (1999), who sees the distribution of affects to new objects as a creative process and therefore regards transference as the psychoanalytic concept that best recognizes the creative aspect of the psyche. For Chodorow, people are compelled to use their emotions and fantasies to interpret the world, and in so doing give it an idiosyncratic stamp of meaning. Because she equates transference with this hermeneutic tendency, she sees transference as the means by which people give their lives unique meaning and therefore as an inherently creative process. This concept of transference seems to be the polar opposite of our definition of the term as an effort to maintain sameness at the cost of novelty. How can we understand this difference?

To equate the bestowing of personal meaning with transference, as Chodorow does, is to violate the meaning transference has always had as the *transfer* of old experience onto new objects. If affective life and meaning are transferred, they are not changed and new meaning cannot be created. When the Rat Man feared Freud (1909) would attack him, he was not creating new meaning; he was transferring old meaning, fear of his father's attacks, onto a new object. In this way, he treated a potentially new object, Freud, as the old object, his father. Therefore, to call the creation of new meaning transference is to lose the essential meaning of the term. By transferring affects from earlier in life to current figures, the patient is precluding the experience of novelty by refusing to see the current situation as new. As an effort to diminish the originality of experience by giving it preexisting form, transference is not creative but conservative.

The distinction between transference and the creation of meaning is critical to the therapeutic process because the therapist tries to resolve transference but aims to create new meaning. If transference is the process of creating personal meaning, why do we hope to resolve it? The very fact that we have a concept of transference resolution indicates that we regard the transferring of early affects onto current objects as problematic; we certainly would not want to pathologize the process of giving personal meaning to life. Therefore, it is fundamentally important to recognize the distinction in the clinical encounter between efforts to understand and resolve transference on the one hand, and the creation of new meaning on the other. This is not to say that Chodorow is wrong in her contention that people are compelled to endow the world with personally created meaning. On the contrary, I agree that people are hermeneutic in nature; we are interpretive beings (Gadamer, 2000). I object only to Chodorow's equating this general human tendency with transference, which by definition opposes the creation of new meaning by sustaining old meaning in the face of new experience.

We can use Chodorow's conflation of the creation of meaning with transference to develop a critical clinical distinction. While transference provides the analytic space with a rigidly defined content, the creation of meaning requires a space with the ambiguity necessary to maximize creative possibilities. That is to say, if the patient is to create new meaning, the analytic space must contain an openness that precludes a defined content. As we saw in chapter 1, such a space is a potential space, a consciously designed relationship the content of which is yet to be created. By contrast, transference closes space by fitting experience into preexisting categories, thus limiting the possibility of new creation. While transference meaning antedates the therapeutic relationship, the meaning of potential space is yet to be determined. The establishment of potential space, therefore, requires that transference meaning be overcome sufficiently so that new meanings are possible. Transference and potential space represent two very different but essential aspects of the therapeutic relationship.

THEORY OF TECHNIQUE

From the time Freud established the importance of the transference, theories of psychoanalytic technique have historically divided the psychoanalytic process into three components: interpretation in the transference, interpretation outside the transference, and understanding of the patient's past (e.g., Meninger and Holzman, 1958; Dewald, 1964; Fenichel, 1945). A plethora of theoretical work has been directed to the relative emphases of these elements and how to use each aspect of the process. A wide range of theoretical viewpoints are united in their common focus on utilizing these constituents to achieve therapeutic benefit. Despite the popularity of this concept of the analytic process, it fails to include a crucial component: the creation of new ways of being and relating. I submit that Winnicott (1971) introduced a fourth, and crucial, aspect of therapeutic action with his concept of potential space. Inclusion of the notion of potential space in the theory of therapeutic action decisively shifts our understanding of how the process works and the nature of the therapeutic field.

When all aspects of the patient's relationship to the analyst are conceptualized as transference, the crucial difference between transference and potential space is blurred. Such a global concept of transference does not differentiate the space in which old patterns are repeated from the opportunity for the creation of new ways of being and relating. Stern (1994) has drawn a similar distinction between the "repeated" and "needed" relationship to the analyst, but in his view, the "needed" relationship has a predetermined content, a concept that removes the possibility of potential space. If the therapeutic goal is to author the self, the relationship the patient needs does not have a content that can be foreseen but, existing only in potential form, must be created in the space opened by transference analysis.

Interpretation of the transference helps the patient see the origins and meaning of her template for relating to the analyst, but all too frequently the patient unconsciously fits transference experience into preexisting patterns so that a sense of fatedness becomes attached to the old configurations (Bollas, 1989; Strenger, 1998). Unable to see alternatives to her historical patterns, but no longer wanting to continue the dysfunctional configurations of the past, the patient not only feels stalemated, but also confused, disoriented, and helpless. The analytic relationship becomes enclosed in a rigid pattern, freezing the analytic space so that no other possibilities are seen. Referred to as the "transference neurosis" in conventional analytic parlance, this clinical situation is the commonplace transference–countertransference stalemate in which the analytic interaction becomes subsumed in a repetition of the patient's history.

Between the relinquishing of the old and the failure to find the new is a void in which the patient has no anchoring points for navigating the interpersonal world (Summers, 1997, 1999). Not only does the patient feel the threat of nonexistence, the analyst cannot avoid the anxiety that the patient's sense of self is slipping away. To diminish this dread, both members of the analytic pair are tempted to believe that if the dynamic were simply better understood it would be relinquished. Yet the perceived void provides the openness needed for the establishment of potential space. As Winnicott (1971) demonstrated, the less structure provided by the analyst, the greater the opportunity for the patient to create her own meaning from the analytic relationship. Often the patient's incipient self-expressions remain undeveloped because the analyst does not see their potentially decisive importance. To interpret such nascent states as transference is to miss their potential to become new ways of being. At this point, repeated interpretations of the transference are counterproductive because they militate against the opening of the space to new possibilities. In other words, interpretation would be operating in transference space, whereas the patient requires potential space to make use of the void. Moreover, to interpret the patient's inability to extricate herself from historical patterns as resistance, to attempt to rectify the frustration by the provision of functions, or even to take an active role in the creation of a new relationship is to interfere with the potentiality of the space created between patient and analyst.

By refusing to impose meaning, the analyst injects a disconcerting ambiguity into the analytic field. The patient believes the process is stalemated and must be moved ahead but does not see that confusion born of understanding is a potential space in which creation can take place. When the patient responds to the lack of structure with confusion and even disorientation, the most productive analytic attitude is to indicate, either in word or deed, that this very uncertainty provides the opportunity for the patient to create a new relationship. The analyst's response to the patient's confusion is some form of, "That's the point. The process is where it needs to be." This attitude not only maintains the void but also provides a boundary that inevitably limits the openness of the analytic relationship without prematurely shaping it.

While the patient attempts to keep the old pattern, the analyst tries to open the analytic field to new possibilities. When the historical patterns give way and the analytic space is opened to new constructions of meaning, the relationship can no longer be characterized as transference, but as an open space receptive to new forms. Successful transference resolution transforms the therapeutic space from the rigidity of transference repetition to potential space.

We have seen the clinical operation of this distinction in the case of Leo. When this young man was seething with rage but feared its expression, he was ensconced in the transference meaning of anger as destructive. Anxious over the damaging effects he assumed to inhere in aggression, he avoided its expression toward me as he had toward his father. When repeated interpretations disrupted his connection between objectionable behavior and his withdrawal reflex, he was perplexed in his attitude toward his experience. As the cracks in his previously rock-hard assumptions had the inestimable effect of stimulating self inquiry, Leo lost his sense of self-certainty. The resulting opacity of his self-experience left him in an experiential void while he grappled with discovering buried affective experience. This unclear state became a potential space in which he eventually was able to create a meaning for anger devoid of the implication of destructiveness.

UNDERSTANDING AS CREATING

When potential space is opened by the relaxation of defenses, whatever arises at this point may be regarded as a free association in the broadest sense. However, rather than material to be interpreted in terms of its meaning in the past, such free associations, being indicators of potential ways of being, point to the future. As we saw in chapter 2, the patient's free associations not only indicate what the patient has been but also point toward what she may become, thus rendering the future dimension an inherent part of the analytic process. As such, free associations are best read at this juncture not as derivatives of warded-off affects but as possible directions for the formation of new patterns. It falls to the analyst to convey that the patient's spontaneous gestures, expressions of new experience unencumbered by previously existing form, are the best guide to what comes next. The analytic task is to detect the project implicit in the spontaneous gestures evoked in transitional space, even though their eventual shape cannot be foreseen.

Uncovering indicators of potential requires a sharply different way of engaging free associations than interpretation of meaning in past experience. As we have seen, associations in potential space are analogous to an infant's spontaneous gestures, or, in Ferenczi's (1911) poetic description, the infant's outstretched arm that seems to be reaching for the moon. An incipient interest, desire, or ambition will emerge in however nascent a form and, once elaborated into its full meaning, has the capability of issuing in new, more authentic ways of engaging the world. However, as the patient is typically only aware of a vaguely defined, unformed experience, the potential of this emerging material is rarely seen by the patient until recognized by the analyst. For this reason, the analyst's vision of the patient, described in chapter 3, becomes critical.

Just as the infant does not know her experience until the parent's gaze makes it real, so the patient does not believe in the reality of her unformed states until the analyst recognizes them. As Benjamin (1995) has shown, the child knows the reality of her desires and interests only when they are recognized by the other. The patient is drawn to the direction of the spontaneous gesture, but, lacking articulation and without recognition from the other, the experience does not feel real. In the analyst's grasp of the patient's associations as potential aspects of the self, these budding states have the possibility of becoming articulated into ways of being and relating. By continually illuminating dimly seen aspects of authentic experience, the analyst not only welcomes and promotes the explication of these previously undeveloped states, but in so doing imparts a sense of reality to them. We saw examples of this process in our discussions of Zelda and Helen. Neither woman believed in the reality of her talents or even saw her interests as desires until they were highlighted in the therapeutic process. Once recognized by the therapist, Zelda's interest in health and the body and Helen's passion for literature attained a reality unknown to them before.

At this point, the patient can begin to symbolize and define the new experience and to develop and enlarge it. If these emerging dispositions are nurtured by the analyst, the patient will elaborate these fledgling states into new forms of engagement, forming a new "grammar of being" (Bollas, 1987). Zelda abandoned her passivity in favor of a creative integration of her femininity with new-found ambition and aggression. Similarly, Helen made the literary arts and intellectual stimulation an integral part of her daily life. The association that launches this movement may be as benign as a dormant interest never before linguistically encoded, or it may erupt as a disturbance of the patient's psychic equilibrium. This emergence may take intense, even destructive forms, but the analyst's job is to identify the glimmerings of the buried self rather than react to its distorted expressions, and the patient's task is to find ways to develop these incipient interests and affects into modes of engaging the world.

I am describing a dialectical process between the patient's spontaneous gestures and the analyst's recognition of one or more of them, between the patient's elaboration of the material highlighted by the analyst and the analyst's further appreciation for the patient's articulation of nascent states into new ways of being and relating. If the analyst sees authentic expressions and the patient is able to elaborate unformed states, the outcome of the process will eventually issue in the creation of new aspects of the self. It may happen, of course, that the analyst misperceives an association as possessing potential the patient cannot respond to. In such cases, the interaction, rather than moving toward the articulation of the nascent state, will become stymied, and the material, rather than being more fully developed, will remain superficial. This natural limit to the evolution of the process provides a built-in brake on the analyst's ability to influence the direction of the treatment. The only reasonable analytic strategy at this point is to acknowledge a therapeutic dead end and encourage further associations.

Nonetheless, the analyst's inevitably selective approach to the patient's associations molds the material in a way that immediately limits the analytic space. This temporary structuring is inevitable in order to focus on the delineation of new forms of being. At this point, the therapeutic space loses a great deal of its openness in order to bring to fruition previously arrested aspects of the self. When the elaboration of unformed states is well developed, the space may be reopened or new transference components may emerge. That is, another dialectical aspect of the therapeutic interaction is the movement between the openness of potential space and the structuring needed to make use of the material that emerges from that space. When the latter is in focus, the space foregoes some of its ambiguity but only until new form is created, at which point the field must be reopened for the emergence of new potential.

The patient's free association process in potential space and its recognition by the analyst is illustrated in the treatment of

Bruce, an aimless young man who had little direction and even less motivation to find a path in life. He had as little enthusiasm for his job as for anything else he did. Bruce could give no reason why he was in his field; he never felt he had made a conscious choice to enter it. As with everything else in his life, he seemed to have simply "fallen into" his job without making a decision. Indeed, there was little in his life he felt was a product of his desire. As we discussed the emptiness he felt in his work, he became aware that he was unfulfilled and did not wish to live a life without meaning. Without any sense of what could make his life fulfilling, he felt lost. He decided that he needed to change his vocation but had no sense of where he could go.

Bruce was not struggling with a vocational choice; his confusion about future employment was simply one result of a life without purpose or direction. The therapeutic space became a void in which he wanted to feel something that would provide a sense of self, but he experienced only the emptiness previously hidden under a façade of respectability. During one session, Bruce's thought emerged: "The only time I really feel good is when I help people." While Bruce regarded this association as a passing thought, I asked him to pause and consider what he had just said. I pointed out that in the year and a half he had been in therapy, this thought was the first in which he had mentioned something that suggested a positive motive, rather than simply the absence of a negative one.

Bruce's association and my underscoring of its importance gradually resulted in his taking seriously his interest in doing for others. After experimenting with several career paths, he eventually became the director of a not-for-profit organization dedicated to providing food and clothing for poor and homeless people. Working in this arena gave a depth and richness to his life that he had never before experienced. While the path from the first thought of wanting to do for others to a life in a charitable organization was not without obstacles and difficulties, it all started with a free association that illuminated a desire he had not before articulated, even to himself. My role was to see that his association reflected a significant step forward that could prove fruitful if its importance was appreciated. While the association came from Bruce, I drew attention to it by highlighting its potential significance, and Bruce responded to my recognition of the remark by extending and developing his interest over the course of the psychotherapy.

A much more dramatic illustration occurred in the treatment of an attractive, young woman. Anna had a highly successful career, but she was so fearful of abandonment that she had become characterologically compliant, generous, and self-sacrificing in both romance and friendships to the point that she was frequently taken advantage of. Fearing aggressive expression, she tended to suppress her desires, but she would typically become resentful of the asymmetry of most of her relationships. Anna frequently commented on her mother's repeated remonstrations to restrain any behavior that might discomfort others. Whenever she had a problem with other children, no matter what the conflict, her mother became panicky and told her that she "would not have any friends." After an extended period of therapy in which Anna absorbed the insight that her life was dominated by the equation between aggression and abandonment she had learned from her mother, she recalled being a feisty, strong-willed, stubborn child who insisted on having her way. Her father had often delighted in referring to her as "a pistol." Her mother's repeated insistence that she submit to others' desires was often in response to Anna's determined oppositional behavior that her mother feared would alienate others and leave her daughter alone in the world. Told not to assert her will for fear of losing companionship, Anna's anxiety about losing relationships grew until her character structure was organized around pleasing others.

Suppressing her rebellious self-assertion, Anna honed her skill so well that in adulthood her social calendar was filled for weeks into the future, but she rarely asserted her will with her friends. Most of these relationships were built around Anna's compliance, and her friends found her "easy to get along with." As we discussed her inhibition, she became frustrated with her inability to extricate herself from this pattern and envied people who voiced their desires, even in the face of conflict with others. When I asked her about those she envied, Anna said they inserted their views in every situation and "pushed back" if others had conflicting desires. Although she often regarded such people as obnoxious, Anna longed for their freedom of expression.

When Anna reached the apex of her frustration, she exploded with a rage previously unknown to her. Initially, she unleashed a vitriolic attack at her mother for promoting her fear of abandonment, but this eruption was soon followed by an outpouring of rage at a list of people who she felt had taken advantage of her compliance. These outbursts constituted a free association indicating a previously buried desire to articulate her desires and interests and anger at their suppression. Viewing Anna's angry outburst as the emergence of an assertive way of being rather than the displacement of long-repressed anger at an old figure, I understood her eruption as an expression of both her buried desire to live without the sense of obligation to others' preferences and a long-suppressed aggressiveness that was beginning to gain expression. This way of construing her behavior was an interpretation not of the meaning of her past but of an incipient move toward a different future. I saw her rage as a step toward the realization of potential long dormant within her.

At this point, I maintained an interpretive posture, but the nature of the interpretation consisted of movement toward future possibilities, an interpretation, that is, of who Anna might become. The meaning of Anna's rage was, in my view, not to be found in its developmental origins because in a very real sense her explosion had no meaning in the past. For Anna, aggression of any type had existed only in potential form until the moment of its eruption. Consequently, its meaning lay not in a repetition or enactment of the past but in the initiation of a new beginning, a step toward the future. This spontaneous gesture was simultaneously Anna's first move toward overcoming her abandonment anxiety and the beginning of a newfound self assertion. As her aggression unfolded, Anna discovered her anger. That is to say, her aggression was created as it was found.

ANALYST AS ATTENDANT

In Anna's recognition that she was frustrated in her efforts to assert herself and not let others take advantage of her, a new form of self-expression was appearing that originated in her associations and my grasp of them. When Anna burst forth with her rage, she did not understand her behavior; she only knew that she could no longer contain her anger. The experience itself being inchoate, she was not sure of its meaning; she only knew that she was expressing something in herself that needed to be articulated. I remarked that she was vocalizing a lifetime of frustration with inhibiting her desires. The intent of my comment was not so much to offer new understanding as to facilitate Anna's ability to give meaning to her angry explosion. This clinical moment is an illustration of the importance of the analyst's vision of the patient in the creation of meaning, but, even more important for the present purpose, it shows the spontaneous and surprising way the patient's new ways of being emerge in the free association process, a development often jarring to both patient and therapist. When these spontaneous gestures appear, the therapist must be alert to see their potential. My welcoming the anger as a new, progressive development reflected my belief that Anna and I were inhabiting a potential space in which her aggressive displays could become elaborated into useful forms of behavior.

The critical clinical decision was my view of Anna's newly found aggression not as transference, but as a use of potential space, a spontaneous gesture with the potential for self creation. The primary basis for this judgment was the fact that the inhibition of her aggressivity had been well understood, and Anna's frustration resulted from the futility of her understanding. As impulsive as her outburst appeared to be, it had been prepared by the hard analytic work of understanding her anxiety over self assertion. The stalemate in which Anna found herself gave birth to a spontaneous, creative gesture, a new way of being that opposed her pattern of compliance. Like creative production in the arts and sciences, Anna's self-creation was a reaction to the ineffectiveness of the existing parameters. In the intensity of her explosion, she introduced feelings that had previously been outside her relationship boundaries. To regard the eruption as a transference reaction originating in anger at an early life figure would have not only conflated the distinction between transference and potential space, but also misinterpreted as repetition what was in fact the beginning of a piece of self construction.

My understanding of her outburst as a step toward a future filled with potential new ways of being was a recognition that Anna had moved beyond transference. Any conceptualization of her anger as the displacement of repressed affect from an early figure would have suggested that she was stuck in the past even as she tried to break out of the mold of her historical behavior. The patient in this situation is often excited about her spontaneous shift to a new way of relating, and Anna possessed this type of enthusiasm. Reducing this forward movement to a pathological enactment would threaten to quash the emergence of a much-needed alternative to her lifelong patterns. For these reasons, patients frequently experience interpretation of the past in these situations as deflating and demoralizing. The therapist who reduces the emergence of new ways of relating to a transference reaction can be likened to the parent whose only response to a child gushing with excitement about some newly accomplished feat is disapproval that the young person seems unable to contain her excitement. My response was to welcome the new development as the emergence of aggressive potential that must be brought to fruition, and Anna's reaction was to feel encouraged to continue aggressive forms of relating.

When Anna apologized for her outburst, I connected her anger to a fear of abandonment. She said that she did not know how to be aggressive and she felt lost, as if she was supposed to pilot a ship without a compass. To my comment that we were now confronting the negative affects she had buried all her life, Anna replied that, ironically, at that moment she was angry at me for "bringing me to this place." I replied that her current feeling was an opportunity to do what she had always felt unable to do: communicate her anger. Erupting at me once again, she said that I did not realize how difficult it was for her to be angry, that to act in this way was to be a different person, and "I don't know who that person is." With considerable wrath, she went on to say that she believed I thought she could simply turn her anger "on and off like a faucet" and that I was expecting too much of her.

At this point, the analysis underwent a period of intermittent verbalization of negative feelings at me and many others in her life, including the friends who seemed to be there only when she was compliant. I responded by illuminating the fact she was now bringing to realization a part of herself that had always existed beneath her surface compliance. Anna feared that she was becoming chronically angry with little provocation, that she would not be able to control herself, and would elicit negative reactions from others. She did not want to become a hostile, abusive person, but she would no longer tolerate being taken advantage of by others. First, I suggested that her assumption was that her only means of self protection was doing injury to others, and that this belief reflected her inability to act aggressively. I went on to say that there was a positive way to view what she was saying. That is, she was expressing a second important value: a desire to remain interpersonally sensitive while she insisted on protecting herself with her aggression. At that point, the analysis became focused on her discovering a way to live on the basis of both values. In this process, she was struggling to create a way of being that she had never before thought possible for herself: a life of caring for others and protection for herself. This key component of the analytic process, in which she worked hard to find a way to be true to both values, is described further in the next chapter.

If Anna's aggressive eruption was a positive development, why did it appear in such an impulsive, explosive burst? The answer is deceptively simple: she knew no other way. From her mother she learned that aggression endangers relationships, that its expression comes at the price of emotional ties. Recall that Anna had been a "spunky," strong-willed child until her mother evoked in her the anxiety that her behavior would lead to a life of abandonment and isolation. Anna interpreted her mother's warnings to mean that aggression was self-centered and damaging to others. If negative affect were not offensive, why would it become a reason for abandonment? To Anna, all this meant that aggression is destructive, and she had no experience to the contrary. Having inhibited aggressive expression all her life, she had no chance to learn how to make use of it to achieve goals. Consequently, she had no experience of deploying aggression within the context of a relationship. That patients like Anna can realize their long-dormant affects only in intense, seemingly impulsive ways has led analysts to set limits on such behavior or interpret its past meaning. Such clinical strategies may be indicated in the midst of transference enactment, but, when the patient is using potential space for creation, emergence of affect, however negative it might be, must be recognized as progress and its kernel encouraged, even if its current manifestation is problematic.

Thus, Anna's aggressive expression was not the discovery of a fixed mental content but the birth of an aggressive way of relating. "Aggression" does not exist separately from this experience; it entails movement to relate in an aggressive manner and an object toward whom the aggression is directed. These characteristics apply to all affective experience: emotions such as interest, enjoyment, and distress all move the person toward ways of relating. The experience of interest, for example, means adopting an interested relation to the world. That is, interpretation in transitional space points beyond immediate experience to new ways of relating. By facilitating the emergence and articulation of Anna's aggression, I was going beyond understanding to the facilitation of a new way of being.

The role of facilitator returns the therapist to the original meaning of the word therapy. The word comes from *therapeutis*, literally "attendants," groups of people who attended to the afflicted in the 12th century. In transitional space, the analyst facilitates psychic healing by attending to the parts of the self that seek to gain realization. As an attendant, the therapist, in this phase, plays a key role in nurturing undeveloped potential.

CONCLUSION

We may conclude, then, that two types of interpretation tend not to be sufficiently distinguished in analytic theory of technique. Within the transference, interpretation is an effort to understand current behavior by grasping underlying motivations and explaining how they came to be, whereas interpretation in potential space is an attempt to bring out dormant potential by stimulating new ways of being and relating. Interpretation within this space uncovers future possibilities rather than the unconscious meaning of what now is. It is this future potential, recognized in the present, that provides the way out of the therapeutic quandary presented by the limits of interpretation.

If understanding is to bear fruit, the analysis must become a space in which the patient is able to realize unearthed parts of the self. The analyst's interpretations of who the patient might become constitute a stimulus for the realization of dormant potential. In this way, the analyst becomes a facilitator, an agent for this process. By keeping the space open and encouraging the patient's experimentation with new ways of being, the analyst continues to play an active role in the patient's articulation of new ways of being and relating. As we have seen, the analyst shifts posture from that of an interpreter of what is to that of a facilitator of what may be. Included in the latter role are interpretations of the patient's potential, or facilitative interpretations. The point at which old patterns are understood but alternatives are not yet developed occurs many times throughout the course of an analysis as patient and analyst achieve depth understanding of particular transference issues and patterns. At the point of frustration with understanding that does not produce change, the analyst is in a position to shift to a facilitative strategy in which the patient's free associations are regarded as indicators of potential alternatives to the old patterns. After new ways of relating become articulated to replace the old patterns, eventually new material emerges that needs to be understood, causing the analysis to resume its focus on interpretation. In this way, the analysis oscillates between the interpretive and facilitative modes.

From this viewpoint, the most critical departure from the past in terms of clinical technique is not the theoretical difference between drive theory and other views of human motivation, nor the consideration of new analytic functions (such as the meeting of selfobject needs), nor even the inclusion of the analyst's impact on the process. It is the concept of the analytic process as the discovery and realization of what has not yet been that decisively distinguishes this view of therapeutic action from the classical viewpoint. At critical points of the therapeutic journey, the therapist's role shifts to that of an "attendant" who nurtures the creation of new ways of being and relating.

Thus the distinction between insight and creation is an artifact of the limited view of interpretation to which analysis has been subject. Interpretation within the transference, being confined to appreciating the existence of current symptoms and patterns, ends at uncovering, but insight that recognizes potential self development initiates creation. In potential space, understanding and creation are inextricably linked as insight is tantamount to the recognition of potential ways of being that are then brought to fruition in the therapeutic dyad. Inherently dynamic, the self, once discovered, moves toward its elaboration if facilitated by an environment that sees and encourages new possibilities.

As incipient states of being are realized, a new component of the self is not simply discovered but created. Moreover, the evolution of various aspects of the self issues in the formation of a new composition, and this process is also a creative act. Bringing together the various pieces of the self in a new way is what Strenger (1998) calls the "project of individuality," which he likens to artistic creation. That is, the outcome of the successful use of transitional space is ultimately the patient's ability to create new ways of being and relating in the world. Adam Phillips (1998) has suggested that the value of life consists in the transformation of what one is "fed by" into the unique self. People come to therapy, he points out, because they are undernourished or are unable to effect a useful transformation of their psychic nourishment. In either case, the patient is a failed artist of her own life, in Phillips's terms. The movement from transference to potential space by Bruce, Anna, and Zelda led in each to an artistic product, the creation of a new self. For each of these struggling persons, the artist was restored.

As we have seen, the art of self-creation requires the emergence of new possibilities. Previously dormant potential is detected, uncovered, and its possibilities explored so that new ways of being can be brought to fruition in the process of creating the self. Therefore, central to the analytic task is the creation of possibilities and their transposition into new ways of being and relating. It is to this process that we now turn.

5

PSYCHOANALYTIC THERAPY AS
THE ART OF POSSIBILITIES

When Anna began to overcome her lifelong pattern of compliance, she immediately feared becoming selfish and disrespectful of others. Clinically, this phenomenon appears with uncanny frequency: on the verge of yielding one trait, people tend to become anxious about falling into the opposite pattern. Patients who contemplate being less aggressive fear becoming excessively submissive, while the aloof individual becomes anxious about dependence, and the formerly clinging patient fears loss of contact. Sensitive people tend to be concerned about selfishness, and the self-centered individual, selflessness. Aggression and passivity, grandiosity and inadequacy, love and hatred, and many other human traits are linked as pairs of antinomies (Benjamin, 1997).

This reversal into the opposite, first noted by Freud (1915), fits with the insight from object relations theory that a child internalizes not an object but an object relationship (Kernberg, 1988). The child's template is a self state connected to an object representation by an affective bond (Kernberg, 1976). Either the self- or object state may be enacted, casting the other in the opposite side of the object relationship. So any expressed pattern is one side of an object relationship. For example, a patient who has a pattern of being a victim has internalized an object relationship of "perpetrator–victim" that can be reversed so that the patient becomes the perpetrator. The upshot of this insight from object relations theory is that pathology is not defined by the patient's tending to be a victim, but by the patient's knowing only the perpetrator–victim pattern; it is of less importance which side is enacted at any given time. Anna feared becoming selfish because a self-involved, insensitive trait was the other side of her submissive–narcissistic internalized object relationship. The two sides exist in a relationship of what Benjamin (1997) calls "complementarity": to move from one to the other is not to change the level of relating but simply to flip the same object relationship to its other side.

The transcendence of old object relational patterns seldom consists of a simple, unidirectional unfolding of a new way of being. More frequently, the patient's effort to jettison one configuration results in the fear of enacting an equally extreme expression of its opposite, and, in some cases, the contrary behavior takes place. The anxiety of reversal into the opposite is the first problem encountered in the emergence of new object relational possibilities. In Anna's case, as she struggled to restructure her relationships, she feared her aggression would explode in uncontrolled outbursts. Her explosion at me, which no longer fit the mold of Anna's past, constituted the appearance of a previously dormant capability in her that had ramifications extending throughout her life.

This response on Anna's part indicates that the problem reflected in her compliance was more than anxiety over the consequences of aggressive behavior; the deeper root of the problem lay in her inability to use aggression to achieve desired ends. Even as she overcame her fear of aggression, Anna did not know how to use it. Her compliance had been an effort to remove all aggression because she did not know how to deploy it in the context of mutuality. When she was not compliant, she burst into explosive, uncontrolled rages. Consequently, she could not sustain a relationship in which her own and others' needs were balanced.

Because a reversal stays within the same object-relational configuration, the enactment of the opposite pole of an antinomy is not more authentic than the original pattern. To become self-centered, Anna would have to bury her sensitivity to and caring for others. Far from being a genuine expression of who she is, a pattern of selfishness would have been an offensive form of behavior that she found alien to her most dearly held values. Submission to others' wishes and an insensitive disregard of them are the poles of the only object relationship Anna knew; consequently, the only change she could envision from acquiescence to others' wishes was unmitigated selfishness, a possibility she found abhorrent.

We now find a second obstacle to overcoming established patterns: however pathological they may be, a valued attribute is usually embedded within them. Compliance reflected Anna's generosity, a characteristic of which she was proud. The problem was that Anna felt she could express her magnanimity only by stifling her need for self-respect, and a switch to unbridled self-interest would violate the generosity of her spirit. For Anna, either trait required the suppression of an important aspect of her self so that neither side of the dilemma was an adequate expression of who she was. Consequently, once Anna unearthed her capacity for self assertion, a disturbing question presented itself: did her newly appearing aggression mean she would lose the very qualities of which she was most proud—her generosity and sensitivity to others? Anna did not know how to pursue her desires without feeling that she had lost her concern for others. In fact, Anna looked and acted bewildered, often simply blurting out, "I don't know how to do this!"

Noting that she was in this dilemma because her generosity had been taken advantage of by others, Anna felt unable to accommodate without subjecting herself to victimization, nor did she know how to set limits without being uncompromisingly obstinate and even hostile. Anna was now confronted with having to decide when she was being taken advantage of and when she might be overly sensitive in protecting herself from exploitation. We now encounter the third obstacle to surrendering a pathological character trait: any alternative is likely to evoke the anxieties the old pattern was designed to soothe. While determined to act on her feelings and desires, Anna knew she would conflict with those who would not be pleased with her lack of compliance. If she were to become aggressive in the expression of her opinions and wishes, would she have to pay the price of losing her friends? Indeed, many of her friends had come to expect and even depend on this pattern of self-denial. On the other hand, if she contained her subjectivity, would she simply be reverting to the passivity she was trying to overcome?

That Anna had never learned to mobilize her aggression in the course of her development explains why, when her anger finally emerged, she feared its explosiveness. Not knowing how to use it to set limits and achieve desired ends, Anna's anger confused her. Overwhelmed by her newly erupting aggression, Anna struggled to make use of it. As Anna became aware of the intensity of her anger, it became clear that her rage was not directed to any one individual nor connected to any particular event or events. A new category of experiencing was now introduced to her that she was striving to organize into ways of being and relating. Anna's anger did not appear as an isolated affect aimed at a specific object, but as an inchoate new type of experience that had the potential to be encoded in various ways. Anna's task was to learn what to do with aggression; many possibilities lay before her. For Anna to make effective use of her negative affects, she would have to create new possibilities, ways of being and relating that she did not yet envision. The creation of meaning out of her nebulous aggression required Anna to imagine and implement heretofore unforeseen possibilities. In this way, the creation of possibilities was an essential step if Anna was to transform her newly emerging aggressivity into a component of her self.

The therapeutic evolution of Anna's assertion of her self-interest is prototypical of the process of unburying long-dormant potential components of the self. A new category of experience appears in inchoate form so that the surfacing of the new material is only a step in the process of self-formation. From a classical perspective, repression is lifted from a distinct experience already formed and directed to a particular object so that the therapeutic action requires only the relinquishing of the defense. However, as we have seen, it is far more common for a category of potential experience to be arrested, resulting in the surfacing of affects that have yet to be formed into organized ways of being. Many possibilities exist for the newly appearing material; a variety of meanings can be created from it. In that sense, the analytic task now becomes the creation of new possibilities.

THE CREATIVE CHALLENGE

Anxieties formerly managed by the old object relational patterns appear as the patient sees a realistic prospect of relinquishing them. Anna's abandonment anxiety emerged intensely as she contemplated asserting her interest. I told Anna, "These deep fears have been with you all your life; they led you to bury your own experience in favor of others. You have always felt that you faced the choice of abandoning yourself in favor of others or being abandoned by others and facing total loneliness." Anna agreed that this choice had unconsciously guided her life and that she had chosen the latter because she feared loneliness more than self-denial. In fact, she became aware of a previously unconscious expectation that others would repay her selflessness with continuous availability and she felt cheated when the expected reciprocity was not forthcoming.

If we define pathology as the disguised expression of buried aspects of the self, we may say that a symptom is an indirect expression of a disavowed component of the self (Summers, 1999). Anna's compliance, reflecting her sense of generosity, helped her form intense relationships but at the price of her personal integrity. To lose the opportunity to give voice to such central components of the self is to suffer self defeat, but the symptom or pathological pattern is the effort of a buried aspect of the self to gain expression, albeit in an indirect manner. Because Anna did not know how to be both self-respecting and generous, her creative challenge could be justifiably stated as: how to be self-assertive and ambitious while living with care and concern for others; or how to be a caring, sensitive person without being a pushover.

Another patient, Shannon, came for analysis because she felt chronically persecuted and exploited by others. A resourceful person, Shannon often discovered new methods and technology that made her work more productive, but she felt that others later used these new ideas without giving her credit. Her friendships were problematic and often ended abruptly when she felt that others were attacking, abusive, or at minimum did not like and were not sensitive to her. Believing that others were only looking for ways to exploit her, she regarded herself as a giving person whose magnanimity was rarely reciprocated. Similarly, she felt the analysis was exploitive, even though she was given a low fee that she almost never paid on time, and accommodations were made to her various demands, such as my accepting her phone calls and frequent change of sessions. Although she was typically late in paying her bill, Shannon felt deeply injured when I pointed out her tardiness. She even exploded with rage at times, accusing me of abusing her and caring only about my income. Shannon demanded that measures be taken to please her in all areas of life, but she never regarded such adjustments as sufficient. Feeling suffocated by the pressure of her expectations, I felt that anything I said could be, and often was, attacked as an example of my ruthless exploitation. Feeling mistreated and under continual attack for the inadequacy of my efforts, I wondered what I was getting out of seeing her. Although Shannon experienced herself as the victim of others' needs, she was, in fact, a perpetrator of abuse. She knew how to relate only on the basis of exploitation and victimization, so her relationships were characterized by this antinomy, the only mutability being the reversal of subject and object. As offensive as her demanding behavior often was, it was the only alternative she knew to being taken advantage of. Shannon's creative challenge was to free herself from passivity without abusing and dominating others.

It would be a mistake to believe a solution can be achieved by finding a "middle ground" between two pathological patterns, such as hostility and compliance, sadism and masochism, or passivity and activity. These antinomies, being complementary poles of the same object relationship, have no midpoint. For example, the inhibition of aggression creates not compassion but docility. When the constraint on aggressive relating becomes intolerable, the suppressed aggression may erupt in an outburst of hostility, and fear of such outbursts may well lead to renewed efforts to restrict aggressiveness. But there will be no "in between" response: compliance and hostility evoke each other. When aggression is believed to be damaging, moderately aggressive responses tend not to occur because they imply that aggression is not destructive.

As we have seen, Benjamin (1997) has shown that to live life on one side of an antinomy is to fail to recognize the partner's subjectivity. If one is always active, the other must be passive, and so the subjectivity of the other is not recognized and mutuality is not possible. Pathological states typified by abuse and compliance contrast with mutuality, the state in which the other is appreciated for her difference. The only solution, in Benjamin's view, is to hold the tension of both sides of the antinomy. If one can be both active and passive, the other will be experienced, respectively, as passive and active, and therefore, the partner's subjectivity will be recognized. Benjamin concludes that it is this ability to share roles that leads out of the trap of antinomy to mutuality.

Benjamin's understanding of antinomies is a major advance in psychoanalytic theory, but she leaves unclear how the reversal of roles issues in the recognition of the other's subjectivity. If one partner is active and the other passive, and vice versa, the other is still experienced as a complement, even if the content shifts. If playing complementary roles does not imply a recognition of the other's subjectivity, why should the ability to change roles in a complementary relationship result in the recognition of the other's subjectivity? Indeed, reversal of roles often occurs in sadomasochistic relationships as the partners switch between sadistic and masochistic enactments, in each of which the other is a complement, not a separate subjectivity. Without such a recognition of the other, the patient remains trapped in the antinomy.

Benjamin does not provide criteria to distinguish passivity freely chosen to receive pleasure from the other from crippling passivity such as Anna's. When Benjamin describes a mutual, as opposed to a complementary, relationship, she depicts a dyad in which each partner chooses the role at the moment, although she is not explicit that the freedom to choose is the decisive difference between antinomy and mutuality. Yet implicit in her view of mutuality is the freedom given each partner by the other to participate in each role: A relationship becomes mutual not because both roles are played, but because the roles are freely chosen.

The essence of therapeutic action, the key to the patient's creating a new self structure, is the resolution of the creative challenge. As we have seen, each pole of the object relationship contains an important aspect of the patient's self, and there must be room in the analytic relationship for the expression of each if the patient is to transcend the pathological pattern. For Anna, this meant being both generous and self-respecting. To live in both these ways constituted a new possibility for both her charitable nature and self-regard: her freely chosen generosity enhanced, rather than eroded, her self-respect, and the latter had no trace of selfishness. For Anna, expression in her daily life of both of these deeply held values was not a "middle ground" of compromise between the two, but the creation of a new ability, the capacity to live in accordance with self-respect and generosity.

To make both traits central to her life, Anna would have to learn to articulate both in a new way. To continue her beneficence in a manner consonant with self-respect meant that her generosity would have to be discerning, continually balanced with concern for the integrity of her self. Similarly, her self-respect could not be lived in the selfish manner of her fantasy but in a self-protective manner that did not inhibit her generosity.

Such a notion of personality change implies that the patient's desire can assume different forms and be satisfied in various manners. While it may seem commonplace to some that a value such as generosity can be lived in different ways, psychoanalytic theory has historically conceptualized desire as an immutable given. Although this assumption originated in Freud's (1915a) biologically based drive theory, its influence has extended to virtually every psychoanalytic school, including much of contemporary theory. Correlatively, to relinquish finally the reified concept of desire and affect generally has far-reaching implications for the psychoanalytic theory of therapeutic action. To appreciate the importance of this break from the past and to locate it in the history of psychoanalytic ideas, it is useful to consider, however briefly, the history of the concept of desire and its relationship to reality in psychoanalytic theory.

FREUD'S CONCEPT OF DESIRE AND REALITY

For Freud (1915a), desire is the psychological expression of a biologically based drive that can gain expression in four different ways: repression, sublimation, reversal into its opposite, or turning around on the self. The first is the primary defense that keeps the wish and all associated mental phenomena unconscious so that it may gain expression only in symptomatic form. The latter two are also defenses, differing from repression only in that they disguise the drive by changing its form. Only sublimation is a healthy outcome as the drive achieves discharge by shifting its energy into a more socially acceptable form. In any of these vicissitudes, the patient must acquiesce to the demands of reality and civilization that do not allow the direct fulfillment of wishes. From this perspective, renunciation is crucial to a mature, healthy personality as wishes must be frustrated to achieve the sublimated expression characteristic of psychic health. It follows that transference love can be resolved only by strict adherence to the abstinence necessary for sublimation (Freud, 1914a). From this viewpoint, a key component of therapeutic action lies in the analyst's refusal to gratify the patient's wish and the patient's learning to accept its infantile nature, resulting in its relinquishment. Therefore, the only outcomes for the patient's desire are either adaptation to reality through renunciation or neurosis.

According to Freud (1914a, p. 168), transference love is a repetition of infantile wishes, but that does not distinguish it from typical adult love. In this conceptualization, the love that was formed originally on the basis of the parent's meeting childhood needs never fundamentally alters its character; it signifies the essence of love between adults. Consistent with his drive theory, Freud believed only the object of desire is changeable; the wish itself cannot be altered. Freud could not dispute the "genuineness" of transference love partly because all love "consists of new editions of old traits" (p. 168). For Freud, the adult form of love, in or out of the transference, is the same as a child's love for the parent. Subsequent generations of analytic theorists, such as Loewald (1960), endorsed the concept that all relations are transference repetitions.

This traditional psychoanalytic view of desire is clearly reductionistic, but equally important is its implicit reification. It is not just that Freud equated adult desires with childhood wishes; he also saw desire as a given, an immutable entity that can either be gratified in the way it presents itself or be frustrated. The only nondefensive vicissitude is sublimation, but, even in that mechanism, change comes only from the transfer of energy to another activity, a process that leaves the underlying wish unfulfilled. Thus, sublimation is another form of renouncing the wish, differing from other defenses only by offering a diluted type of gratification.

In Freud's view, the childhood wish has a defined content with no potential to be other than it is. Therefore, once the analysis uncovers the childhood wish, the process reaches psychological rock bottom, requiring only "working through" via repetition for the wish to be finally given up (Freud, 1914a). There is no consideration in this perspective that desire per se is malleable and includes alternative ways of relating to the world. The upshot is a rigid, limited concept of the person–world relationship. Reality, such as it is, simply forces a choice between repression and sublimation.

While this concrete concept of desire undoubtedly originated in Freud's biological assumptions, it is not necessarily changed by a shift away from drive theory. The reification of desire has left a legacy with which psychoanalysis is still struggling. In contemporary ego psychology, for example, although the clinical technique is focused on a gradual interpretation of the defenses "from the surface down," the goal of analytic inquiry is to uncover the wish presumed to lie unchanged from childhood to the present (e.g., Busch, 1995). Contemporary Kleinian thought likewise regards the aggressive drive as an immutable given that can be made conscious but can never be altered (e.g., Segal, 1981). Self psychology represents a shift in this sense as it emphasizes the transformation of "archaic selfobject" needs into ambitions and ideals through the therapeutic process (Kohut, 1971). Although this school has a more flexible view of desire than does classical Freudian thought, it still regards "archaic selfobject needs" as psychological substances that either retain their form into adulthood or become transformed into a predetermined incarnation of a "mature" selfobject need. For example, grandiosity can become only ambition and idealization only ideals; there is no other possibility for early narcissistic needs. Thus, even though self psychology recognizes the possibility of changes in childhood needs, their potential is limited to only one possibility. In this way, self psychology retains residual effects of Freud's reification of desire.

Relational analysis has taken another step toward a flexible view of desire with its conceptualization of affect as a fluid process influenced by the current environment. Mitchell (1988) argued against Freud that childhood desires are continually altered by environmental contingencies throughout life, including the current adult world. This type of thinking moves psychoanalytic theory away from the reification that has limited its concept of desire and the relationship to the world. Nonetheless, the relational view sees the flexibility of desire only in response to the vicissitudes of the "relational matrix" (Mitchell, 1988). Desire being only reactive, it remains captive to environmental changes. Such a notion contains no concept of desire as possessing the creative capacity to influence the environment. While the relational view conceives of desire as malleable, its capacity for change lies in its sensitivity to environmental vicissitudes; creative choice is not imputed to desire itself. So the challenge remains: how can psychoanalysis revitalize its notion of human desire to expand its concept of therapeutic possibility?

PHENOMENOLOGY

Here is another instance in which psychoanalysis can be aided by the findings of phenomenological philosophy. Husserl (1913) showed through his phenomenological descriptions that one cannot understand what something is only by looking at its immediate, concrete presentation because that represents only one appearance of its reality, that is to say, one of its possibilities. To understand the essence of a thing is to know what it can and cannot be, its system of possibilities.

Heidegger (1936) followed up Husserl's insight by pointing out that we make the reality we "find." The tree was always potentially lumber, but wood was not one of its realizations until humankind saw that potential and the lumberjack brought it to fruition. Being is created in the relationship between person and world. In one of Heidegger's examples, he points out that the sun is experienced commonly as a source of warmth, but to the scientist it is a measurable group of gases. Both are true; both are possibilities of the thing. The essence of the sun is that it can be viewed in these and other ways, but it cannot be experienced in *any* way one pleases. Anyone who tried to treat the sun as food would go hungry.

There is a clear affinity between Winnicott's (1971) concept of potential space and Heidegger's (1936) analysis of the person–world relationship. Heidegger's view of the nature of a "thing" accords with Winnicott's concept that potential space contains certain givens out of which different realities may be created. Crucial for Heidegger is that the various concepts of the thing are created, just as for Winnicott what comes out of potential space is created. Whether we experience the sun as a source of warmth or as a group of gases, we create these concepts within the limitations of the sun's givens. During the greatest part of human history, the view of the sun as a ball of gases did not exist. That this concept was created by humankind in relatively recent history makes this view of the sun no less real than any other. This capacity to create a "thing" is not just a fact about science; we create things as part of who we are. A tree can be an object of aesthetic pleasure, a source of wood, an interference in the building of a road, a source of shade, or an object of a botanist's investigation. All these possibilities are created out of the thing we call a "tree," but only one embodies the perspective of natural science.

Heidegger made the further point that in the confrontation with the thing we are "thrown back" to ourselves: We find our self as we confront the thing. As the lumberjack turns the tree into wood, he realizes a potential in himself. If we appreciate the beauty of the tree, we realize our aesthetic potential. In each case, as we create a new possibility for the thing, we realize a new aspect of our self.

AFFECT AND CREATION

This understanding of the person–world relationship applies to the emotions as well as to cognition. Just as a thing may be conceptualized in a variety of ways, each emotional state can be experienced in different ways. Alternative modes of experiencing a particular affect, whether it be hope, fear, surprise, love, hatred, or any other, are different ways of being in the world. We do not find forms of being like archeological relics waiting to be uncovered, but we create them from the affective dispositions we find in ourselves, more like the three-dimensional artist's creations from his materials. While strangulated affects contain the latent possibility for their expression, the untapped potential is not a defined way of experiencing a specific affect but an unformed capability that may be realized in different ways. To be brought to fruition, this undeveloped capacity requires a situation that can evoke the affect. But we must be careful because it is equally true that we do not create a new possibility the way the painter fashions a new form on a blank canvas. The ultimate form the affect will take is limited by the affective disposition. Therefore, it would be an unwarranted reductionism to presume that the form taken on is solely a product of the interpersonal environment. The situation sets up the conditions to which a response is created, but this creation cannot be reduced to the situation and is not predictable from it.

The findings of child developmental research show that affects are generated in creative ways that cannot be predicted by environmental factors (Tomkins, 1962, 1963, 1978). According to neuroscientific findings, experience is not passively recorded but actively categorized. Affects are not stored as replicas of previous experience but are put into categories creating the potential to be mobilized by new experience (Modell, 2000; Edelman and Tononi, 1991). The creation of a new affective experience is not like the development of a negative into a photograph. On the contrary, affects spread by a creative process in which the child finds an analogy between different but similar situations. The affective potential for new experience can gain expression in different ways and by different sources. When stimulated, affective potential will become realized either by fitting the experience into a preexisting mental slot or by creating a new category. In either case, a new type of affective experience has been realized. Between the unformed potential and the situation, a new reality, a new way of being, has been created. This new reality has been neither uncovered in a defined form, nor concocted in fantasy, but created out of the interaction of person and world.

Thus desire and fantasy are not psychological "rock bottom" givens that constitute building blocks of the psyche, but ways of being, expressions of self potential. Even the most primitive fantasy is a response to a feeling of frustration or deprivation. In the psychoanalytic situation, we find intense, persistent, often uncontrollable desires and fantasies motivating current symptoms and patterns. Given the pressure of such motivations, it is understandable that we tend to think of them as the root cause of symptoms. In fact, transference fantasies and desires are responses to depriving and problematic situations; they differ from other desires only in their apparent tenacity, a characteristic that makes them seem like psychological "givens."

Moreover, the concrete form of an affective state is only one of its embodiments. Whether the affect is love, aggression, excitement, fear, or any other, the person and situation in which the state is embedded saturate the affective experience. It is a different experience with a different meaning to be angry at the boss for criticism, the child for spilling milk, the parent for saying no. Anger at the boss contains a sense of personal injury; at the child, frustration often mixed with understanding; and at the parent, rebellion perhaps with a sense of injustice. To take another example, excitement can take many forms, have a variety of different meanings, and be manifested in different ways, some of which may be dangerous, others innocuous. Such an affect can mean joy at victory, the ebullience of accomplishment, or anticipation of discovery, among other possible meanings. One cannot assume, therefore, that the particular way an affective experience is presented is the only manner in which it can be felt. Any embodiment of the desire may appear to have only one means of fulfillment, but to adopt such a view is to confuse the desire itself with one of its concrete expressions in a particular context. It is crucial that the psychotherapist understand that any verbalized desire has the potential to be expressed and adequately fulfilled—not merely sublimated—in unforeseen ways.

The classic concept of penis envy is a good example of the misconception that a fantasy created to cope with a deficit is causal. Freud regarded penis envy as the rock bottom cause of women's sense of inferiority. From Freud's perspective, the woman's desire for a penis, rooted in female anatomy, was an unalterable biological given. Because the girl can only wish for something unfulfillable, she has no choice but to renounce the longing. Benjamin (1995), however, noted that the girl who is not recognized as a source of power or desire by the father representing these qualities will long to have the power possessed by the man, and this longing may well be embodied in penis envy. But this envy of the phallus signifies only the desire for a sense of agency; such a longing can be expressed and lived in many ways. On the other hand, if the girl is recognized by her father as a source of desire, she will have a sense of her own power and no reason to envy the penis.

It is true that affects revealed in analysis are commonly reified, frozen repetitions, but that is why they are pathological.

Persistence and rigidity of desire are symptomatic of unfulfilled desire, an arrested need of the self. Indeed, what makes an affect pathological is precisely the reification that results in the relentless pursuit of one particular means of its fulfillment. Often, to defend against awareness of an affect that has become threatening, the patient is compelled to repeat the defense whenever a suggestion of the affect in question appears. That is why the repetition compulsion has received so much attention in psychoanalytic discussions of psychopathology (Freud, 1920). The repetition compulsion is not the norm but the product of a psyche stuck in the illusory effort to obtain what was missing in childhood. Freud's mistake was to equate the pathological form of the desire and the accompanying anxiety with its essential nature.

Freud's (1917) formulation of the Wolf Man is a poignant illustration of this point. The patient suffered from a number of obsessive rituals, such as praying and making endless signs of the cross before going to sleep, kissing religious pictures obsessively, and breathing out noisily whenever he saw a beggar. He also was tortured by blasphemous thoughts, such as "God is swine! God is shit!" that tormented him with guilt. At age three and one quarter, he was seduced by his sister; three months later he was abandoned by his parents who were replaced by a governess who taunted him. After these events, he became nasty and even sadistic, torturing insects and often cutting them into pieces. The patient's hostility, possessing the clear intent to injure, was defended with the desperate obsessive rituals that had to be repeated continually out of fear the aggression would erupt. While Freud interpreted these symptoms as defenses against the aggressive drive, the appearance of the child's hostility and sadism after traumatic events clearly indicates that these destructive affects were a reaction to loss and abuse. The automatic, repetitive, driven quality of the patient's hostile aggression was not an inborn drive but a reaction to threat. Every inkling of aggressivity took on a sadistic meaning because he was wounded by the losses and frustration of his life. His sadistic reactions became the only way he was able to utilize his aggression. In this way, he lost the flexibility to endow his aggressivity with different meanings.

Evidence of this principle has been demonstrated in Parens's (1979) study of childhood aggressivity. From his observations of children, Parens showed that the original purpose of inborn infantile aggression is mastery of the environment. Play and exploration are both aspects of this initial purpose of aggressive behavior. Parens's careful observations of children's aggressive behavior showed that hostile aggression is a reaction to frustration or deprivation and tends to be employed to handle particular situations. If the environment is responsive to the source of the child's displeasure, the aggressive behavior terminates. If frustration is not excessive, aggression is a flexible, adaptive response that is used for environmental mastery in a variety of ways. If, however, the environment fails to help the child remove the source of frustration, hostility builds and this type of aggression ensues. In this situation, hostile aggression becomes repetitive and grows into a chronic, automatic response to negative experience, even minor degrees of displeasure. In this constellation of events, aggression acquires destructive intent, and therefore defenses are often erected to protect against its expression. When the defense fails, the underlying hostile aggression tends to burst forth in uncontrolled fury. This repetitive, driven hostile aggression then becomes the only type of aggressiveness available. Thus, Parens's work shows that the drivenness and automaticity of hostility may appear to be an "impulse" but is in fact a distortion of inborn aggressivity in response to threat and endangerment. When an affect such as aggressivity serves the purpose of protecting an injury, it loses its flexibility, its capacity to adapt to different situations, and attains a driven quality.

We have seen an example of this reification of an arrested affect in the way Anna was unable to deploy her aggression. Her mother's anxiety in response to her assertive childhood behavior resulted in an overwhelming conviction that any aggressive behavior on her part would result in abandonment by others and lifelong isolation. This equation being the only meaning that aggression had for her, Anna was driven to avoid all self-assertive acts because she saw no other meaning in them. Once aggression took on the meaning of destructiveness to relationships, she was compelled to avoid it, thus preventing herself from having other experiences of aggression. Unable to envision an alternative way of understanding the forceful expression of her states and affects, Anna lacked any ability to adapt her aggressivity to individual situations. Although Anna was frozen into a unidimensional meaning of aggression, the potential for other forms of its expression and deployment was not destroyed.

A similar point regarding the nature of pleasure seeking is found in the differing theoretical viewpoints of Kohut (1984) and Fairbairn (1944). Both theorists observed that the pursuit of pure pleasure for its own sake arises only under conditions of psychic breakdown, a state Fairbairn called the "fractionated ego" and Kohut referred to as the breakdown of the self. In normal development one sees not the operation of the pleasure principle but the pursuit of a tender, affectionate relationship unless the original need is excessively frustrated. According to both theorists, when this deviation of the developmental process occurs, the normal desire for emotional bonds devolves into a single-minded devotion to tension discharge. This desperate need to fill the gap in emotional relating may take a disguised form, such as substance abuse or an eating disorder; however the need is pursued, a search for soothing replaces the original desire. The capacity for a variety of emotional relationships is lost in favor of the driven need to exploit others in order to allay anxiety. Just as we saw with aggression, the originally flexible affective need becomes distorted into a single, unidirectional meaning applicable to all forms of interpersonal relating. The capacity to use multiple affective experiences to adapt to and transform different situations is greatly diminished.

If the symptomatic appearance of the affect were its essential nature, then the only road to freedom would lie in renouncing the longing, and the goal of psychoanalysis could only be the transformation of neurotic misery into common human unhappiness. This was in fact Freud's (1895) conclusion. But missing from this view is an appreciation for human affect as a process, the possibilities of what it may be, and the way reality may be influenced to accommodate it. Applying Heidegger's (1926) concept of the person–world relationship, we learn not to equate the symptomatic wish with the patient's desire. Viewing desire as a process, as a way of being, shifts the analytic aim from renouncing desire to exploring and fostering its other possible meanings. The repetitive, unidimensional affective discharge, or defense against it, characteristic of so many patients, is a symptom. A critical aim of psychoanalytic therapy, irrespective of individual goals, is the transformation of the concrete, symptomatic manifestation of affect to the creation of new possibilities for its expression.

THE CREATION OF POSSIBILITIES

As we have seen, deprivation and frustration tend to distort affect into a single-minded effort to follow an unbending but fruitless search for gratification or result in a persistent defense against its painful recognition. As long as the effects of the early traumatic experience endure, the need to heal the wound dominates affective expression. It follows that the return to the original flexibility is possible only if the emotional injury is healed in some way by the therapeutic process. That is to say, there must be sufficient gratification of the patient's longing to motivate the relinquishing of the defense. Because the desire itself must be reached, not simply its symptomatic expression, the therapist must find a way to contact the desire embedded in the symptom or pathological pattern.

Shannon's therapeutic voyage illustrates the potential of concrete desire to find new possibilities by using potential space to create previously unknown avenues of being. As we have seen, Shannon felt victimized by those who continually disappointed her, and this pattern was repeated in my inability to meet her every want. Although her presenting problem was the feeling of exploitation, Shannon demanded constant attention and responsiveness to the point that she attempted to control my every therapeutic move. I repeatedly remarked that only by her tenacious demands did she feel any chance of my responding to her as she needed. Although Shannon agreed with this line of interpretation, she continued to insist on my continual availability and responsiveness to every moment of tension, and she did not elicit that type of reaction on demand. Whenever she felt that I would not be able to provide the synchronous responsiveness that would obliterate the boundary between us, Shannon fell into despair. Possessing a fragile self, she felt that only a fused relationship could make her feel whole (Summers, 1999). I indicated to her that efforts to maintain vigilance of my behavior made sense because she looked to me for what she needed—unlimited availability, emotional resonance, nurturing, and understanding—and yet she did not trust my ability to provide them. I told her that I understood she believed I could benefit her only if our differences were obliterated. Without this merger, she felt left alone, abandoned, and unable to cope with the world. Consequently, the only way she could understand my establishing boundaries was to assume that I was purposely trying to hurt her. In each such instance, she felt I was cruelly inflicting pain on her. I told her that these reactions explained her chronic sense of victimization because whenever others did not accommodate her need for fusion, she felt they were intent on injuring her.

Shannon regarded anything less than the erasure of boundaries as diluted interpersonal contact that missed her need for affective connection. Her sense of fragility and correlative dread of abandonment did not allow her to consider any other possible ways of benefitting from the therapeutic relationship. To suggest that her desire could be met in some way other than merger was to threaten Shannon's lifeline, her only thread of hope, and would have left her feeling not only misunderstood but abandoned once again.

While Shannon regarded her desire as a need that must be met to avoid psychic death, I saw in her very demandingness the belief in a potentially helpful object (Cooper, 2000). Her sense of hope being invested in object seeking, Shannon was laying claim to me through her efforts to control my behavior. The possibility of an affective connection depended on her expectations being met in some way, that is, on Shannon's being able to exact something from me. The very longing itself suggested the capability for emotional connection, but if this potential were to be realized, she would have to form a relationship the only way she knew: The need for fusion would have to be met, perhaps not as she wanted it to be, but to a degree that would feel meaningful to her.

Thus, I attempted to meet her demands as best I could: I saw her four times a week and was available to her for phone calls. Allowing her to comfort herself on the couch as she needed to, I let her know in innumerable ways that I understood her need for the nurturance she had never received. I told her that I knew that what counted for her was to feel at one with me in order to relieve her fear of being abandoned. In some sessions, she was peacefully silent and later told me that she had felt as comforted as a small child sleeping near her mother. In other sessions, she spoke of her emptiness, a longing that could never be filled, the feeling of being a bottomless pit. Often she despaired that she would be alone forever. I told her that I knew she needed to feel we had no boundary, that she wanted us never to separate. Although her experiences in the sessions and my comments invariably soothed her anxiety at the moment, the ending of each session evoked intense anxiety and rage, as she felt abandoned to the hostile outside world. Shannon often entered the next session seething with rage, verbally abusing me for abandoning her: How could I let her go like that? Why was I so cruel to her? When she berated me, I acknowledged that I had failed her owing to my limitations and that she must feel that I was purposely trying to injure her.

Vacations, of course, were much worse. Each vacation became the primary topic of discussion months before it occurred and for an extended period after my return. These periods of anticipation and postvacation trauma lengthened until they virtually consumed the therapy. I repeatedly pointed out to Shannon that each separation, especially vacations, confronted her with an awareness of the separateness between us that she found intolerable.

The limitations of the connection, manifested in every separation, interruption, and misunderstanding, prevented the enduring fusion Shannon sought and led to deep injury and rage at me for failing her. On each such occasion, I told her that she felt her survival depended on my being there for her at all times, and, when I was not, the injury was so painful she felt I was persecuting her. This experience gave us the opportunity to understand that her chronic sense of victimization resulted from ruptures in her pursuit of fusion. I registered that she often did experience us as one, but these fusion experiences were disrupted, and it was the interruptions that she found intolerable. My understanding of her state as a valid need even as I was unable to meet it inevitably calmed her by reconnecting us.

In each phone call or session she felt a connection, albeit temporary and fragile, that would vanish shortly after it ended. No matter how disturbing the ending of each such contact, Shannon came away with a momentary experience of fusion. As these moments of contact gradually began to have some impact beyond the sessions, Shannon started to feel some continuity in her experience of me and in her sense of self. Initially perplexed that the therapeutic process was proving beneficial despite its limitations, Shannon realized that in her experiences of fusion, which she called "moments of being," she felt a sense of life inside her, as though a baby were being born. Despite the pain she felt whenever these moments were erased by disruptions, Shannon realized that her deeply buried self was being reached. It was this awareness that led her to see that she could have a gratifying relationship without the obliteration of self–other boundaries.

The moments of fusion and our discussions of them eventually led to a continuity of experience that Shannon called "connecting the dots." She felt something useful but recognized that what she found satisfying was not the merger she sought because, ultimately, she had to come back to her self separate from me. Although she expressed disappointment and frustration at each such awareness of separateness, I noted that in verbalizing her displeasure without rage or intense anxiety, she was showing the beginning of an ability to have affective exchanges with me while recognizing a boundary between us. Shannon acknowledged that she felt more able to manage the frustrations of not only her relationship with me, but also much more problematic interactions in the outside world, most of which were not comforting. Correlatively, it was as though a fog had lifted from her vision of me. Gradually ceasing her efforts to control my behavior, she accepted my externality. Although she still felt a loss when I was not in tune with her desire of the moment, the gap no longer threatened her sense of self. Consequently, she no longer felt persecuted in response to every confrontation with the limitations of the relationship.

The unique relationship she experienced in the therapeutic dyad showed Shannon that her desire had possibilities well beyond the rigidity of boundary obliteration and therefore, she had the capacity to form connections in a variety of ways. Utilizing previously dormant potential, Shannon began to create relationships with differing affective intensities and degrees of intimacy. It was at this point that Shannon started to relax her demands of me and even showed less interest in our relationship. She initiated new relationships and was largely successful because she did not expect others to be in perfect emotional synchrony with her. For the first time in her life, Shannon sought out people with whom she wanted to form friendships. Drawn to those who shared her desire for affective connection as well as her interests and emerging sense of humor, she established a variety of relationships. The most important were with people whom she felt a kindred spirit. But perhaps most noticeably, she found value in more limited relationships in which she might share only a particular interest. To her surprise, Shannon discovered that people with whom she could have deep, absorbing conversations offered her rewarding experiences even though the relationship might be largely intellectual. She also developed a spiritual life and found a group to share it with. Although these relationships varied widely in intensity, Shannon benefited a great deal from each of them. Without the need for fusion, the persecutor–victim pattern faded away as Shannon became satisfied in different types of relationships.

The essence of the therapeutic movement for Shannon consisted of the creation of relationships of varying intensity, the gratification from which rendered unnecessary the search for fused bonds. If she could not have the experience she wanted at a particular moment, Shannon pursued an alternative. Her longing for affective connections was no longer a concrete, reified entity that could only be met in one way, but a desire that had various possibilities, any one of which might be realized at a given time. Ultimately, her deepest change was the development of the capacity to create ever-new relationships of varying types and the means for finding fulfillment in them. Whereas she had formerly seen only one way to have a meaningful relationship, she now found various avenues of relating to other people.

THEORY OF THERAPEUTIC ACTION

The new possibilities of which Shannon now availed herself emerged after she felt a response to her longing for fusion. Sensing that her desire was not only understood but gratified, albeit in a limited way, Shannon felt a new sense of self building within. This connection soothed her pain, and, to a degree healed her wounded psyche. It was this experience of "moments of being" that led to the abatement of Shannon's insistence that her desire for fusion be directly gratified. She began to relinquish her demandingness as she felt an emotional connection formed from moments of merger. The very fact that the longing for fusion was met at moments, along with the experience of limits and frustration, provided Shannon with a meaningful emotional exchange without the enduring fusion she sought. This mending experience meant that erasing the boundaries was no longer the only way Shannon could feel an emotional bond. The driven form of the desire subsided as the need to heal the wound was obviated. My contribution in this phase was to facilitate Shannon's exploration of new ways of relating. We can see then that once the concrete embodiment of Shannon's desire declined, she spontaneously created new avenues of self expression.

Some analytic formulations of this type of therapeutic progress would view Shannon's changes as a product of internalizing the analytic relationship. From both ego psychological and self psychological viewpoints, the patient internalized the analyst's functions so that she became able to do for herself what had been done for her. The classical self psychological view holds that the key to therapeutic action is optimal disillusionment in the analyst (Gedo and Goldberg, 1973; Kohut, 1984; Akhtar, 1996). According to this position, as the patient becomes disillusioned in manageable doses, the transmuting internalization process transforms the originally unrealistic strivings into more realistic life goals. Indeed, Shannon's treatment included a mixture of gratification and frustration. As much as she felt gratified in what for her was a unique bond, she was equally frustrated by my inability to provide for her needs in the way she sought. According to the theory of optimal disillusionment, the disappointments induced Shannon to give up her archaic longings and transform them into more realistic strivings.

Undoubtedly, Shannon absorbed a great deal from the analytic encounter, but internalization is an insufficient concept to capture the changes she made. Rather than passively absorbing my interventions, she reacted to my affective resonance with her longing by creating relationships she had neither experienced nor witnessed. The essence of Shannon's therapeutic changes consisted of her use of the therapeutic process to create relationships of different kinds with different degrees of meaning; she had never before experienced bounded relationships as meaningful in or out of the analytic setting. For the therapeutic dyad to be employed in this way, it had to be transformed at various points into potential space so that Shannon could create these new forms of relating. The concept of internalization cannot account for Shannon's newly developed ability to create relationships that had not been part of her experience. Establishing friendships based on common interests did not reflect the internalization of something experienced in the therapeutic dyad, but the exercise of a new capability. This distinction directly bears on clinical strategy in that the therapist who views the creation of possibilities, rather than internalization, as the key feature of therapeutic action takes pains to shift the analytic relationship to potential space at pivotal points in the process.

To be sure, the concept of optimal disillusionment, along with Bacal's (1985) more recent reformulation of that notion as "optimal responsiveness," emphasizes a mixture of gratification and frustration in therapeutic action that overlaps the view presented here. The latter shares with self psychology the idea that the therapist's empathy with and frustration of the patient's desires are central to therapeutic action. The difference is that the self psychological position, even in amended form, relies on the notion that Shannon modified her overriding longing to make it more fulfillable. This concept assumes that Shannon's pressured desire for fusion was the continuance of a childhood state that had never been tamed by deprivation. However, we have seen that such a demanding expectation of others is not the normal developmental process but a product of excessive frustration. Shannon's history bears out this formulation: the multiple traumas she suffered led to overwhelming pain that she desperately sought to calm with a fused bond. Furthermore, the blossoming of new possibilities in a variety of ways cannot be accounted for by a theory of therapeutic action that relies on the transformation of an originally driven desire into a more subdued version of itself. Missing from such a model of therapeutic action is an explanation for the creation of new possibilities. Because new ways of being and relating are indeed created by the patient, as we have seen with both Anna and Shannon, one is led logically to the conclusion that the therapeutic process, when successful, taps dormant potential. The crux of the difference between the view of therapeutic action set forth here, on one hand, and the self psychological and ego psychological models, on the other, is that the former sees a key role for the analyst in bringing to fruition incipient states of being. In Shannon's case, the gratification she felt from moments of fusion stimulated her capability to utilize tender affects to form a variety of emotional connections.

To regard the therapeutic progress of Shannon and Anna as the realization of long-dormant potential is to apply to the analytic process the understanding of normal development set forth above. As we have seen, a child deploys affects flexibly and endows them with different meanings in changing circumstances unless deprivation and frustration increase to the point that this capacity becomes compromised. This potential for affective diversity was lost in both Anna and Shannon as they coped with traumatic childhood experiences by seeking desperately to protect the wounds inside from reopening. The search for fusion was Shannon's way of attempting to heal her deep sense of fragility, the rawness of an incomplete self. For her part, Anna was driven to protect herself against abandonment by using compliance to defend against interpersonal conflict. Both Shannon's and Anna's therapeutic experiences brought to fruition long-dormant potential for variegated affective experience. For Shannon, moments of fusion and intimacy soothed the injury and began to heal it, thus obviating the desperate search for a fused bond. Once her need for emotional relatedness was no longer saturated with the craving for merger, Shannon was able to exercise her latent capacity to explore a variety of ways to form meaningful emotional connections.

In Anna's case, the therapeutic space provided the opportunity to assert her desires even in an aggressive manner without losing her concern for others, and this experience tapped her potential for self-affirmation without sacrificing her altruism. Anna's anger became available to her for self-protection, the function it serves in normal children, as Parens (1979) has shown. Anna was able to fit aggressive expressions into her interactions with varying degrees of intensity, so this type of reaction became a flexibly used adaptation to situations of threat or endangerment. In this way, Anna realized her potential to pursue her desires and confront conflict, but this capability was exercised only after she was able to bring her aggressivity into the therapeutic relationship. Anna's ability to be angry at me was a pivotal step on her journey to become self-defining and, ultimately, gain control over the direction of an interaction. It was equally significant that she engage me in this way while maintaining her altruism. Ultimately, then, Anna used the therapeutic space to learn to pursue self-interest without compromising her natural generosity.

Opening the therapeutic space to Anna's expression of desire was analogous to meeting Shannon's longing for fusion. The experience of self-affirmation, including the deployment of negative affect in a positive relationship, rendered unnecessary Anna's compliant defense against self interest just as the meeting of Shannon's search for merger obviated her craving for the obliteration of self–other boundaries. Once Anna had the experience of becoming enraged in the therapeutic space without compromising her deeply held value of generosity, she was free to deploy both her self assertiveness and her altruism as she needed. Anna was then able to create ways of assertive relating to replace her formerly rigid compliance. In this way, Anna's capacity for pursuing her desires was finally being realized.

Another view would hold that Shannon was forced to renounce her longing in the therapeutic process and sublimated it with different types of relationships. But this explanation misses the essential fact that Shannon's desire was met, however imperfectly, and led to new forms of its appearance and gratification. When she accepted the boundaries of the relationship, Shannon did so in the context of a uniquely meaningful relationship that enabled her to form satisfying relationships with varying degrees of intensity. These other relationships were not sublimations of her "real" desire but alternative ways of engaging it.

If desire were the concrete, reified entity of Freud's conceptualization, its fate would be limited to either direct gratification or renunciation. That Shannon was able to transcend her need for fusion without its being fully met indicates that desire is inherently pregnant with possibilities that can be pursued in a variety of venues, only one being the concrete fulfillment the patient seeks. Freud (1911) believed that, when desire conflicts with reality, one must relinquish the desire; but from a nonreified view of desire as a process, one searches for a new relationship between desire and reality rather than abandoning the desire in toto. The creative challenge is not just to find alternative avenues for expression of the desire but to find means of fulfillment that fit the exigencies of reality. As we have seen, Shannon neither renounced nor completely fulfilled her desire but created a number of different ways of engaging the relationship between her desire and the limitations of reality.

Recall that Anna's creative challenge was to find a way to live in accordance with the coexisting values of magnanimity and self-respect. She needed to find a way to be generous without allowing herself to be exploited by the people who take advantage of beneficence. Anna feared she would lose her most preciously held value, the part of her self of which she was most proud, if she were to abandon her empathic attitude toward others. She realized, however, that to be giving without being exploited meant that she would have to be aware of how others responded to her new-found ability to assert her desires. To sustain her charitable attitude, Anna gave everyone the benefit of the doubt, but once she found any evidence of a willingness to take advantage of her, she withdrew her largesse. Expressing her will in virtually all interpersonal encounters, her sensitivity to others' feelings was exercised only with those whom she judged to be accepting and even appreciative of her desires. Friends who were intolerant of the "new Anna" quickly left the scene, and she showed little remorse for losing them, although she did express a great deal of bitterness and consternation that she had previously regarded them as friends. In this way, Anna created a new means of expressing her altruism.

All her life Anna had believed that to be a giving person meant endless compliance. From the therapeutic process, she discovered that she did not have to abandon her ethical beliefs in order to protect herself against exploitation. Anna thought that benevolence had only one form, blanket compliance, and therefore she found herself in the predicament of having to choose between magnanimity and self-respect. In treatment, she discovered a new way of being generous that was consistent with her need for self-respect. In this way, she both maintained the humanitarianism that was so important to her and defined its limits. In doing the latter, she used her aggression when needed to protect her integrity. Although steadfastly refusing to become hostile, she was quick to anger when she felt attacked, devalued, or taken for granted. In this self-created way, Anna transcended the polarity of compliance and hostility: she was not self-subjugating, but neither did she regard herself with more importance than others. The selective beneficence she exercised toward those she judged trustworthy was a way of giving to people that contrasted decisively with the blind, indiscriminate benevolence of her past. Anna's altruism, articulated in her new way of relating, was qualitatively different from its former expression as compliance.

SPREADING PSYCHIC CHANGE

This way of thinking about the analytic process has implications for the theory of transference. What the patient transfers onto the therapist is not a definitive form carried from childhood to adulthood, but a desire with many possibilities, only one of which appears as the current transference manifestation. There is no reason to dispute Freud's (1912) insight that the adult desire is rooted in childhood conflict, but it does not follow that the longing of the adult patient is to be equated with the child's desire. If such an equation were valid, Shannon could only have been satisfied with a reversal of her history to a maternal relationship. The need originated with a feeling of childhood deprivation, but the form it assumed in adulthood was met by the recognition and acceptance of deeply buried aspects of her self. Despite the fact that this type of connection is not the same as the baby's need for a sense of oneness, Shannon felt her need had been responded to, albeit not completely fulfilled. Never having experienced a nurturing maternal relationship, Shannon transferred her unmet desire for an intimate connection onto the therapist, and she enacted this need the only way she knew. But, as we have seen, to Shannon's surprise, she found through the therapeutic process that her desire could be fulfilled in a variety of ways. Transference, then, is one current manifestation of a childhood desire that can be expressed in a variety of ways.

This recasting of the transference should not be taken to mean that patients such as Shannon do not suffer from anxiety about "perfectly normal needs" (Mitchell, 1988). That Shannon required momentary states of self–object merger to transcend the desire for fusion suggests that the quality and intensity of her desire was not a typical need for others but an unmet longing from earlier in her life. But the mastery of transference was not achieved solely by understanding the connection with its childhood roots; it required a responsiveness that freed the desire and opened it to other possible forms of gratification. Transference resolution is tantamount to the ability to use the therapeutic relationship despite its limitations. To put it another way, the transference is finally transcended when the patient creates new uses of the therapeutic space.

Essential to overcoming the transference is the patient's ability to create alternative ways of being and relating. This view of therapeutic action offers us a way to understand the phenomenon often referred to as the "nonspecific effects" of psychotherapy, that is, significant behavioral changes that may be quite dramatic even though they have been only lightly touched on in therapy or perhaps not discussed at all. Such generalized "effects" are the patient's creation of new possibilities after the reified version of the desire has been relinquished. Anna, after she rebuilt her personal relationships, began to assess her career for the first time since she started working. Although quite successful in her field, Anna felt her work was meaningless. Having tasted the freedom of following her desires in relationships, Anna strove to live in accordance with what she felt was most important to her in all aspects of her life. Since learning to influence her relationships by pursuing her desires, Anna could no longer tolerate the drudgery of a day-to-day existence that did not reflect the values on which she wanted to base her life. Realizing that she was not obligated to continue on a vocational path she had never consciously elected to pursue, Anna embarked on a new career that required additional formal education. She returned to school, obtained a graduate degree, and pursued a life in social service that she felt reflected her most highly valued qualities. In this way, the capacity to create authentic ways of living was transferred to the vocational arena. Despite this complete turnaround in her employment situation, Anna's career was never a therapeutic topic, and her decision to change her work life was discussed only after it was made. What would in common parlance be called a nonspecific effect of the psychotherapy was Anna's application of her ability to build her life on her affective experience to different situations. This extension of the capacity to realize new possibilities to areas not even discussed in the treatment explains the far-reaching and "non-specific effects" of psychoanalytic therapy; simultaneously, it demonstrates the inadequacy of the concept of internalization to account for such changes.

Shannon, for her part, brought her therapeutic experience into other relationships not by direct repetition but by her willingness to create limited relationships, even though the latter were different from the patient–therapist interactional pattern. Although I never overtly discussed with Shannon the possibility of forming relationships of varying intensity, she constructed a number of different interactional models by using the capacity for limited emotional connection developed in therapy. If therapeutic action were only a matter of specific insights, Shannon could not have made these changes. The fact that patients can effect such far-reaching alterations without extensive therapeutic discussion is explained by the fact that the therapeutic process can stimulate and facilitate the capacity to create new ways of being and relating. The construction of such a capacity is incomprehensible within a concept of therapeutic action limited to awareness of motivation, even if enlarged by internalization or the building of ego functions. Creativity in the growth process makes sense only if one thinks of psychotherapy as the art of creating new possibilities.

CONCLUSION: "WORKING THROUGH" AS THE CREATION OF POSSIBILITIES

In conventional psychoanalytic language, the movement from insight to behavioral change is explained by the concept of working through (Freud, 1914a). As discussed in chapter 1, this concept means an insight must be repeatedly gone over until it becomes integrated in a way that leads to the alteration of old patterns. In agreement with Mitchell (1997), I view this notion as lacking any substantive change-producing factor. In its original form, working through did no more than add time and repetition to insight. Although, as we saw in chapter 1, some recent writers have suggested that something must be added by the patient to integrate insight, no new factors have been introduced. There is little explanation by Freud or subsequent psychoanalytic theorists for how time can produce a therapeutic effect that insight alone does not provide (e.g., Grossman and Stewart, 1976). Psychoanalysis has always struggled to define how insight leads to change, and this problem is debated to this day. The reconceptualization of human emotion based on the phenomenological concept of mind suggests that this difficulty may be rooted in the reification of mind and emotion. If affect is conceptualized as a concretely fixed entity, then working through can mean little more than repetition until the patient renounces desire, and, as we have seen, this explanation for change is problematic. On the other hand, if one sees the patient's affect as a single manifestation of a desire with many possibilities, then the process traditionally labeled working through becomes a matter of creating new possibilities for affect.

Viewed in this way, working through connotes the process we have seen in both Anna and Shannon. In both cases, the understanding of historical patterns had minimal impact until a fundamental need was met (in Anna's case the expression of aggressivity, and in Shannon's, the longing for fusion). The recognition and meeting of the patient's desire, as we have seen, obviated the unidimensional, concrete form of the affect. Shannon's emotional contact without fusion and Anna's aggressivity without injury made possible the realization of dormant potential for affective expression. With this affective flexibility, both women had a variety of ways to meet their respective needs, and the drivenness of presenting patterns abated. At this point, the symptoms disappeared and were replaced by new and more flexible ways of being and relating. The insights that had begun the process were not "worked through" as much as they constituted a first step in the creation of new possibilities.

We can learn from the therapeutic journeys of both Anna and Shannon that when new ways of relating evolve from an old desire, the symptomatic expression of the desire tends to give way to these new modalities of expression. So, Anna, after understanding her anxiety of abandonment, used the potential space of the psychoanalytic setting to become aggressive within a needed relationship. When she was able to reconcile her altruistic value system with this newly discovered assertion of desire, the anxiety of abandonment was overcome, and new possibilities for aggressive expression came alive. Similarly, when Shannon experienced a relationship that was both meaningful and limited, she was able to form bonds with varying degrees of intensity, thus transcending her fixation on a fused relationship. Working through does not adequately capture the creation of such new ways of being and relating. Rather than working through insights into her motivation and past, each patient used them to create new ways of realizing desires embedded in the old patterns. And that is why the creation of possibilities is the essence of the therapeutic action of psychoanalytic therapy.

6

THE ANALYST'S PROCESS
THE MIND OF THE OTHER

To this point, we have considered the creation of the self from the viewpoint of the patient and in that context have seen the key role the therapist plays in this project. The fact that the therapist's subjectivity has not yet been discussed in detail is an expository artifact as his experience of the interaction is brought into the therapeutic engagement at each stage of the undertaking. We have seen the involvement of the therapist in the creation of potential space, the analyst's vision of the patient, and the creation of new possibilities. Let's now take the opportunity to reflect on the therapist's subjectivity from each of these points of view.

THE EMERGENCE OF POTENTIAL SPACE

As we have seen, for potential space to take over the analytic relationship, the therapist must contribute to an openness in which new ways of being can be created. It might sound strange to hear that the therapist contributes to "formlessness," but to abort the typical interpersonal flow of experience requires constraining the natural tendency to "match" affective expressions. We saw in chapter 1 that the therapist diminishes the involvement of his subjective experience to minimize the structure of the analytic space, but we did not note then the strain this limitation puts on the therapist. To inhibit the tendency to match the patient's affects is an unnatural feeling that can easily result a mounting tension. Nonetheless, the therapist's task is to bear the tension evoked by his affective responses in the interest of keeping the space open to the widest array of possibilities.

Opening the therapeutic space leaves the patient without structure, thereby evoking the anxiety of living without guideposts. Not being sure what her navigation points are, the patient has no guidelines for his behavior and turns to the therapist to relieve his free-floating feeling by filling the space. Is this not the therapist's responsibility? The patient is suffering from, perhaps even agonizing over, a threatening disorientation. How does the therapist stay indifferent to such anxiety and unresponsive to the patient's pleas for some comfort? To do so is to feel cold-hearted and even sadistic as the patient suffers from a sense of nonbeing. It is not uncommon for the therapist's unresponsiveness to evoke the guilt of not responding to the patient's pain. However, to meet the patient's request is to fill the space, thereby reducing its potential for creation. Caught between guilt and a therapeutic responsibility to create space, the therapist is in a quandary. To respond to the patient's expectation of tension relief is tempting, but to yield to it is counterproductive.

The responsibility to maintain potential space at the cost of the patient's anxiety is the most troubling experience for the therapist in this phase of the therapeutic endeavor. To withstand the pressure to ameliorate the patient's fear of the void requires that the therapist maintain the conviction that sustaining this most distressing form of anxiety will ultimately prove beneficial. The benefit is expected to appear in the creations that may emerge eventually from the unstructured therapeutic space. Thus, while the patient's suffering is current and real, the value of this suffering is a future projection. Inevitably, the therapist will wonder if the price is too high, and there is frequently a temptation to provide relief by giving a form to the space, but if the belief in the purpose of the void is maintained, the opportunity for creation is maximized.

CREATING THE SELF AND THE THERAPIST'S RISK

The foresight to envision how the patient's interests, passions, and potential capacities might become a "self" is not a traditionally conceptualized therapeutic role and is not typically a component of clinical training. Consequently, the therapist has little formal education that can be relied on to help the patient actualize such a vision. Furthermore, with the exception of Loewald, no major analytic theorist has conceptualized the fashioning of a vision of the patient as an analytic role. As a result, there is little scholarly work available for guidance. Thus, the therapist can easily feel that she is navigating without a compass.

To invest in a vision of the patient entails a greater risk than the making of an interpretation in the usual manner. If experience shows that the therapist's offered understanding is inaccurate or ill timed, the consequences are not typically far reaching because the therapist can backpedal and reconsider the material from a different viewpoint. By projecting a vision, however, the therapist is not only adopting a posture based on who she believes the patient might become, but is also making a guess as to one of its possible directions. If the therapist's understanding includes a claim about the patient's possibilities, her projection may not be borne out by the evolution of the patient's growth process. What if the patient's potential as viewed by the therapist does not appear to be materializing? What if the expected future does not come? These are the anxieties confronted by the therapist who views her role as abetting the development of the self. Projecting future possibilities from the patient's potential sheds the safety of the traditionally conceived interpretive stance, and it is likely that this exposed stance explains why many therapists are reluctant to assume this role.

Furthermore, when we must form an extrapolation of who the patient might be, we are likely to feel the anxiety of imposing our preconceptions on the therapeutic process. Deeply etched in the heart of all analysts is the principle that we should not influence our patients' development with our own values and biases. When we form an image of the patient, are we not pushing our own version of the patient and trying to convince him to become the way we want him to be? This anxiety and the guilt to which such influence often leads is one more source of consternation for the analyst who recognizes that her image of the patient is an intrinsic part of the process. The therapist is caught between not wanting to mold the patient according to a preconceived image and recognizing she must have an idea of who the patient can be to help him.

The best antidote to imposing an agenda on the therapeutic outcome, as we saw in chapter 3, is rooting the analyst's image in the patient's free associations and interactions as they emerge. While this attitude is the most beneficial position the therapist can adopt, it does not completely eliminate the anxiety of undue influence. The question is always there, in the background or foreground of the therapist's mind: how much am I imposing myself on where the therapy is going? Although the dilemma cannot be escaped entirely, to conduct therapy without a vision of the patient is more perilous still, because lack of awareness of the therapist's image of the patient will most likely result in unexamined influence. The more the therapist is cognizant of her formulated image of the patient and the basis on which it was constructed, the more she can be receptive to material that does not fit it. As we saw in chapter 3, the therapist's vision will be challenged by the evolution of the analytic process and continually reformulated in accordance with it. If such shifts do not occur, the therapist should suspect that she is holding on to a rigid image of the patient. The changes in the therapist's vision, on the other hand, are indices of her willingness to respond to the patient rather than insist on a preconception of who she is.

The other horn of the dilemma is that having a conception the patient's possibilities and relying on that belief is to risk imposing oneself on the patient. Recognizing that our therapeutic ambition can easily distort the analyst's ability to view the material, Freud (1912) warned us that the greatest peril faced by the analyst is his desire to cure the patient. If we have too much at stake in a particular therapeutic outcome or way of understanding, we may lose our ability to consider all the material and follow its lead. Despite Freud's warning, when one views the analyses he conducted as described by his patients, it is clear that he often had a particular formulation of the patient's material in which he had invested his understanding (e.g., Grinker, 1940; Kardiner, 1977). As Kardiner (1977) pointed out in his description of his own analysis, once Freud uncovered what he believed to be the oedipal origin of Kardiner's neurosis, he ended the inquiry and persisted in repeating interpretations that Kardiner did not find helpful. In addition to simplifying the patient's dynamics, such premature closure eases the analyst's anxiety of not understanding. By insisting that Kardiner was resisting his interpretations of homosexuality, Freud did not have to consider other possibilities, and his uncertainty was allayed. From the current perspective, openness to possibilities is the very essence of the process and therefore a primary analytic task is to sustain the anxiety of ambiguity, rather than seek to extinguish it. The temptation to wrap the material in one or another tight formulation to achieve a premature sense of clarity is a siren that the therapist, like Ulysses chained to the mast, must resist. Nothing less is required if the analyst is to maximize the possibilities of the analytic relationship.

At this juncture of psychoanalytic history, it is commonly recognized that every therapist has a theoretical viewpoint with which she organizes a patient's material. Less often acknowledged is that embedded in the analyst's perspective is a vision of who the patient may become. Any guiding principle employed to understand the patient applies not only to present and past but also to her future, as we saw in chapter 3. The idea that therapists need a conceptual framework to understand their patients, therefore, is tantamount to the claim that therapists have their own visions of their patients. Precisely speaking, it is not that the clinical strategy advocated here requires more of the therapist than does an "interpretation only" approach, but that there is a need to recognize the judgment about the patient's potential that is inherent in all clinical understanding. Including the therapist's vision in clinical theory simply makes conscious what is implicit in any clinical approach, interpretive or otherwise. The distinction is not between therapists who conjecture versus those who limit themselves to understanding but between clinicians who make explicit their vision as opposed to those who deny they have one.

Projecting into the future is not an easy task for stock market analysts, and it is that much more difficult to speculate on the future of a person. The therapist has no statistical analysis of the patient's market performance, but she does have an informed sense of the patient's history and current patterns. Because she must rely on her impressions enough to formulate a concept of who the patient might become, the therapist has a heavy burden placed on her understanding. It is this investment in a vision of the patient's possibilities that defines clinical strategy in the post-interpretive phase.

We saw an example of the risk of this clinical approach in my willingness to welcome Zelda's aggressive explosions as a positive move toward the exercise of her desire and ambition. I saw her as potentially aggressive and ambitious but inhibited by the anxiety of abandonment. But how could I be sure of what I was seeing? Maybe I imagined aggression and ambition in her because I wanted her to rise up against those who had suppressed her development. Her passivity and compliance bothered me, but was I imposing my value of assertiveness on an unwilling victim? I wrestled with that question, but I also had to remind myself that Zelda was miserable; if her compliance was working for her, how could we account for her depression and restlessness? Gaining no pleasure from her life, Zelda was filled with agitated energy lacking form or direction. Her desires changed by the minute as she flitted from one activity to another, none of which ever fulfilled her. This futile energy suggested a desire to gain more from life without knowing how to go about finding direction. I read her restless behavior as a communication of unarticulated dissatisfaction.

Accepting Zelda's outburst as a positive step that would move the process along was a risk built on the belief there was a healthy ambition buried within her virulent rage. The tension I felt was rooted in more than a perilous clinical challenge. The depth of her anger was indeed frightening: it erupted in such a sudden and explosive manner that it had an eerie quality. The challenge was to sustain my conviction that her outbursts contained the aggression she needed to nurture. As unsettling as her rage was, I could not in good conscience object to it after I had sought throughout the therapeutic process to unearth whatever aggressive potential she might have. I managed my anxiety by reminding myself that I was getting what I had been attempting to find. In maintaining this posture, I relied on my knowledge of Zelda and the dormant capabilities I had sensed in her since I had known her. My faith in her desire and ability to exercise her intellect and realize ambition was not blind; I kept in mind her energy, her longing to breakout of the "empty-headed bimbo" mold, and the intellectual and self-reflective capacity I had come to see in her. Nevertheless, I was putting faith in my conviction that these unrealized competencies could be brought to fruition in the analytic process. My challenge was to sustain my belief in this possibility as I absorbed the depth of her rage.

KNOWLEDGE AND FAITH IN
THE THERAPEUTIC PROCESS

My experience with Zelda oscillated between taking a leap of faith and the knowledge of her that I could fall back on. We might call this back and forth movement the dialectic between knowledge and faith in the therapeutic process. In formulating my vision of her as possessing potential ambition and use of intellect, I placed my faith not only in my judgment that she possessed these capacities but also in her willingness to use them. While I felt confident that I had evidence of unrealized abilities from her work in the sessions, I continually questioned how I could be so sure, even if she had these capabilities, of her will to use them. The counterpoint to my doubts was the emptiness, dissatisfaction, and agitation Zelda felt in her current life. This disquiet, the very ennui of her day-to-day existence, convinced me that she sought to live from the depths of her psyche, to utilize her potential. My interpretation of her restlessness as a symptom of a buried self longing to be born did not come wholly from my subjectivity; it had an evidential basis in Zelda's behavior. The latter constituted the data on which I based my assessment that she sought expression of unfulfilled parts of herself. In this sense, I based my conviction on knowledge. Nonetheless, there was no direct logical inference from her disquiet to my vision of her. On the basis of what I experienced with her, I put my faith in her unborn potential and desire to use it. My belief in her sustained both of us through the emotional roller coaster of affective eruptions and frequent self doubting. I overcame my self-questioning by holding firm to my judgment of her capabilities.

It also helped to remind myself that the very fact that Zelda had no history of using her aggression and ambition is what made their development so important. If she had historically harnessed her aggression on behalf of realistic goals, aggressive behavior would not have been so important in the creation of a new self. I had to have faith in something that had not yet happened if new possibilities were to emerge to replace her *ennui*. That is to say, the anxiety I felt in putting faith in the eventual appearance of new ways of being was intrinsic to the project of self creation. Reminding myself of this fact helped me endure the anxiety and strain of placing faith in the emergence of ways of living that Zelda had never experienced.

Zelda's therapeutic voyage illustrates the extent to which therapeutic outcome depends on the therapist's belief that the patient has potential that can be fulfilled. This faith in who the patient can become is what Loewald (1960) meant by the spiritual dimension of psychoanalytic therapy. His point was that no experience or knowledge of the patient is decisive in the formulation of the therapist's belief in the patient. Our experience with the patient cannot tell us definitively who the patient will become; it can only give us indicators that we can use in fashioning our vision. Therefore, Loewald concluded, the success of the therapeutic project depends partly on the analyst's spirit, his faith in the patient's capability of making forward movement.

The therapist's experience, then, includes a deeply felt appreciation for all aspects of the patient and the conviction that she can overcome conflicts to transcend current patterns. Ultimately, the therapist does not just discern the patient's potential; she *believes* in its power to provide a rewarding future. Such faith does not come easily because the patient's pathology stands between unrealized possibilities at the patient's core and the analyst's effort to achieve a depth understanding. The resolute belief in the possibility of a more enriched life issues in a continual seeking for the kernel of health believed to lie, like a buried treasure, under the patient's pathological patterns. The patient, of course, is not sure such a core of health exists and resists the effort to pursue it. The patient's fears of the emergence of the buried self tests the therapist's convictions at every step of the analytic voyage. In the face of opposition from the patient, the therapist must dig deep within herself to sustain the belief in the patient's ability to forge new ways of being. This battle can be difficult in some cases, as we saw with Shannon, and the therapist may require a great deal of forbearance to manage the strain of the therapeutic interaction while seeking to uncover buried potential. To a considerable extent, the success of the project relies on the tenacity of the therapist's spirit.

Often it takes time for the therapist to ascertain something in the patient on which she can rest such a positive prognostication, but there may come a point when the therapist ceases to believe she is going to find a foundation on which to base any such belief. In this situation, the therapist does not have a vision of the patient's potential for growth that can sustain the analytic relationship over the stubbornness of the pathological patterns. The outcome of the therapeutic endeavor so depends on the evolution of the therapist's belief in the patient that it is hard to imagine a positive result with a therapist who cannot see the potential for a new self. Consequently, the therapist who has ceased to believe in the patient's potential has to decide whether to continue the treatment in hopes of finding a cornerstone on which to found an authentic regard for the patient's possibilities, or refer the patient elsewhere. The success of the therapeutic endeavor relies on the therapist's vision; I see no other option.

Moreover, once the therapist begins to reach the deeply hidden potential, she cannot expect a welcome response from the patient. The buried *in nascendu* aspects of the self, having never been recognized or used by the patient, are feared as unknown and possibly dangerous potentialities. This is why previously inexperienced aspects of the self, once touched, erupt in unexpected and often frightening ways. The therapist's initial idea of the patient's emerging potential tends to be more benign and anxiety-free than the patient's new capacities as they actually appear. We saw a good illustration of the patient's tendency to violate analytic exceptions in our discussion of Zelda. It is precisely the spontaneity of the reaction that provides a sense of conviction that the patient's expression is authentic. The vitriolic nature of Zelda's anger and the fact that it surprised both of us made clear the response came from her. Indeed, if the patient's development were to follow closely the analyst's preconceived idea, we might well wonder if newly emerging affects constitute the patient's unconscious compliance with the therapist's presumptions. The therapist is greatly aided in managing his feelings by keeping this principle in mind.

Management of the therapist's anxiety-filled and often disoriented reaction to the patient's spontaneous outburst becomes a key factor in the ultimate success of the patient's emergence. Critical to the therapist's containment of her response to the patient's jarring outbursts is the ability to sustain the perspective that the unexpected, even if appearing in a shocking form, is precisely what is to be anticipated if the patient is to create something new. Adopting this attitude helps the therapist refrain from the temptation to relieve the pressure she feels by retaliating, a reaction that would only interfere with the therapeutic project. The more the therapist is able to keep this conceptualization in mind, the more she is able to help the patient transform the initially spontaneous outburst into newly effective ways of being and relating.

The assessment of potential has a profound influence on the therapist's clinical strategy. Optimistic clinicians tend to see the patient as capable of more change and achievement than therapists who tend to be pessimistic. The former group will interpret with an emphasis on being able to overcome conflicts, with a presumption that the patient is capable of ways of relating different from historical patterns. In counterpoint, the therapist who ascribes a "limited prognosis" will be less venturesome in her interpretations and will not see the purpose of addressing certain conflicts because she will not believe that they can be overcome. If the therapist judges the passive patient capable of deploying aggression, she will look for ways to elicit potential aggression; if she regards the patient's aggression to be dangerously destructive or the patient to be either lacking in aggressive potential or the ability to use it, she will not make the effort to draw the patient's dormant aggression into the analytic interaction. The result is a Pygmalion effect in the consulting room.

To be sure, as we saw in chapter 3, our vision often changes over the course of psychotherapy. Unanticipated passions and capacities tend to emerge and submerge leading to a continual reformulation of the analyst's vision. Although the vicissitudes of the therapist's image tend to diminish her anxiety about the integrity of any particular therapeutic direction, the oscillations create a different sort of problem. The unexpected events and sudden shifts in the course of the therapy can take a heavy toll on the therapist's emotional equilibrium. Understanding the patient tends to provide a sense of clarity that operates as a psychic organizer for the analyst who navigates the therapeutic relationship in accordance with the principles by which she understands the patient. Surprises dictate a reorganization of the therapist's grasp of the patient's dynamics, and to rethink continually one's understanding puts considerable strain on the therapist's emotional capacity. The extension of the analyst's understanding to the future only increases her emotional burden. But the analytic process requires just such an imaginative undertaking. The current approach requires no more of the therapist than is inherent in the role of using potential space to create a self. An occupational hazard of this endeavor is the emotional upheaval of having one's psychological moorings frequently jostled. To keep this in mind is to maintain a perspective that helps stabilize the therapist's emotional roller coaster.

POSSIBILITIES AND THE THERAPIST'S MIND

Recognition of the importance of creating new possibilities requires that the therapist be open to and actively seek pregnant meanings and variants of seemingly clear affective states. As we saw in chapter 5, the therapist must engage the patient's desire not as a given, but as a concrete embodiment of one among other possibilities. This stance diminishes the therapist's sense of safety because the reification of desire makes affect a given, a defined entity on which the therapist can build his understanding of the patient. However, if manifest desire is regarded as one form of a potentially multifaceted process, this presumed clarity erodes, and the analyst is left with a less certain foundation on which to build his comprehension of the patient. This greater sense of ambiguity issues in a feeling of *angst* that is endemic to the therapist's role. We noted that the therapist's vision contains a strong component of existential questioning, but the recognition of desire as a process rather than a given leads to another existential burden. To wit, the analyst must confront the fact that she cannot regard the patient's affects as defined entities on which to build; many are likely to be reexperienced and even redefined over the course of a successful process. In this arena, too, the burden of navigating without a compass is very real. The lack of clarity felt by the therapist can easily feel so overwhelming and disorienting that there is an understandable desire to avoid the onus of maintaining an openness to multiple possibilities by placing the patient's experience into reified, simplistic categories. Patient behavior that bears resemblance to stories from the past can quickly be fit into preexisting slots to serve this end. The more that complex material can be reduced to simple mental filing cabinets, the less one feels the responsibility of considering a variety of possibilities.

This tendency to simplify the therapeutic process is more than a matter of avoiding complexity and ambiguity. The reduction of experience to preset categories tends to relieve the intensity of the clinical encounter. Lear (1998) provides a good example of this function of analytic simplification in his discussion of the Rat Man. Lear avers that both Freud and the patient were perplexed at the intensity of the Rat Man's fear that Freud would do him injury. Freud's quick interpretation that the patient was projecting his fear of his father onto his analyst relieved the anxiety for both members of the dyad by circumventing the patient's experience of Freud. Freud's haste to dissipate the Rat Man's fear precluded consideration of other possibilities. Freud never considered that he might have done something of which the Rat Man might well be afraid. For example, Freud never entertained the possibility that his effort to analyze may have been experienced by the patient as an attack, an intrusion into his privacy. The point is not that Freud privileged the here-and-now transference, but that he precluded all possibilities except the one truth he believed captured the single meaning of the patient's fear. By recasting this fear as belonging not to himself but to the Rat Man's father, Freud got himself off the hook and avoided the difficulty of searching for different ways of understanding the patient's fear.

Lear's discussion of the Rat Man illustrates the way an analyst can use her interpretive role to diminish the complexity of his task and thereby reduce the anxiety of ambiguity. To sustain this anxiety is a psychic strain that therapists understandably wish to avoid but that they must hold in order to allow a full range of possibilities to come into play. The binding of open analytic space by conceptualization is an inevitable outcome of understanding, but for that very reason the analyst must be careful not to use interpretation to effect premature closure. Even a seemingly well-intentioned and accurate interpretive strategy can be employed to diminish the analyst's fear of being overwhelmed by an array of possibilities. This is what Freud did with the Rat Man, and the anxieties Freud avoided are no less real today. The clinical stance advocated here of opening potential space and allowing multiple possibilities to unfold strains the analyst's psychic equilibrium considerably, a problem that analysts of previous generations were able to avoid.

THE ANALYST'S EXPERIENCE AND THE FRAGILE SELF

Working with a patient like Shannon takes a considerably greater toll on the therapist's emotional life than working with patients like Zelda and Anna. Shannon seemed to benefit little from interpretations. My words did not appear to register with her, so I was frustrated and unsure if my work with her could bear fruit. Warding off pessimism, I decided that the ineffectiveness of my interpretive work could be looked at in two ways: either as a problem of Shannon's character or of my agenda. There was a struggle inside me between these two positions. My dilemma was that if I adapted to Shannon, would I be immersed in a regressive relationship with no way out? And if I did not, would I ever have an impact? Ultimately, I decided to suspend my agenda in favor of hers because I felt that my insistence on understanding was not going to reach her need for a nurturing relationship. The problem, of course, was that in doing so I was adjusting my clinical strategy on the belief that she had a potential for self realization that would emerge out of a deeply regressive relationship if I could make contact with it.

By my subordinating the interpretive stance, my belief in her was tested in a deeper way than was true for Zelda or Anna, and the risk was greater. In accommodating Shannon's longing for fusion, I was putting my faith in a hoped-for future response to my ministrations. But what if she never responded? How would I disentangle myself from her dependence on me? I resolved to engage her needs despite this anxiety. I knew I was taking a risk, but I believed in her ability to respond to a relationship that connected with her buried self. This is the leap of faith required of the therapist who makes an adaptation to the patient in an effort to stimulate the creation of self by reaching the patient's hidden core.

Even with Shannon, my faith was not blind. I undertook a risk on the basis of indications in the patient's behavior suggesting the ability and desire to attach. Shannon's demands were difficult to bear; nothing seemed to satisfy her. I often felt helpless to find something she would respond to, but in her claims on me, she was showing not only her need and desire for an attachment but her hope for a positive relationship and her belief that she could have a useful connection with me. As offended as I was by her sense of entitlement, I saw in it the cry for a relationship in the only way she knew. So it was Shannon's plea that gave me the courage to meet her needs. I trusted that she would eventually grow into a relationship of mutuality with me if she could first feel that I believed in her and that her most significant affects were being engaged.

I find it more difficult to preserve belief in patients who show little interest in or ability for an emotional connection. I believe that many emotionally removed patients are capable of attachment, but I find myself struggling to sustain this belief in the face of emotional distance. No matter how offensive a demand might be, I tend to be inspired by the desire, whereas I do not feel myself stirred by a patient who seems distant from human connection This type of subjective response is not the same for all of us. Other therapists might well respond more hopefully to the distant patient and less optimistically to entitlement. Therapists, who have their own personality traits, are moved differently by different issues and their emotional reactions greatly influence their belief in and vision of the patient's possibilities. It is often difficult to predict which patients will strike a responsive chord in any particular therapist. What does seem clear is that only if the therapist finds a way to believe in the patient's potential can she engage the patient as a person with the potential to create a new, more meaningful self, as I did with Shannon, Anna, and Zelda.

To emphasize the therapist's faith and risk is to recognize the existential component of psychoanalytic therapy directed to the creation of the self. The therapist risks her convictions, her most deeply held beliefs about what people are capable of and who an individual might become. To be sure, the judgment is made from the way the patient engages the therapeutic process, that is, from the evidence in the patient's ways of being and relating. However, the therapist extrapolates beyond the historical patterns to as-yet-unfulfilled possibilities. This subjective judgment is an inferential leap beyond the patient's behavior and therein lies the risk in being the agent for the patient's self creation.

CONCLUSION

We have seen that therapists who undertake the project of self creation and the performance of tasks are embarked on a mission that requires the confrontation of issues that differ from the traditional analytic role, and for which they have not been trained. We have seen that a therapist trying to envision the patient's future is faced with difficult existential choices and risks. There are many temptations to escape the ensuing dilemmas, but the therapist who gives play to the widest variety of patient possibilities feels the *angst* of ambiguity develop in the potential space of the therapeutic field. These choices become an important part of the therapeutic endeavor as the dialectic between knowledge and faith permeates analytic interaction. The therapist attempting to facilitate the creation of self feels the strain of having to choose among myriad possibilities and the investment in a vision always open to change.

Having completed our theoretical discussion of how the therapist promotes the patient's creation of self along with our understanding of the emotional strain the process places on the therapist, we are now in position to consider how this model applies to specific clinical conditions frequently seen in the consulting room.

PART TWO

CLINICAL APPLICATIONS

Having delineated a model of psychoanalytic therapy designed to help the patient create new components of the self in PartOne, we now turn to the application of this paradigm to specific clinical pictures. The syndromes chosen are not meant to represent an exhaustive list of problems to which this approach can be applied; nor is it assumed that the clinical strategy advocated here can be used to ameliorate the symptoms of all patients who fit into these categories. Four common clinical syndromes were chosen because they are likely to be familiar to most practicing analytic therapists and because the model has been effectively used to diminish symptoms in patients whose problems fit these categories. Somatic symptoms, depression, and narcissistic injuries are among the most frequently seen problems facing the contemporary therapist. Although the grip of bad objects is not analogous to the other syndromes, this problem is included here to highlight both its commonality and difficulty. In a variety of clinical pictures, the therapeutic process frequently leads to stubbornly adhesive bad objects that seem refractory to therapeutic intervention, often leading to a stalemate in the therapy. This problem has proven so difficult for so many therapists that it seemed fitting to include a chapter on the way the current model can be used to address this vexing psychological configuration.

7

THE DISOWNED BODY

When Breuer and Freud (1895) treated hysterical patients, they encountered people whose bodies seemed to be mysteriously out of their control. Such symptoms as paralysis, coughs, and bodily weakness without physical basis all seemed to reflect a body acting as though on its own. The clinical problem was to bring the body back under the control of the patient. When Freud (1923) defined the aim of psychoanalysis with his famous, pithy statement, "Where id was, there ego shall be," he made clear that command of the body was the very essence of psychoanalytic therapy. Thus, in a very real sense, mastery of the body and bodily urges has been a goal of the psychoanalytic process from the beginning of the field.

For Freud, of course, regulation of bodily experience meant primarily control over the drives. This drive-based view of motivation led to the theoretical elaboration of ego psychology and the central role of ego mastery in the outcome of psychoanalysis. Ego psychologists such as Hartmann (1939), Hendrick (1942), and White (1963) postulated independent ego energies with the motivation to effect the environment and organize the psyche irrespective of tension reduction needs. Rapaport (1951, 1957) made ego mastery over id impulses and environmental influences the goal of the psychoanalytic process.

The ego psychological approach led to the formulation that bodily expression of symptoms represents a failure in ego control mechanisms due to the inability to mediate linguistically affective tension or a failure of the internalization process (e.g., Fenichel, 1945). That is, affective pressure unmodulated by defenses or adaptive mechanisms may seek direct discharge in bodily

159

symptoms. This formulation of somatic expression as unmediated affective display has become so commonplace in psychoanalytic theory that it is expressed not only by classical ego psychologists, such as Fenichel (1945), but also by more contemporary writers, such as McDougall (1985), Khan (1974), and Gunsberg and Tylim (1998). For all these theorists, affects dislodged from symbolic discourse gain immediate, nonlinguistic expression through somatic symptoms.

This way of understanding somatic symptom formation assumes that unstructured, directionless energy is the original form of affective experience, whereas psychic organization is a secondary phenomenon grafted onto this originally disorganized affective life. Such a theoretical construction is central to the way psychoanalysts have traditionally conceptualized the dynamics of somatic symptoms. Yet evidence from research on early affective life calls into question this developmental assumption.

DEVELOPMENT AND OBJECT RELATIONS THEORY

It is now recognized that basic affects are inborn (Tomkins, 1962; Demos, 1992). Whether or not one agrees with Tomkins's particular enumeration of early affects, it is clear that states such as interest, enjoyment, surprise, distress, anger, fear, and disgust do not have to be learned. An infant will react to environmental circumstances in any of these ways without having witnessed them. As inborn responses to the environment, the baby's affects influence greatly the developing relationship between child and the early figures in his life (Demos, 1988, 1992). Painful cries, enjoyment of stimulation, and interest in novel experiences are organized affective responses that fit environmental circumstances and, over the course of development, become elaborated into more complex affective states. Far from being disorganized, affects, in whatever form they assume, are differentiated responses to situations. Even in the first days of life, affects are not tantamount to somatic symptoms. Rather, affects use the body to convey what is cared about, what matters. When the infant is excited, he expresses an excited relatedness to the world; when angry he relates to the world aggressively. If something captures his attention, he shows interest. If the mother is responsive to the child's affective states by correctly identifying them and providing an "optimal zone of affective engagement," the child uses his affects to form a relationship between himself and the world (Demos, 1988, 1992).

Many developmental studies have demonstrated that affective life is, from the beginning, organized around relating to others (Lichtenberg, 1983; Stern, 1985). According to Bowlby (1969), this need serves the adaptive purpose of keeping the young child close to the protector. Whatever the specific evolutionary origin, the child needs and seems prewired to form an attachment to the caretaker and feels threatened without it (Ainsworth, et al., 1978; Bowlby, 1988). Very early on, the baby and caretaker form patterns of relating with rules that the child comes to expect (Beebe, Jaffe, and Lachmann, 1992; Beebe and Lachmann, 2002). The overwhelming developmental evidence points to the conclusion that the child is preprogrammed not for a pleasure-seeking life oblivious to reality, but for interaction with a real person through a relationship mediated by affective states.

These findings support a key precept of object relations theory: the child seeks not pleasure but a reality-oriented relationship to early objects. Fairbairn (1944) observed that pure pleasure seeking is pathological, a symptom of an ego defect rather than a natural state of the human organism. Kohut (1977) later made the same point in the language of self psychology: the child is motivated not by impulsive energies but by the desire to carry out the nuclear program of the self. Thus, according to Kohut (1984), affection and assertiveness are natural states that flower with the proper self-selfobject milieu, but if these natural tendencies are thwarted, they may be transformed into lust and hostility.

Children are not just motivated to form relationships; they are also interested in the world of nonhuman objects. Indeed, we now know that neonates possess considerable mental capability for exploring the world from the first days of life. They can detect contingencies and patterns; they plan and are capable of voluntary motor control (e.g., DeCasper and Carstens, 1981; Demos, 1992). Most important, infants are motivated to use these capacities, being limited in doing so only by their musculature. Infants quickly attempt and often succeed at learning to do voluntarily what is originally done involuntarily (Tomkins, 1978). Apparent disorganization signifies a self organization restricted by the child's muscular and motor limitations (Demos, 1988).

The developmental research on the autonomous nature of children's curiosity about and elaboration of the world supports the notion that they are inherently motivated to exercise their capacities to form a self. By fueling the desire to become the self, affects play a critical role in this inborn motive (Summers, 1999, pp. 45–53). Therefore, if self potential is to be realized, it must be possible for affects to be used in accordance with the needs of the self. For example, aggression must be available to fulfill ambitions, and affection must be accessible for intimate relationships. The child must be free to pursue his interests. As Benjamin (1995) has emphasized, such affective freedom is possible only if the caretakers' accepting and approving gaze recognizes and nurtures the child's spontaneous affective expressions.

When facilitated by the caretaker, affects define the ways in which we are able to care. As we have seen in chapter 5, affects spread to experiences possessing both similar and dissimilar characteristics to the original affective situation. In this way, affects magnify and become the medium through which the self forms its ways of relating to the world. The organization of these affective states, each of which defines an aspect of the person-world relationship, becomes the self. Rather than existing in isolation, affects are embedded in a self structure that implicates a world of objects.

THE PSYCHOANALYTIC CONCEPT OF OWNERSHIP

Rapaport's (1951, 1957) theory that ego autonomy is achieved through the counterbalancing of drives and environment led to a problematic account of the "ownership" of the psyche. If, in fact, each puts a brake on the other, this constraint does not produce autonomy because there is no subject able to be autonomous with respect to either source of pressure on the psyche. If the drives withstand the pressure of the environment, no subject takes ownership of the effects of the environment; *mutatis mutandi*, the reverse is true. Rapaport's introduction of ego control mechanisms did not resolve this difficulty because such mechanisms are impersonal and distant from the psychic events they are supposed to control. Thus, the ego as an apparatus of tension control is not a center of subjectivity and cannot assume ownership of psychic events. As Benjamin (1997) has noted, ownership requires a subject, and the concept of subjectivity cannot be embraced by ego psychology.

In contradistinction to ego psychology, the findings of developmental research and the clinical–theoretical concepts of object relations theory that we have briefly reviewed *do* provide the foundation for a psychoanalytic concept of ownership. As we have seen, if caretakers are responsive to the child's psychic states, affects become elaborated into ways of being and relating. For example, if the child's excitement about learning a task is echoed in the parents' response, this enthusiasm becomes available to the growing child in response to the exercise of emerging capacities. Accomplishments then are met with positive feelings that spread to a variety of successful experiences. In like manner, any affect that is welcomed by the early caretakers becomes a characteristic ways of relating to the environment and thereby a part of the self organization.

In this situation, a person is free to utilize affects to realize capacities and define the significant relationships between the world and others. Affects free to be used in this way form the basis of a self that has the freedom to react and create on behalf of its aims; that is a self that is owned. Ownership of the psyche, then, is achieved by utilizing authentic affects in being and relating. It is the *authenticity* of affect, as facilitated by the early caretakers, that is the crucial factor in ownership of the psyche. In other words, if authentic affects are free to gain expression, no superordinate control apparatus such as an "ego" is required. Indeed, if a mechanism is needed to control affective expression, then the affects in question are derivative expressions of frustration in early development. The shift in psychoanalytic developmental theory from original formless energy to organized, if primitive, relatedness to the world through affective exchange suggests a correlative change in the concept of ownership of the self. Appropriation of the self is achieved by living in accordance with one's authentic experience rather than through executing a control apparatus. The question then arises: if affects are originally reality related, how is it that clinicians see so much distortion, disorganization, and illusion in the affective lives of patients?

THE PSYCHOPATHOLOGY OF AFFECTIVE LIFE

Developmental research and clinical theory converge to show that the child's affective states require a resonance with the caretaker such that the child feels her affects are not only welcomed and appreciated, but also "real" (e.g., Lacan, 1949; Kohut, 1971; Winnicott, 1971). It is only through the responsiveness of the other that the child has a sense of her own reality. For this reason, the concept of the "mirror" has gained much attention in recent psychoanalytic thought (e.g., Lacan, 1949; Kohut, 1971). If the child's affects are ignored, she feels that they are somehow invalid or defective. Even more poignantly, if the child evinces an emotional response that is met with an overtly negative response from the caretaker, the affect will be experienced by the child as threatening the bond. Believing that an affect will cost the love of the parent or even the relationship itself, the child will bury such an affect in order to maintain the caretaker connection.

To the extent that the environment militates against the genuine expression of experience, defenses are erected to protect authentically experienced self states. Winnicott termed the latter the true self, and I have referred to such hidden affective potential as the buried self (Summers, 1999). For example, if the caretaker cannot tolerate anger, the child feels that the relationship is threatened by aggressive expression, and the anger will be disavowed in order to secure the child's tie to the adult on whom he depends. If excitement evokes anxiety in the parenting figure, the child will squelch potentially excited states to fit the exigencies of the relationship. Under these and similar circumstances, the child splits her engagement with the social world from the affective experience that jeopardized the caretaking bond. The affect may be completely buried or reduced to a muffled, attenuated form.

As Breuer and Freud (1895) and Freud (1915) told us long ago, if an affect is denied entrance into consciousness, it seeks expression in another form. Emotions push for release, but if direct expression is not possible, derivative forms of expression must be found. The clinical evidence that patients continually seek an outlet for buried affects confirms Freud's idea that unconscious states attempt to gain entry into consciousness, but Freud's explanation was that "drives" seek gratification by reducing "tension." If affects are no longer assumed to be derivative of drives, this explanation must be altered. As we have seen, the child has a motivation to exercise and develop inborn capacities; affects are a crucial component of this movement. An affect that is disavowed cannot mediate the self's relationship to the world, causing the loss of an important potential component of the self. The result is a constriction of self-development.

The search for an outlet for arrested affective states leads to the distortion of emotional life manifested in so many patients. If the child's affects are neglected or met with negative reactions, his anger will build. But, if his anger is similarly opposed or ignored, the child will often act out his anger in behavior—by breaking rules, stealing, or defying parental authority or by hostility to weaker figures, such as siblings (Parens, 1979). The viciousness and sadism of which some children are capable is an unmet reaction to frustration of the need for parental responsiveness and the inability to express frustration and anger directly (Parens, 1979). Some children will defend against their hostility by becoming overexcited. Unbridled rage or uncontrolled excitement are two possible reactions to the suppression of spontaneous affects. Any such indirect, distorted communication of affect is tantamount to the psychopathology of affective life. Such pathology may take many forms, among which is the somatization of the affect, our focus here.

PSYCHOPATHOLOGY OF THE BODY

Affects are clearly bodily experiences. In addition to the measurable level of neurological excitation that inheres in affects, the latter are experienced in the body. When the mother enters the room, for example, the infant's excitement is a bodily reaction: he gurgles and wriggles his whole body. Similarly, distress is emitted not only with an anguished facial expression but also with a convulsion of the entire body. Although as the child grows, the connection between body and affects will become more subtle, affects always retain a bodily component. Due to this connection, when the infant owns his affective states, he owns his bodily experience.

Gunsberg and Tylim (1998) have proposed that the psychopathology of body ownership is rooted in parents who appropriate the child's body for themselves. While this dynamic is undoubtedly a factor in some instances, parental "hijacking" is not the only possible cause of disowned bodily experience. Any early environment requiring the child to divorce affects, and therefore bodily experience, from engagement with the world can result in disowned bodily states. For example, if anger is experienced by the early attachment figures as injurious, the child learns to suppress all aggressive responses with the result that one aspect of bodily experience is disowned. If sensual experience and pleasure evoke reactions of disapproval or even disgust in the caretaker, the child soon learns that such positive states threaten the parental bond and this aspect of bodily experience will be removed from consciousness. A wide variety of such parental reactions may lead the child to suppress particular affective experiences or even affective life itself.

Owing to the link between feelings and the body, any such burying of affective experience issues in bodily tension. As the affect can achieve expression only through the soma, the body must be used to prevent its articulation. A psychic battle is therefore waged within the physiology of the patient. To suppress anger, for example, means to contain aggressive expressions by countermeasures of both the psyche and the musculature. As affective experiences are now divorced from human interaction, the body learns to contain the tension of somatic urges that cannot be brought to fruition. The upshot is a split between bodily experience and ways of relating to the world, a cleavage within the psyche that isolates bodily experience from the interpersonal realm.

The tension produced by this conflict is not to be confused with the conflict which Freud believed to be the root of neurotic symptoms. For Freud (1923), the tension was rooted in the conflict between the need for endogenous drive discharge, on the one hand, and the constraints of reality and the superego that prevent immediacy of relief, on the other. In the current conceptualization, by contrast, the tension of psychic conflict expressed in somatic form originates in the motive to utilize inborn affective capacities. The conflict is with an environment that prohibits significant affective expressions, resulting in bodily frustration. According to the view proposed here, somatic symptoms may originate in the prohibition of a variety of affective dispositions, whereas Freud's formulation limited the source of all neurotic symptoms to the repression of sexual or aggressive drives. Furthermore, the pressure for affective expression in the current view is the motive to exercise capacities, to become fully human by articulating the variety of affective possibilities with which one is born. This position embraces a much broader concept of possible sources of somatic pathology. Freud's narrow concept of the "return of the repressed" is replaced here by the "return of the capacities of the self."

Because of the intimate connection between the body and affects, unarticulated body experience contains the meaning of the experience from which it has been disowned. As the container of disavowed affects, the body bears the meaning of those aspects of experience that cannot be brought into the social world; one might say that the unconscious lays dormant within the body. When the indirect entrance of the buried self is concretized in the body, the soma becomes a vehicle for communicating strangulated affects. It is this somatic expression, which replaces the linguistic conveyance of meaning, that we call the symptom: The somatic symptom represents the bodily imprisonment of arrested affective potential. In one sense, Freud's idea of the unconscious meaning of repressed affect has stood the test of time: the bodily symptom results from stifled affect and contains its unconscious meaning. However, it fits the clinical facts, in opposition to Freud's drive theory, to conceptualize the distortion of affect as a disavowed affective experience resulting in the splitting off of a part of the self.

This split-off aspect of the self, then, cannot be deployed for ways of being and relating. The self suffers a severe constriction of its capabilities as a product of buried affective potential. For example, if aggression is disavowed, the self cannot pursue goals, realize ambitions, achieve mastery over conflict, or engage in competition. The aggressive disposition remains as a bodily tension, contained within a psyche that operates without the use of aggression for these purposes. The possibilities for the self are in this way severely compromised. The same is true for all major affective categories, such as excitement, interest, shame, disgust, or joy. Without the availability of affective experience, the self becomes constricted in the ways it can engage the world.

This explanation accounts for the fact that analysts often look in vain for a specific symbolic meaning of the bodily symptom. While the pathological picture seldom has a specific symbolic content that can be equated with a traumatic event, the symptom does represent the expression of a category of self-experience that is not otherwise accessible. Modell (1991), employing Edelman's theory of memory, has shown that affects are stored as *categories* of experience, not as discrete states. For example, if the caretaker is threatened by the child's anger, this affect is encoded under the file of "threat." As a result, the affect is buried, divorced from the interpersonal world. The self develops without a repertoire of angry responses, and aggression, not being an option, remains only as untapped potential. The affect category "anger," rather than being a specific memory or fantasy, becomes unconscious. Any situation or event that has the potential to evoke anger will be avoided because "anger" is connected to "threat," not because it stimulates a specific memory.

But the anger still exists and will often find some indirect means of expression. If the mother is threatened by anger, for example, the child may attack a younger sibling who is less threatening or break or destroy possessions the mother values. The child may misbehave at school and be brought in for consultation as a "behavior problem." The possibilities are endless. Whatever form the symptom takes, it captures anger and therefore has meaning. But it does not typically reflect a particular incident or fantasy. That is why patient and analyst so frequently seem on an endless and fruitless quest for something in the child's past that is never uncovered. They are trying to unravel a symptom that corresponds to a general affect category rather than to a specific incident or transaction.

The same analysis applies to the somatic expression of a disavowed affect. To continue with our example, a child who is unable to express his anger may complain of stomach aches or pain in various parts of the body. As adults, many such patients visit medical clinics with various pains, such as headaches, back and neck pain, gastrointestinal disorders, or ulcers. The analysis of one patient, who was pathologically compliant, revealed an intense and frightening degree of rage at his father, who had not only been verbally abusive to him as a child but cheated him in a business deal as an adult. On entering analysis, the patient was aware of no ill feelings toward his deceased father in the past or present. He had spent his adulthood trying to gain his father's approval and consciously was aware only of positive feelings toward the older man. When the anger was uncovered in the treatment, the patient remembered that he had developed an ulcer at age 10. The parents and the doctor had decided that he was under "too much stress" and bought the boy a backboard and basket to play basketball to "relieve the stress." The patient never questioned this solution until he recalled the incident in analysis. At that point, he began to feel the full intensity of his anger toward his father, and the emergence of his long-suppressed aggression evoked a lengthy series of memories of verbal abuse that went on all his life and led to the patient's feeling of defectiveness.

The manifestation of the disowned body is found not only in psychosomatic and hysterical symptoms but also in a variety of other pathological outcomes. For example, submission as a desperate effort to achieve interpersonal contact in concrete bodily form becomes masochism. In an extreme form of sacrificing the self to gain recognition from the other, the masochist believes that he must disavow any agency, suppress his own will completely, in order to achieve object contact (Berliner, 1947, 1958). Sexual gratification can be obtained only when the body submits, when pain is inflicted, since pain evokes the illusion that all desire and agency have been wiped clean from the psyche. The suppression of all agency becomes concretized in the passive body that can gain pleasure only in its very submission.

It is difficult to say why in some people disavowed affects erupt into bodily symptoms, while in others the outcome is an interpersonal expression of the unarticulated part of the self. The question of "symptom choice" has puzzled clinicians for decades, and I cannot add to the time-honored debate here. Alexander (1943), puzzling over this issue, hypothesized that some sort of congenital weakness in a part of the body was the source of the specific somatic symptom. Whatever the validity of such a theory, what we can say is that given the inextricable link between affect and the body, any suppression of an affective category has the potential to gain expression in a somatic symptom. It also bears noting that the distinction between somatic and hysterical symptoms, on one hand, and apparently "nonsomatic" disorders, on the other, is not as clear as it may appear. Even in cases in which the symptomatic outcome is not clearly somatic, there is often a bodily component. Anxiety symptoms, for example, are experienced in the body: sweaty palms, racing heart, and hyperventilation are all bodily expressions. The rage of the borderline patient is often an overwhelming bodily reaction that cannot, at times, be controlled. Even depression typically includes a loss of bodily energy. In point of fact, virtually all psychopathology has a bodily manifestation.

For Breuer and Freud (1895) bodily symptoms represented specific repressed psychic content, whereas the theoretical advance of the various self theorists lies in the reconceptualization of repressed material from specific events, memories, or wishes to unrealized capacities. When a child sacrifices authentic expression of affects for the maintenance of early relationships, the upshot is the removal of an affective category from the development of the self, resulting in an arrest of self-potential. The disowned affect reappears as a symptom, and, if this reemergence takes on bodily form, a somatic symptom will result.

Somatic symptoms originate in the sacrifice of a major part of affective life in order to sustain an attachment to a caretaker. The body becomes the recipient of the strangulated affect and a passive vehicle for its expression. This part of bodily experience, rather than being authored by the self, is experienced as a victim of unseen and unknown forces. While the passively experienced body is not owned, bodily ownership cannot be regained simply by turning passivity into activity. One of Benjamin's (1997) major contributions to psychoanalytic theory is her insight that reversal of passive into active or vice versa does not constitute ownership: masochism turned around becomes sadism, an equally "driven" state. Benjamin argues that to achieve ownership such antinomies must be transcended so that the patient is capable both of active and of passive forms of expression. What must be added to Benjamin's formulation is that enacting passive and active states does not constitute ownership: the ability to be alternately masochistic and sadistic is not ownership of the psyche. For example, borderline patients typically oscillate, often suddenly and even violently, between helpless passivity and belligerent activity without owning either state. Missing for such patients is the ability to deploy activity and passivity to create and sustain the self. Self-realization requires activity when certain affective responses need expression and elaboration, and passivity when affects call for being the recipient of others' actions. When active and passive positions can be freely used to achieve one's aims, then the self may be said to be owned.

Understanding somatic symptoms as the derivative expression of arrested capacities rather than the discharge of affect suggests that analysts search not only for symbolic content but also for indications of unrealized affective potential. The purpose of the search for the disowned body is to uncover hidden content as well as to open up a space in which new possibilities for affective expression may emerge. The buried affective potential, which exists largely as a domain of potential bodily experience, must be discovered and brought into the analytic dialogue. Once it enters the analytic space, the aim is to transform it from an incipient affective state to a way of being. Here we see the concrete difference in clinical posture emanating from the difference between viewing somatic symptoms as strangulated affects and seeing them as disowned parts of the self. From the latter viewpoint, a key analytic goal is to create new possible ways of being and relating from previously dormant incipient affective dispositions.

This difference between the classic analytic posture of understanding and the goal of achieving ownership is nowhere clearer than in the very first "analytic" case: Anna O. Elsewhere I have discussed this case in detail (Summers, 1999). Here I provide only the briefest summary to highlight the difference between an analytic posture of uncovering repressed contents and the aim of achieving ownership of the body. As is well known, Breuer found Bertha Pappenheim in a state of severe bed-ridden hysteria, an extreme case of losing control of bodily experience (Breuer, 1895). Her symptoms included paralysis, a persistent cough, anorexia, hysterical blindness, muteness, and even hallucinations. In an autohypnotic state, the young woman was muttering to herself in a seemingly incoherent fashion. It is less well known that Breuer was impressed by more than her pathology: he took note of Bertha's prodigious intellect, articulateness, fault finding, independence of judgment, and compassion (Hirschmuller, 1989). Breuer was convinced that her desire and capacity to help people would serve her well in life and that her compassion "should be exercised at the earliest" after treatment was ended. Breuer also recognized that Bertha's training to be an Orthodox Jewish homemaker left her intellect "undernourished."

Breuer was the first to take her seemingly incoherent speech seriously. He repeated her words back to her, she told him what was bothering her, and together they traced her symptoms to their beginnings. According to Breuer's account, with each symptom she relived psychic events in reverse order until she recalled the pathogenic traumatic event, and at that point, the symptom disappeared. Although Bertha achieved considerable symptom relief, she was hospitalized on three separate occasions after the treatment ended and was not completely restored to functioning until she moved with her mother to Frankfurt. There she was accepted into the social circle of her mother's family, the Goldschmidts, a group of wealthy, cultured, sophisticated German Jews who appreciated her prodigious intellect and wit. Exposed to their social consciousness, especially feminism and social welfare, Bertha flowered, devoting herself to helping society's dispossessed members—pregnant teenage girls, refugees, homeless teens, and unmarried women. She also became a feminist scholar, studying the history of Jewish ghetto women and translating the works of Jewish feminists.

Although Breuer's treatment of Anna O had remarkable success in relieving her symptoms at a time when psychiatry was having precious little influence on hysterical symptomatology, she remained symptomatic and intermittently dysfunctional until she was accepted into the Goldschmidts' social and intellectual circle. Breuer concentrated on the derepression of traumatic events and their strangulated affects, but the Goldschmidts served a very different function: they helped Bertha realize long-dormant capacities. They nourished her gifts and her natural disposition and character traits. Bertha ultimately found fulfillment in the utilization of exactly those traits Breuer had noticed on first meeting her, but it was the Goldschmidts, not Breuer, who helped her find avenues of expression for her intellect, her critical judgment, and her compassion. When these traits were nourished, Bertha regained ownership of her body, and her hysterical symptoms finally disappeared.

Breuer separated the development of Bertha's character and talent from her treatment, and the limits of his effectiveness may be directly attributable to this division. Psychoanalysis can learn an invaluable lesson from Breuer's experience. Bertha's frustration with her imprisoned life was expressed mostly through her bodily paralysis and dysfunction. Breuer knew that her strict upbringing was not healthy for her, but he was so focused on symptom relief by way of the derepression of strangulated affects that he disconnected the suffocation of her character and talents from the treatment. Bertha Pappenheim's experience with her relatives, who valued her gifts and helped her bring them to fruition, shows that such a divorce was unwarranted. When her capacities and most highly cherished values were allowed to flourish, her affective life was freed to gain expression in her ways of living. With her desires and affects directing her life, Bertha regained ownership of her body, and her symptoms disappeared forever. It is clear from this case that the analytic task in the treatment of the disowned body is to discover buried affective potential and facilitate its articulation into ways of being and relating so that the patient can assume ownership of his bodily states. Now let us see how this theoretical shift affects the clinical strategy in the treatment of somatic conditions.

CLINICAL TECHNIQUE

A more contemporary example of this process can be seen in the analytic treatment of Jenny, a 74-year-old woman who had been married to her second husband for 20 years when she became highly symptomatic. She felt weak and dizzy, her body was filled with pain, and she broke out in a rash. Jenny was initially hospitalized medically, but no physical source of the symptoms was discovered; when transfer to the psychiatric unit was recommended, she refused and left the hospital. Although she could not say why at the time, she did not feel she could return to her husband, Joe. The thought of reentering her marital situation intensified her anxiety, and, when relatives suggested she stay with them, she was greatly relieved and immediately assented. She was living in this new situation without knowing what her future plans were when she sought outpatient psychotherapy.

Jenny presented as highly anxious, as though afraid of some unnamable danger. She said that she needed someone to be available continually to her and asked to be seen five times a week. She stated clearly that the thought of returning to Joe nauseated her, but she had never lived on her own and feared she could never manage her life without the support of others. She was satisfied living with relatives but did not know how long she could do so. No option felt safe. Acknowledging that she had lived in fear of impending danger all her life, Jenny realized that she did feel protected in each marriage, although she was never quite able to reach the degree of safety she sought. In both unions, however, Jenny experienced a profound feeling of dissatisfaction. With her first husband, George, she felt ignored. He spent little time at home and focused his life on his business and friends. Ultimately the marriage ended when she discovered an affair.

The second marriage took place shortly after the first ended and was not much more satisfying, but at least Joe was faithful, seldom critical of her, far more supportive than George had been, and he seemed to have a great deal of affection for her. Nonetheless, he was an isolate who relied on Jenny for their social life. Jenny, who had always been gregarious, took complete control of the couple's social calendar and enjoyed their parties and social gatherings. The problem was that, when alone with her husband, she could not get him to engage in conversation. Nonetheless, he insisted that she spend every evening and all her weekend time with him. Jenny felt lonely and frustrated throughout the course of the 20-year marriage. When confronted with the possibility of returning home after her hospitalization, she found the thought of going back to the long, lonely, tedious nights unbearable.

Jenny had been living her life on the assumption that she had little talent or value and that her only role would be as an appendage to a man. It never occurred to her that she had anything to offer anyone, and, after a lifetime of believing that she was incapable of functioning on her own, she was terrified of the thought of living by herself. Desperate to feel safe, she had felt no freedom to decline either marriage proposal, even though she felt no strong affection for either man. Although she was relieved to be married in both cases, her unhappiness began to grow almost as soon as the ceremony ended.

At the risk of simplifying a complicated developmental process, it may be said that Jenny had been given little attention by either parent. The fourth of five children, she had a sister one year older who was born with one leg, an event that precipitated a depressive breakdown in her mother. After being notified of her third child's disability, the mother fell into despair and lost much of her motivation to live and function. Although she had periods of improvement, Jenny's mother never seemed to recover fully and spent most of the rest of her years in a withdrawn depression. Because of his wife's difficulty functioning, Jenny's father brought in the paternal grandmother to care for the sister so that the mother could care for the other children. According to the family's accounts, in an effort to relieve her misery, the mother had another child as soon as possible; and Jenny was born one year after her disabled sister. Although delighted to have an intact child, the older woman was too distraught to assume maternal functions for any of the children. The result was that no one was responsible for Jenny, who, to this day, has no memory of her mother from childhood. Her father, busy building his business, paid little attention to the family and left the upbringing of the children to Jenny's depressed mother and grandmother. When her next sister was born one year after her, Jenny was even more neglected, and she spent much of her childhood lost and isolated.

Despite her depressed mother and unavailable father, Jenny was a vivacious, gregarious, fun-loving child. She remembers playing endless games outside; among her favorites were roller skating, baseball, and games she invented. Her constant companion in all these activities, in addition to the neighborhood children, was her younger sister, with whom she was tightly bonded for the first 18 years of her life. As we discussed her childhood, Jenny wondered aloud what had happened to the playfulness she had so enjoyed in childhood. She felt that a key part of her personality was somehow "lost." When asked if she could recall when her life had become overly serious, Jenny, who had never thought about the question before, immediately associated to ages 12 and 13, when she first became interested in boys. She had assumed, without being aware of it, that she had to stifle the active, aggressive part of her personality so that boys would like her, as her mother said. An outstanding athlete, Jenny gave up all athletic pursuits at that time; they were not resumed until her children were grown. Her mother was explicit about the behavior that would attract boys and men: passivity, pleasing others, nurturant activity, and, above all, putting the man's desires before her own. The idea was to be a good wife and, if going to college would help her achieve that goal, it was a good idea, but not for any other reason. Her mother acquiesced to sending her to a prestigious college because a good education made her more marriageable. Jenny now realized that she had transformed herself into a passive person with the goal of making herself desirable, while holding in abeyance the rest of her personality.

This trend was crystallized when she met George. The marriage to her humorless, demanding, affectless husband consolidated her inclination toward compliance and erased the last vestiges of playfulness and self-initiative that Jenny had been able to sustain for brief periods. George could not tolerate her humor and spontaneity, and the focus of Jenny's life gradually shifted to pleasing George. However, nothing she did seemed to satisfy him, and as his criticisms increased, Jenny worked all the harder to gratify him until her life became overburdened with the effort to perform tasks to his standard. The pattern of devoting herself to meeting the needs of her spouse continued with Joe, who, although a more accommodating personality than George, had little capacity for fun, humor, or social activity.

Jenny had always felt incompetent despite having graduated from an elite college and, after her first marriage confirmed this feeling, never believed herself capable of functioning with any degree of independence. On college graduation, Jenny panicked that she might never marry. Despite an excellent record at an outstanding institution, she gave little thought to her future except as wife and mother. In the marriage, she ceded all decisions to her husband and assumed a generally subservient role that she never questioned. She did feel protected against some unknown danger by this arrangement but gave little thought to her unhappiness. Jenny tried to devote herself to being a good wife and mother, but she felt an emptiness that diminished her motivation and had difficulty finding the energy to keep up with three children and a demanding husband. Often forgetting details and at times confused about her children's schedules, she was regarded as inept by her husband, an attribution that confirmed her self-perception. Openly critical of her, George was away for increasing periods of time during the course of the marriage, the couple grew increasingly distant, and, when Jenny finally discovered an affair, the marriage ended. After the separation, she discovered that he had had numerous extramarital relationships.

As I asked her about the distress she felt at the idea of going home, Jenny recounted the relationship with Joe. He had never spoken much, and many people wondered how she was able to live with his silence as long as she did. Jenny said that she attempted to cope with the lack of contact by getting involved in her own work projects and by trying to become an independent scholar, but Joe objected to her spending time away from the house. Her efforts to work were a constant source of conflict for the couple, and Jenny never felt that the issue was resolved, despite the completion of her first book after considerable delay and consternation. Although she was interested in the work, she felt that a primary motivation was her desire to escape the boredom of being with her husband and find a way to stimulate herself. After her book was finished, she had no subsequent venture in the offing and so found herself once again at home with Joe. She tried engaging him but at this point he was not only naturally reticent, but also suffering the physical and emotional effects of aging and had lost the few extrabusiness interests he had when younger. Jenny wished to engage in activities on her own, but Joe, lonely and with failing health, begged her to stay with him. She felt guilty when she undertook a project that did not include him, but he had no desire to do anything. At this point, her frustration mounting and feeling trapped in a virtual cell of isolation, Jenny began to feel a variety of somatic pains, had frequent spells of dizziness, and her rash broke out.

In therapy, Jenny began to realize that she had sacrificed important capacities and interests for the sake of both marriages. This understanding then led to the further insight that the suffocation from the two betrothals was a prime reason she could not return to Joe. In her words, "Just living outside the house, I can breathe." Jenny said that she felt that she had escaped jail; she used the prisoner metaphor throughout the course of the therapy to refer to her past. She was explicit about her desire to regain her childhood self, the self who could "play," a process that she called "reclaiming" that part of herself. I added that, by repossessing an important part of who she was, she was becoming free to create new ways of relating to others.

From the initial focus on Jenny's sense of imprisonment in her second marriage, the therapeutic process led inexorably to her lifelong feeling of endangerment. Jenny could say only that she felt that she was deficient in her ability to act in the adult world. Believing that others had the social and vocational competence she lacked, she concluded that by being attached to a man, she could survive under the protective umbrella men provide. This self-doubting seemed always to have been unrealistic for this highly intelligent, well-educated woman, but, in her current situation, it seemed almost delusional. She had substantial savings on which she could live for the rest of her life, but this reality did not keep her from feeling that she needed a man to support her. Confronted with the fact that her continual belief that she required a male protector could not be a financial need, Jenny began to face the origins of her conviction that she was incompetent and helpless to control her fate. This belief was rooted in her identification with her mother's helpless dependency, and we then began to address her feminine identity. In Jenny's mind, men had the capacity to engage the world, whereas women, such as her mother, were unable to cope with life.

Anxious at the idea that she could surpass the dysfunctional life of her mother, Jenny felt fated to the same unhappy, dependent, crippled existence as her mother, and she had come close to carrying it out, although without her mother's severe depression. When I asked her about the deep-seated conviction that she would be unhappy like her mother, Jenny surprised us both by associating to her sister, and she said she felt undeserving. I suggested that she felt guilty about having been born with a healthy body and that she could not allow herself to be happy while her sister was maimed and her mother depressed. Jenny had a powerful reaction to this interpretation; she felt that we had struck something true and deep in her. She responded especially to the idea that she felt guilty about her sister, for she sensed that this guilt explained her conviction that she was undeserving of happiness. As she thought about this dynamic, Jenny noted that, although she had had a great deal of fun as a child, she had always sensed a vague sense of guilt beneath her enjoyment. More significantly, she noted that during her happy childhood was an underlying belief that her enjoyment would eventually dissipate and her ultimate fate was a life of pain. Childhood had always felt like "living on borrowed time, and the debt would have to be paid." Her childhood fun, she now realized, had an unconscious feeling of illegitimacy, as though she were violating a family rule. Brought to consciousness now was the injunction, "Do not be any happier than your mother and sister." She had managed to escape this dictate in childhood by telling herself that childhood was not the "real world" and that her enjoyment would be temporary.

Marriage symbolized entry into adulthood, life now being "for real," and imprisonment was her way to pay off the "debt." She did so by marrying two men who expected her role to be suffocatingly limited. The marriages were motivated by her identification with her mother and her guilt over having an intact body, as well as the related feelings of incompetence and the need to be protected from danger. While all these insights were epiphanies to Jenny, she had great difficulty using them to live a different kind of life. She wanted to be free of guilt while exercising her intelligence and capabilities, but, despite her new insights, she found these feelings to be stubbornly resistant. I suggested that to use the analytic interpretations would be to violate the terms of her childhood "contract" to be unhappy. She felt a resonance with this statement because she had noticed, without explicit awareness, that she was able to accept analytic insights as long as she kept them at a distance, as though playing a game.

To improve her life in a meaningful way would be to cease paying off the "debt" Jenny owed for her healthy body and spontaneous personality. By keeping the therapy as an "as if" activity, she was able to appear to engage in it, but, if now she were to change the way she behaved, therapy would become "real," and she would be confronted with the possibility of being happy, of overcoming the misery that afflicted her mother and sister. The thought was both frightening and exhilarating; Jenny now indulged herself in the fantasies of what her life would be like if she were free to do as she pleased.

Jenny interpreted my focus on the power of her need for safety to mean that I believed her to be capable of more self-reliance than she had ever shown. She was not wrong. On the basis of her considerable intellectual gifts, exceptional capacity for insight, and keen judgment, I had a vision of her as competent to organize and live her own life without constraints imposed by others. I persistently interpreted her doubts as guilt and anxiety over finding the happiness that eluded her mother and sister. I suggested that we had abundant evidence of her intelligence in her education and scholarly achievements, but she had never included her intellectual gifts in her self-image owing to her guilt over her sister's disability and her identification with her mother. I often commented that her interpretation of my behavior suggested a long-dormant potential to believe in her own capacities, but she could not be convinced of her strengths until she knew that I knew she had them. My vision of her ability to make judgments and decisions for herself gave impetus to her long-dormant wish and capacity to use her intelligence to pursue her interests.

Believing that we now had a solid understanding that needed to be implemented, I shifted my clinical stance from understanding to creating, that is, from transference space to potential space. I asked Jenny what she would do if she were free of guilt and identification with her mother. With growing excitement, Jenny said that she felt robbed of her adulthood, and she animatedly recounted a series of cultural, artistic, and intellectual interests she would love to pursue. When I noted that she seemed to be impassioned about these pursuits, Jenny said that she was inspired not about the activities per se, but by the thought that she might actually live according to her desires and thereby reclaim a significant part of her self. When I asked her about this new resolve, Jenny said that she finally saw how much of her life she had given over to guilt and, being in her 70s, she felt she could ill afford to lose any more of it. I commented that we could regard her "instinctive" exhilaration as a beginning step toward renewing the spontaneity she had lost long ago. At this time, Jenny began to expand her social life; she saw friends with whom she had been out of contact for many years because her husband wanted her to be with him. She now felt free of such constraints and resumed many friendships.

Most important, Jenny began to shift her motivation. No longer willing to behave from guilt or a feeling of unworthiness or inadequacy, she looked closely at her desires and felt that she had the right to pursue them. This transformation of her motivational structure from obligation and compensation to desire was the decisive change in her life. Acting in accordance with her affects, she felt her life to be in synchrony with her experience for the first time since childhood.

Jenny decided that it was ultimately up to her to allow herself to feel happy about what she was doing and that she could no longer afford to forego her own desires for an illusory feeling of safety. Nonetheless, she felt guilty about leaving her lonely husband by himself, especially after he developed a major illness. Jenny had been seeing him on a regular basis, but, when he became ill, she felt she wanted to help him. She was conflicted, though, because she feared being drawn back into the vortex of her guilt and compliance with her husband's needs. She knew that he needed her, and she could not bring herself to treat him with callous disregard. Viewing her husband as a basically decent, honest person who cared deeply about her and whom she wished to help, Jenny feared an insidious loss of her hard-earned gains if she moved back in with him. So she decided to have a rare frank discussion with Joe in which she let him know she would like to return home, but she had found the former situation intolerable and would need to have the freedom to pursue her writing, friends, and other interests. Joe, delighted at the prospect of her return, agreed to what she wanted immediately, and his spirits lifted palpably. The couple negotiated a living arrangement in which they ate most of their meals together and spent considerable time in each other's company, but in which Jenny had enough time to herself each day to work on her projects and engage in her own activities. During the last few years of their life together, he never objected to any of her endeavors. She spent time writing, seeing friends, pursuing her cultural interests, and working on new projects as opportunities presented themselves.

Jenny found the time with Joe to be the most difficult in this period, but she was willing to be with him out of respect for his needs, out of companionship appropriate to a 20-year marriage, and because she respected him and his accomplishments. She felt she had arrived at a satisfactory balance between her continuing obligation to her sick, elderly husband and leading the life she desired. Although she would have preferred a life without obligation, Jenny felt she could live with a less-than-perfect arrangement as long as she had her own time. In addition, it was rewarding for her to be able to contribute to Joe's last years.

Her changes extended beyond new interests to a general awareness and expression of previously disavowed affects. For example, she was able to articulate her anger about the severe limitations of her previous life, although she did not blame either husband because she recognized that she had chosen her compliance and made her own trade-offs.

In the midst of this dramatic reversal of her former lifestyle, Jenny's somatic pains disappeared completely. From the inception of the psychotherapy, Jenny noticed a reduction in severity of her somatic pains, but it was only now, as she became aware of and utilized her affects as guides to her behavior, that they vanished. We never discussed the specific meaning of any individual symptom. Jenny felt, and I concurred, that the symptoms were the expression in her body of the tension resulting from the disavowal and suppression of a great deal of her affective life. That is, no individual pain represented any particular affect, but all the somatic symptoms reflected the lack of ownership of her life. Her inability to experience spontaneity, joy, excitement and pursue her interests had led to tension that was communicated somatically. Her anger was a part of the suppressed experience, but no symptom directly symbolized her anger. Nor did we need to uncover symbolic meanings to achieve symptom relief. The pains were symptoms not only of strangulated affects, but of a lost self. When Jenny resumed ownership of her self, when she acquired the freedom to live according to the dictates of her experience, the tension was gone and the symptoms disappeared along with it.

She attributed her new-found happiness to the freedom to follow her passions whatever they might be. Jenny felt she had reappropriated the spontaneous, fun part of herself from childhood and given it adult form. It was this sense of owning her self, of being the author of her behavior without the inhibition of abandonment anxiety and guilt, that she felt had changed her life. Freed from the weight of these inhibiting factors, Jenny felt she enjoyed life for the first time in her adulthood. Her life felt lighter, and she could feel the freedom in her body.

Jenny had not simply substituted the therapeutic relationship for her marital dependence. In her therapeutic journey, she made difficult decisions, became critical, outspoken, and ultimately capable of utilizing her own affects, which gained expression, inter alia, in criticisms of me, the therapist. This behavior was in contrast to that in both marriages, where she had no control over life, her affects had been split off, and she had been led to comply externally without a sense of authenticity. The therapeutic relationship fostered reliance on her affective states, such as excitement, enjoyment, and anger, as opposed to the compliance that characterized her two marriages. With regard to clinical technique, we can see from Jenny's therapeutic progress that her symptoms abated after she was able to use her affects and follow her passions. Once she became conscious of what she felt and transformed her affects into ways of being and relating, Jenny owned her self and the pressure on her body was relieved.

CONCLUDING NOTE

Jenny's therapeutic voyage demonstrates the importance of the shift from transference space to potential space in the elimination of somatic symptoms and the corresponding emphasis on the future, the therapist's vision, and the creation of new possibilities. At key points in the process, the psychotherapeutic field was transformed from a focus on understanding her current plight to the creation of alternative, more authentic ways of living. The process by which Jenny reclaimed her lost spontaneity and other disavowed affects demonstrates some of the important aspects of potential space in the therapeutic action of psychoanalytic therapy. As Jenny and I recast the therapeutic space, it became organized around the future: we addressed what Jenny could *become* rather than who she already *was*. When she entered psychotherapy out of desperation, Jenny could not believe that anything in her life would ever be different from what it had always been. Without a future-perfect sense, Jenny lived a string of endless present moments she could only endure. The insights she gained into her past and present were not initially alterative, but they did provide the environment within which she was eventually able to project herself into the future which allowed her to live in the future perfect. This sense of futurity, in turn, made it possible for her to use the insights into her present and past. The therapeutic process in this case illustrates the importance of the future as well as the mutual influences of the three temporal modalities.

Jenny's ability to live in the future perfect was made possible in large part by my vision of her as a woman with the potential to live a different life. I saw in her keen insight, intelligence, judgment, and interests possibilities for the creation of a self organized around what mattered to her. This aspect of the changes was particularly striking given that Jenny began psychotherapy when she was 74 years old. Instead of resigning herself to a life that could not be altered so late in the life cycle, she explored new possibilities. Ultimately, then, Jenny created a new self founded on her authentic affects rather than on the escape from danger. Once her affects became the building blocks of her life, the symptoms left, never to return. The course of Jenny's psychotherapy demonstrates the principle that therapeutic action lies in the use of the therapeutic space to create something new, rather than solely understanding something old.

Moreover, Jenny created new possibilities for herself that included the sense of obligation she felt toward her second husband. She crafted a lifestyle that allowed her spontaneity, pursuit of her passions, and fulfillment of what she regarded as a moral responsibility. This life style change, which she would have never before contemplated, was one reflection of her new-found ability to create new opportunities rather than resign herself to circumstances.

The key to the therapeutic action was in Jenny's using affects as her guide. In so doing, she created new meaning for her life: her passions and interests now had priority, and she organized her life around the feeling of authenticity. Her physical symptoms disappeared not solely because they were understood, but because the understanding led to the creation of a self in which her affects played a central role.

This is not to say that all somatic symptoms can necessarily be removed by this method, or by any form of psychoanalytic therapy. It is to say that bodily symptoms are often a product of affects arrested in the developmental process and, when that is the case, the use of transference and potential space first to understand and then to create new ways of being and relating can effectively eradicate the symptoms at the root. Furthermore, this model can be applied to other conditions in which arrested affects constrict the growth of the self, even if the resulting symptoms are not somatic. Jenny felt suffocated for most of her life; and, while her symptoms presented in physical form, many other people would become depressed under her circumstances. Let us now turn to the application of our model of therapeutic action to those patients.

DEPRESSION
THE COLLAPSED SELF

Perry, a highly successful businessman in his 30s, became morose while home sick with a bad case of the flu. Although he had always seemed a confident person, he now found himself preoccupied with the possible failure of a routine deal. The potential sale was not especially large or difficult and, in fact, was like many he had completed in the past. He could not understand why he was so afraid the contract would not be finalized, but he felt helpless to cease his constant ruminating over the possibility that some last-minute obstacle would prevent the final signing. Although he had concluded many more complex transactions and the outcome of this contractual agreement would not significantly affect his highly successful business, Perry was obsessed with what he regarded as the potential catastrophe that the final agreement would not be concluded. It was mysterious both that Perry feared the failure of the transaction and that he regarded that possibility as having dire consequences. Worried his business was on the brink of collapse despite its spectacular growth, Perry was consumed with anxiety and he began to think of himself as a failure. If his business collapsed, he feared, his career would be over and his life would be a waste.

Throughout his career, Perry had been extremely conscientious worker. Routinely putting in 60- to 70-hour weeks, he had always risen early and toiled late. As a result of uninterrupted successes, he and his partners had become wealthy in their early 30s. But, during this bout of flu, he feared returning to work and for the first time in his life did not want to get out of bed in the morning. After the illness, he did resume his business activities but without any of his former emotional investment. Feeling little interest in his work or any other aspect of his life, Perry was sad and hopeless, cried often, and had difficulty sleeping; his appetite was minimal. He had great difficulty concentrating. Although intellectually he knew that he would not be materially affected if the prospective deal was unsuccessful, he could not escape the emotional conviction that such a "failure" would be the beginning of the end. Consumed with catastrophic anxiety, Perry berated himself repeatedly for his condition and especially his lack of motivation. Nonetheless, he could not force himself to regain interest in his work. Fraught with anxiety, lacking motivation, and feeling sad and empty, he sought psychotherapeutic help.

As we discussed his anxiety, Perry came to the grudging awareness that he had always privately feared that his business would collapse but had disavowed his trepidation. His current preoccupation with failing, he now came to realize, was the conscious manifestation of an underlying anxiety that had plagued him all his life. In the therapeutic process, he came to the realization that he had never entered a business negotiation without painful anxiety and insomnia. Despite the seemingly obvious nature of these symptoms, Perry insisted he had been oblivious to both their importance and pervasiveness.

As we attempted to arrive at an understanding of this fear of failure, it became clear that he had not really chosen his vocation. His father wanted him to be a real estate developer, and he had never considered any other career path. Recognition of his overpowering need to comply with his father's expectations, in turn, led to a thematic focus on the importance the older man held in his life and the family in general. Perry regarded his father as a self-made man, the pillar of strength in the family whose fabulous business and financial success were achieved by his resourcefulness, intelligence, and resilience. Greatly admiring his father's rise from modest origins to affluence, Perry had competed for his father's affection and approval with his two older brothers.

Perry painted a picture of his mother as a weak woman who was so easily disturbed by problems of any sort that she either denied their existence or sought comfort in her children. For example, Perry suffered many injuries and illnesses as a child and spent much time recuperating at home. He had had a broken leg, a fractured ankle, a major head injury, several cuts requiring extensive stitches, and a variety of serious illnesses, each of which kept him home in bed for a prolonged period. On one occasion, he fell out of a moving car and sustained numerous injuries, including a traumatic blow to his head. In each case, his mother reacted with a bizarre, contradictory response that bewildered her son. On one hand, she denied the seriousness of the injury and refused to treat her son as sick or injured. On the other hand, although seemingly oblivious to his injuries and illnesses, she became so anxious that she sought solace from Perry even as he lay ill or injured. Despite this need for Perry to comfort her, his mother always denied that Perry got hurt "any more than any other child."

Because his mother was so easily disturbed by any untoward circumstances, often requiring comforting herself, Perry had put his emotional investment in gaining his father's approval to secure the only parental bond he could rely on. His father was consumed with the growth of his own company, and he coveted business achievement for his sons, all of whom knew that their father valued no other career path and measured life success by material wealth. Perry spoke with his father daily, sought his counsel frequently, and took pride in feeling he was the favored son. The importance of succeeding in his father's eyes indicates that Perry's fear of failure was connected to his anxiety over losing the paternal attachment. Perry was greatly relieved when he recognized that he feared losing his father if even a single contract did not turn a large profit. Perry acknowledged that his business career had brought him no satisfaction. The only positive feeling he could identify was a sense of relief when a deal was completed. As the next sale approached, his anxiety built until the agreement was finalized, at which point his distress abated until the next transaction. Not being able to win, he could only "not lose."

As we discussed Perry's childhood accidents and illness, it occurred to him that being home with the flu as an adult evoked his childhood helplessness at being unable to rely on his mother. During his recent flu episode, Perry could not make progress on his latest venture, and his feeling of helplessness resulted in anxiety that grew until it became debilitating. This childhood anxiety, in turn, triggered the need to please his father and the consequent fear that, if his prospective transaction was aborted, he would lose the paternal connection on which he still depended.

Perry's childhood history suggested that he had never felt that his mother recognized or empathized with his experiences. Since his mother was highly anxious and easily threatened by any distress he suffered, Perry learned to bury his affects in order to please her. He grew adept at living according to what his mother needed for her emotional equilibrium; he lived, in Winnicott's (1960) phrase, from "the outside, rather than from the inside out." If he was agreeable and complied with her needs, he felt a connection with her but lost self-respect. Consequently, he took no pride in his superficial maternal relationship. Unable to form a meaningful relationship with his mother, he attempted to gain a strong sense of himself by working to earn his father's approval, but even when such efforts were successful they left an underlying sense of emptiness. Thus, a disquieting undercurrent of *ennui* and dread had always run beneath the surface of Perry's life, troubling affects that were assuaged only momentarily by his achievements.

When Perry was home with the flu, his lifelong adaptation broke down. The helplessness of being unable to be effective at work and the weakened state of his body disrupted his character defense against emptiness through professional accomplishment. Perry's depressive episode, then, seemed to be rooted in his need to sustain an external or false self defined by his status as the preferred son. This self masked the absence of an authentic, affectively rooted self. When he was unable to continue this self-protective style, however temporarily, his feeling of emptiness emerged and his life seemed purposeless. Once Perry consciously experienced this feeling of meaninglessness, he felt hopeless and helpless. The self constructed to effect personal and vocational functioning while protecting against awareness of the hollow feeling beneath had fractured, revealing the underlying emptiness. The emergence of this lacuna in his sense of self was tantamount to the depression with which he had presented to psychotherapy.

Perry was unable to conceive of a different existence and had never seriously contemplated alternatives. Feeling hopeless and helpless to free himself from a life that offered only dissatisfaction, anxiety, and temporary episodic relief, Perry lost his motivation to continue on his former path. As his conscious sense of self was tied to a life that issued in agony, anxiety, and emptiness, Perry could express his pain and craving for authentic self-expression only through depression. Lying in bed, withdrawn from his life, he was protesting a prison he did not know how to escape.

I have found the structure of Perry's symptom onset—the crumbling of a lifelong interpersonal pattern that had protected a gap in affective experience—to be characteristic of many acute outbreaks of depression. Dysphoria is a common reaction to the breakdown of adaptive strategies divorced from desires and interests. Other depressed patients, however, do not suffer such dramatic, acute episodes. Aware of feelings of emptiness and dissatisfaction from childhood or adolescence, they are unable to erect a socially approved adaptation to protect against awareness of the gap in their affective experience. An example of such a case of chronic depression was seen in our discussion of Helen in chapter 2. Helen did not conceive of herself as possessing a future; she lived without a sense of purpose. Perry and Helen both suffered from a lack of authentically derived meaning in their lives. The difference between them was that Perry had a defensive, although highly adaptive, false self that protected against consciousness of his emptiness and promoted adequate functioning. When Perry's lifelong interpersonal strategy broke down, he felt much the same as Helen had all her life. Her lack of futurity was mirrored in Perry's sense of hopelessness. Both cases show how symptoms of depression stem from the helplessness of being unable to live in accordance with incipient affective states and the sense of futility deriving from the failure to direct the course of one's own life.

This formulation of the depressive experience is similar to the self-psychological view. Stated briefly, for Kohut (1971, 1977), failure of the early environment to provide the empathic selfobject responses needed for self-development results in an undernourished self lacking in strength and vigor. From this perspective, depression is the product of such an enfeebled self, lacking in vitality and deficient in its efforts to manage life tasks. With this formulation, Kohut changed the psychoanalytic understanding of depression from guilt over desires to the shame of a weak self unable to withstand the blows of the world and forge an effective path through life.

The self psychological formulation of depression shares with the view advanced here the notion that depression is rooted in a flaw in the self rather than in guilt over wishes. One might well say that both Helen and Perry suffered from enfeebled selves. In this way, the concept of depression set forth here is concordant with Kohut's shift from classical guilt theory to the centrality of shame and weakness or, as Kohut (1984) put it, the revision of psychoanalytic theory from Guilty Man to Tragic Man. The essential difference between the two ways of viewing dysphoric conditions lies in the conceptualization of what the self lacks and what it then needs to achieve vitality. The emphasis in self psychology is on the role of selfobject responses in bolstering infantile grandiosity and idealization, facilitating their gradual relinquishment, and eventual internalization in the form of ambitions and ideals (Kohut, 1971). From my perspective, the fault that issues in depression is the lack of authenticity per se. Because neither Perry nor Helen lived in accordance with their genuinely experienced affects, neither felt a sense of ownership over his or her life. Whereas Perry had constructed a compliant self to hide the lack of authenticity in his life, Helen had no such well-crafted adaptive structure. Neither, however, had built a life on the basis of passions, interests, and affects. The result in both cases was a state of emptiness and lack of meaning in life that we call depression. My emphasis in understanding depression is not on the failure of the environment to provide specific narcissistic functions but on the lack of provision of the environmental conditions needed for the creation of an authentic self. The consequences of this difference are decisive for clinical technique, as we shall see shortly.

DEPRESSION AND THE SELF

When a child is required to restrict her authentic affects to maintain early attachments, she does not believe her experience is valuable, interesting to others, or able to sustain relationships (e.g., Demos, 1983). In such circumstances, defensive strategies are devised to sustain connections to the early figures and ultimately navigate the social world at the cost of genuine affective connection. It would divert us too far from our topic to delineate all the possible adaptive-defensive strategies that may be used for this purpose. Some of the most commonly used techniques include compliance, aloofness, intellectual precision, and self-aggrandizement. Whatever the patient's survival tactic, its disconnection from lived experience means the patient can derive little gratification from it. Because relinquishing the defensive posture triggers the threat of abandonment, however, the patient feels helpless, fated to a life divorced from her affects and interests. Typically, this defensive stance becomes the stable pattern we recognize as "character." For example, a grandiose posture that seeks continual approbation and admiration is an adaptation to helplessness that forms the narcissistic character structure, as we will see in chapter 10.

Despite the underlying emptiness beneath the surface of any of these defensive postures, some degree of interpersonal satisfaction if often achieved. Inflated views of the self, substance abuse, and the obsessive search for approbation through achievement, status, or appearance are among the most typical maneuvers to fill inner emptiness through external means, but perhaps the most common strategy is to attach to another person whose connection completes the sense of self. Such a blurring of self–other boundaries can provide both a feeling of wholeness that masks the lack of ownership of one's states and the helplessness to control one's fate.

This use of objects by the depressive-prone personality (labeled archaic selfobjects by self psychologists) explains why more traditional psychoanalytic formulations emphasize object loss as a key component of the depressive picture. In Freud's (1917) account, mourning became melancholia when the lost object was internalized and attacked within. This way of conceptualizing depression is accurate at one level: depressive states are frequently precipitated by loss of a loved one. For object loss to result in the self-depletion that characterizes depression, however, the object must have served the function of completing the sense of self. When the object is necessary for the sense of wholeness, its loss results in the collapse of the structure dependent on the object, revealing the sense of depletion that we refer to as depression. That is, the severity of the grief reaction to object loss is understandable only if the object has completed an unrealized self. The root of the depression, then, is not the loss of the object per se, but the incompletely developed self that led to the clinging tie to the object which, in turn, makes the self vulnerable to collapse when the object is lost.

Whatever the particular defensive strategy, its breakdown when it cannot be sustained reveals the poverty of authentic motivation and meaning hidden beneath the veneer. For example, others may no longer offer the approbation, or the idealized object relationship may become disrupted, laying bare the emptiness and helplessness beneath the surface, and the patient collapses into a state of depression. Finding no meaning in life, the patient has little interest in the world and often loses appetite or, in a desperate effort to protect against awareness of helplessness, may overeat, becoming obese or bulimic. There being no genuinely experienced emotional investment in the world, the ensuing feeling of meaninglessness may result in exhaustion and excessive sleep, but if the helplessness becomes conscious, the ensuing anxiety can lead to insomnia. Regardless of whether any particular case of depression is manifested in lethargy or anxiety, the depressive reaction results from the inability of an interpersonal strategy to sustain the defense against the absence of an authentically developed self.

Depression is not the only symptomatic expression of the failure of an affectively rooted self to develop. A life that is not authored is the soil in which depression grows. We have seen another reaction in the somatic symptoms discussed in the previous chapter. In whatever nuances or different forms it may assume, depression always means that the subject does not feel in possession of his own life. Although Perry was professionally and financially successful, he felt fated to live a life of others' choosing. His feeling of not possessing his life left him with an emptiness that blossomed into a paralyzing depression when he was home ill. Perry's depression, then, is most usefully conceptualized as the eruption of his dissatisfaction with a life organized around seeking approval from his father by achieving in the business world, a goal divorced from his affective life. His depressive symptoms, although painful, were not simply "pathological"; they were the way unrealized aspects of his potential ways of experiencing could gain expression. The upshot of this understanding for Perry and me was that he could not free himself from his depression until his life was lived as his own, in accordance with what mattered to him. We now come to the process through which this decisive transformation can occur.

THERAPEUTIC ACTION

The first phase of Perry's psychotherapy consisted of arriving at the following understandings: (1) his depressive symptoms were tantamount to the emergence of the underlying emptiness he had hidden from himself with his spectacularly successful business achievements; (2) his accomplishments were motivated by his attempt to gain his father's approbation; and (3) his mother's lack of empathy and sensitivity had led to an early need to organize his emotional needs around his father. We were able to see that beneath the false self built around being his father's favorite was a core sense of emptiness that he felt helpless to overcome. When the therapeutic process brought us to the acute awareness of this vacuum in the self, Perry felt unsure of what direction he wished to go; he saw no alternative to his lifestyle of continually enhancing business and financial success. Nonetheless, to follow this path felt to him like a Sisyphysean task: he experienced his achievements as the product of an endless cycle he felt driven to reenact, but he did know why he was doing so and found little meaning in the process.

Perry's response to this confrontation with the emptiness of his pursuits was to feel caught in a storm that took away all his navigation points. He did not want to continue the well-traveled path of his life, but he saw no other route that appealed to him. Lacking direction, he felt disoriented, much as Helen had felt all her life. In this phase, the therapy sessions were consumed with Perry's confusion. I observed that his behavior reflected the emptiness that underlay his business life. He agreed, saying that no matter how successful the deal, he gained only a temporary feeling of having "won," and, as the relief of completing the transaction wore off, he was left with an empty feeling. In passing, he noted that his happiest moments were his vacations with his family in the country. Perry had always attributed this pleasure to the feeling of being freed from the burdens of work, but, as he talked about his time in those pastoral settings, he felt there was more to his sense of contentment. He described in detail his country pursuits, of hiking and fishing, but, most important, was playing and conversing with his three children. He relished the opportunity for a way of life emphasizing family relationships, which was not available to him during his hectic work life.

As we discussed the intensity of his experience on these vacations, I told him that in depicting scenes from these trips, he was conveying the only passion he had expressed in therapy. In response, Perry voiced a wish that his life could be as bucolic as his excursions into the countryside and, as he did so, it occurred to both of us that he was expressing a long-dormant but authentic desire that he had never considered before. He loved the time he spent with his family in the country, but, because it did not fit the direction that he felt fated to, he never contemplated making this source of pleasure a central component of his life. The desire for a provincial life that centered on his family seemed authentic, whereas his impulsion for business success was driven by his fear of failure rather than by any inherent interest in the activity itself.

As a result of these conversations, Perry began to speak to his wife about his unhappiness with his current lifestyle and his wish to live a rural life. His spouse, who had never felt that she belonged in the materialistic upper-middle-class suburb in which they lived, was excited about the possibility of moving and immediately began to investigate areas to which they might relocate. Eventually, the couple took trips to look at land for sale in locations where they often vacationed, and Perry began to ponder how he might make a living in those locales. His wife, ahead of him in her readiness and enthusiasm, began to tell people they were moving. Perry, however, was not so sure once he confronted the reality of such a dramatic change. In addition to the questionable employment situation, Perry was also concerned about living without the stimulation of the city. When he visited properties with the goal of buying for permanent residence, he became aware of what he enjoyed about urban life. While he felt no need for status symbols, he realized he was enlivened by city life and the challenges of his work. The task of surmounting difficulties to make his projects flourish appealed to him even as he dreaded the pressure to succeed. The idea of country life appealed to Perry, but he realized he would miss the excitement of working with people and the social opportunity of urban living. As the prospect of moving to a rural area became more real, he felt a mounting fear that his life would lack intellectual stimulation, a recognition that showed him the value he placed on testing his mental abilities. Even if he could find a way to make a living in the country, Perry thought, he would feel isolated and deprived of the opportunity to exercise his intellect. Thus, by discovering his reluctance to make the dramatic shift to a rural existence, Perry became aware of the great importance he attached to testing his mental acumen.

At this point Perry became even more confused, because, after seeming to conclude that his work life was empty, he now felt he would miss it. Although Perry appreciated the fact that his business afforded him the opportunity to test his abilities, it was equally apparent that intellectual challenge did not relieve the emptiness. He feared that if he moved to the country he would trade one problem for another. His wife was disappointed when he informed her that he could not envision himself being happy with a rural life style despite his love for that environment. This realization left Perry in a quandary: he felt a void in his current life, but without any visible alternative, he felt as trapped as before he started therapy.

I emphasized to Perry that in contemplating a change to rural living he had discovered his need to utilize his intellect. I suggested that uncovering this positive aspect of his business activities did not mean that his current life was meaningful, only that it afforded him something he needed despite the emptiness of its goals. Perry was disappointed that he saw no clear path out of his dilemma, but I indicated that, even though a permanent rural life did not appeal to him, in seriously considering it, he had discovered some powerful interests and needs. I went on to say that the draw of the countryside had revealed a value system and set of desires that had not only been unconscious, but also unfulfilled. Perry was struck by the word unfulfilled. It meant to him that he had diminished the importance of freedom and family life and that perhaps his life was lacking these values. He now connected the nagging dissatisfaction that had haunted his life with the suppression of his most deeply meaningful desires. Aware of a gap between his aspirations and his daily life, Perry concluded that the emptiness that had plagued his life under the veneer of success was a product of the divorce between what mattered to him and how he lived.

At this crucial point, he expressed in the therapeutic setting a long-dormant set of values and beliefs that had been unconscious but became apparent as he considered changes to his life situation. A pastoral, spiritual, and family-oriented life symbolized what gratified him most without the oppression of a success/failure barometer. The value of this type of life, buried under the need to avoid the anxiety of loss by means of material and professional achievement, became articulated for the first time when Perry took seriously the idea of making a decisive lifestyle change.

In this way, we discovered a great deal about Perry from the evolution of his interest in a rural life style. This idea was a concrete representation of his yearning to make freedom and familial relationships central to his life. Having relegated the latter to the periphery of a life centered on business success had left him with a feeling of *ennui*, but Perry did not know what was missing until we were able to unpack the concrete longing. It now became clear that his passion for the countryside emanated from authentically held values and desires, but to equate these values with living in the country would be to simplify a central and newly emerging segment of Perry's self. This previously disavowed part of his self-organization was gaining expression as the longing for a rural life but was not to be equated with it.

Perry's struggle over urban versus rural living reflected the conflicting sides of his self: the longing for freedom and family life opposed his need for mental stimulation and challenge. Our understanding that Perry's desire was not as simple as a suppressed longing to live an idyllic life in the country led to a deeper exploration of what lay beneath the veneer of his social adaptation. Each side of the conflict embodied a cluster of Perry's desires: urbanity symbolized his love of intellect, challenge, excitement, risk, and opportunity for achievement; the rural, his passion for family, the building of relationships, and the freedom to pursue interests for their own sake without the judgment of success or failure.

These revelations led us naturally to question why Perry's buried desires had surfaced as an attraction to the rural life style. Perry seemed surprised by this question because he had long equated an urban environment with oppressive expectations to succeed and therefore understood personal freedom as requiring escape from the competition of city life. I offered the idea that his equation reflected the very problem he was trying to overcome: he associated urban living, which held an important appeal, with the onus of proving himself to his father. He had never questioned this connection.

Perry then related the following annual emotional cycle. Every year as he returned from summer vacation, he felt the pressure of achievement begin to build as soon as he approached home. The anxiety of possible failure grew immediately and continually until his next trip away, and the cycle continued until he finally succumbed to the pressure by becoming depressed. As a result of this affective oscillation, his unexamined assumption had been that being in the business world meant a life of meeting a financial standard requiring the virtual absorption of his life. It never occurred to Perry that he could operate in a competitive professional environment without devoting his life to spectacular success, the very goal that caused him so much anxiety. I highlighted the fact that he had symbolized his desire for freedom and family life in a fantasy of a pastoral life style that, in fact, seemed not to fit the complexity of his needs.

The creative challenge for Perry was to meet apparently conflicting needs: freedom, the opportunity to appreciate activities for their own sake, and the building of family relationships, on one hand, and the experience of mental challenge and excitement, on the other. The emerging goal for Perry and me was to find a way for him to live in greater freedom than his former life afforded without sacrificing the excitement he found in social engagement and in the mental effort of solving complex problems. His business life enlivened him through the test of his ability and ingenuity but at the cost of liberty of affective expression, a price he could no longer pay.

I questioned Perry's assumption that the exercise of his mental capacity per se entailed oppressive expectations. He immediately associated to childhood memories of being "tested" by his father on math problems, puzzles, and games. Perry had been quick and adroit at these activities. His father relished his son's abilities and often gave him ever-more difficult "brain teasers" to see how far Perry could go before he was stumped. Perry recalled ambivalent feelings when he was called on to perform in this way: he enjoyed the test of his mental acuity and attention from his father, a rare experience of exclusive interaction between them, but he also hated the pressure to perform and the feeling that his father's attention was contingent on his cleverness. I noted that he seemed to feel similarly ambivalent now about his work performance: He enjoyed using his intellect, but felt overburdened by expectations and fear of success. For the first time he became aware that during his father's quizzes he had feared failure, which would incur the older man's disapproval. He immediately saw that the childhood feeling was echoed in his current anxiety about performing to a standard. These historical connections led to the recognition that, because achievement for Perry had always contained a combination of excitement and anxiety, the effort to accomplish filled him with a sense of impending doom.

Perry often dreaded the analysis, not because it might dredge up pain from the past but because, no matter what direction it might take, he felt his job was to be insightful, find the proper emotional roots of his problems, and resolve them. He thought of me as a judge of his performance rather than a partner in the process. The connection with his father was obvious, and he did not require me to make it. The analytic process made him extremely anxious because in every session he thought there was more he could and should have done. When I showed him something about himself, he appreciated the insight but wondered why he had not seen the connection himself and felt diminished at his lack of creative understanding. For example, I told him that he had unconsciously assumed that the pursuit of goals is inherently oppressive, and his response was that he should have been able to see this dynamic himself. I commented that this reaction was the very problem: in the therapeutic process, he believed he should be able to attain the insights himself, and, when he failed to do so, he regarded his performance as subpar and ultimately felt deflated by his failure to meet the standard he set for himself. Perry's reaction to the interpretive atmosphere of analysis was to feel judged, tested, and oppressed, and in this way the therapeutic dyad had become embroiled in the very patterns we were trying to overcome.

For Perry the problem was, how could he embark on self-exploration without feeling as though he was being tested and therefore fearing judgment? The problem mystified him, and he had two highly significant reactions to the conundrum. On one hand, the more the problem seemed to be insurmountable, the more tempted he was to take it on and the greater was his determination to overcome it. On the other, he felt that the therapy had become an onerous task that he wished to jettison in order to make his life easier. I interpreted this conflict as Perry's two warring sides, which had been represented previously as the battle over the desirability of urban versus rural living. The piece of himself that wanted to overcome the problem was his desire to exercise his prodigious intellect, the part that enjoyed his father's puzzles; the other side of himself sought freedom from judgment, resented his father's "tests," and coveted a bucolic life. His core conflict invaded the therapeutic process. He was torn between engaging the therapeutic dilemma, and its accompanying anxieties, and freeing himself from those same anxieties by abandoning the challenge of unknotting the problem and losing the possibility of achievement. To give up therapy was to free himself from the pressure of confronting conflict, but at the price of his engagement with me and, by implication, with the world. Facing the problem, on the other hand, meant embracing a life that held the possibility of accomplishment but at the risk of still more onerous expectations.

Perry, of course, could not imagine tackling a problem in the absence of a tyrannical standard of performance. This dilemma fortified his conviction that mental effort was inextricably linked to unmeetable goals, a conclusion that intensified his frustration. He saw no way out of the impasse, either within himself or between us, and his enthusiasm and motivation for our work together diminished. I commented that his current state in the therapeutic encounter replicated the psychic collapse that had originally led to his entry into therapy. When Perry's sense of helplessness about being able to direct his own life had become unbearable, he fell into a depression; now, seeing the same problem in our interaction, he felt an analogous loss of energy and motivation.

The analysis appeared to be stalemated, but, in fact, despite the apparent conundrum in which we found ourselves, Perry and I were not in the same position as we were at the start of our work together. In this situation we were able to apply the Platonic distinction between the start and beginning (discussed in chapter 4). We had found a highly significant although disavowed part of Perry's self that he longed to make a part of his life; the quandary was how to bring to fruition that "pastoral" aspect of himself without undernourishing his need for mental stimulation. When this conflict emerged in the therapeutic relationship, we were in the position, as described in chapter 4, analogous to the moment in a Platonic dialogue when Socrates has debunked all efforts of his interlocutor to answer the question at hand. With no new knowledge obtained, it appears that the dialogue has been fruitless, but, in fact, the frustrating process has established the opportunity for a new idea to be introduced, a task Socrates fulfills in order to begin the advance toward new knowledge. Analogously, Perry knew that the split in his self-organization had resulted in an alienating feeling of futility and helplessness, an important piece of self-awareness that put him in a different position from the starting point of the therapy. Although he did not know how to heal the split, his frustration with it opened him to the possibility of adopting a new perspective if one were offered.

Perry and I had now reached an understanding he found meaningful and even enlightening but felt helpless to use. Therefore, I took steps to transform the transference space into potential space. First, I highlighted the fact that, although Perry felt that continuation of the past was no longer tolerable as demonstrated by the intensity of his desire to live both aspects of himself, he did not know how to create a different future. I told him that the limbo in which he found himself was a kind of void that had now consumed the therapeutic situation. Not knowing how to go forward and not wanting to return to the default position of attempting to meet suffocating standards, Perry agonized in this state of suspension. Despite his insistence that I rescue him from this intolerable ambiguity, I persisted in my position that the void was a necessity. Then I shifted my inquiry from understanding the past to contemplating possibilities in the future.

When he asked me how he could resolve this intractable problem, I asked him what it would be like to engage me in a therapeutic dialogue without giving himself a grade. He immediately responded that efforts to overcome problems would be fun; the enjoyment would be there without the rigid criterion of success that spoiled his efforts to exercise his intellect. He felt that confronting a challenge was, however, inherently a test of his mental ability, and, therefore, anxiety-filled assessments were inevitable. When I asked for associations to "challenge to his mental ability," Perry responded with a concatenation of mental events involving memories of school tests, his father's puzzles, graduate school, business problems. In all these memories, Perry had ambivalent feelings: he detested the pressure he felt from his father, but ultimately was excited to work on the problems. I said that this flow of associations reflected his enjoyment in problem solving and that this passion made understandable his reluctance to leave the business which he experienced as endless opportunity to overcome obstacles. He replied that he felt fulfilled in business at those moments when he was immersed in the joy of working on a challenge free from the anxiety of evaluation.

When I observed that the therapeutic relationship repeated his split between doing and enjoying, he saw that he could resolve the dilemma only by appreciating and taking pleasure in the therapeutic process as he worked on it. Perry looked at the therapeutic predicament before him and saw that to relax and enjoy the moment was to overcome the split. He then felt excited about this possibility; he was taking a step toward resolving the dilemma. It was stunning to Perry that the problem dissipated for the moment as he lifted the gravity from it by confronting the problem for its own sake and removing potential judgment. We may say that, as Perry thought about the therapeutic conflict and found the solution to be enjoyment of the experience for its own sake, he was creating a new way of being in therapy. While immersed in the moment, Perry experienced both the excitement of mental stimulation and the freedom to follow this desire in the way he chose. For the first time in memory he enjoyed the stimulation of a mental challenge without the oppressive pressure of an external judgment. By absorbing himself in his enthusiasm for solving the problem, Perry transcended the conflict, however momentarily, between testing his mental abilities and the freedom to pursue his desires irrespective of tyrannical judgments. By searching for the solution in a new way, he was finding it or, as we might more accurately say, creating it. Perry had made an important advance toward the creation of a new way of being.

Although Perry's pivotal experience may have seemed to occur suddenly, a great deal of arduous analytic work had gone into the preparation necessary for its appearance. The understanding and emergence of Perry's "rural" side, the repeated interpretive understanding of the conflict between the two sides of his self-organization, and the opening of the void for potential new experience were all requirements for the establishment of an analytic space in which such a moment could take place. The experience itself was significant because it broke through the dichotomy that had plagued Perry's life. Of course, the existence of this moment in itself did not produce enduring changes, but it did show Perry that transcendence of the split was possible.

In the short term, the pleasurable moment faded, and Perry immediately felt that he was not doing enough to improve and needed to work harder at resolving his psychic conflicts. I interpreted this return to the default position of his life as a guilty reaction to the enjoyment of the moment, a harsh reminder that his father's voice remained an active force. In that session, Perry struggled with the tension between returning briefly to an appreciation of the therapeutic process and believing that he had to try harder. After I interpreted the latter in many sessions as the plague of his father's voice, Perry began to recognize it as such. He felt the conflict as a battle between his desire for the enjoyment of life, on one hand, and the father inside who insisted on Perry's living under an oppressive evaluation, on the other.

These two positions oscillated for months as Perry grappled to overcome his lifelong pattern of evaluating every step in addressing problems. Seeing the powerful impact of his father's judgments in this battle, Perry strove to overcome this influence, but, as he was not able to relinquish these internalized standards, he found his efforts to be subpar. At this point, however, rather than despairing, he saw that he had another side, a need to express his desire to enjoy the pleasure inherent in experience. I pointed out that we were facing the lifelong clash between his relatively undeveloped "pastoral" desire "to be" and his impulsion to follow the directives of his father's voice "to do." Perry responded that he wanted to master the dilemma without any concern for his father's injunctions. In the present, he said, he was considerably gratified by immediate appreciation of his experience, free from his father's influence. Such moments of enjoyment, he went on to say, represented the success he was having. He then conveyed his anger at his father for his stifling upbringing and at his mother for her denial and inability to comfort him, his distaste for his current work environment, and his love for escape from his day-to-day existence. None of these sudden and jarring associations appeared to be connected to enjoying the battle against his father's influence. The striking feature of this concatenation of associations was the intensity with which Perry enjoyed expressing the affects. As there appeared to be no content that evoked the string of associations or connected them, the unifying thread seemed to be the depth and freedom of affective expression. The emergence of Perry's ability to enjoy solving problems resulted in an explosion of affects, both positive and negative, some of which had precious little to do with the topic at hand. Perry delighted in talking to me without any concern for "performance"; his string of seemingly disparate associations was an exercise of his new-found affective freedom. The therapeutic space was being transformed from an either/or dilemma to an expanded arena in which problem solving was an expression of freedom rather than the antithesis of it.

In the gratification he derived from ever-more therapeutic moments, Perry was creating new ways of experiencing the therapeutic relationship. As a result of our understanding the dilemma of the therapeutic relationship and the subsequent opening of the space, he was able to confront his conflicts with assessing his performance. Once Perry gained full appreciation of his "pastoral side," he was unable to fill the void by becoming consumed with the drive to material and professional success. Confronted with the inability to go either forward or backward, he created a new experience: the pleasure of mastering the challenges before him. The key to the change, therefore, was his ability to transcend the either/or split by creating a unique experience that gratified both sides of his psyche and motivated him to apply this creative approach to his life.

Although Perry was delighted with his new approach to therapy, the most significant change he sought was a life that fulfilled his formerly conflicting desires. While in therapy, "urban" and "rural" were metaphors; in life they were real. To extend his new experience in the therapeutic space to the rest of his existence, Perry needed to find a way to live the benefits of both passions. To include the part of himself we called "rural" without abandoning his need for achievement, Perry decided to shift the balance between work and personal life. Determined to realize his aspiration for freedom, he was no longer satisfied with full partnership in his business because he felt imprisoned by the burden it imposed. After seriously considering leaving the company, he negotiated with his partners and crafted an innovative arrangement that allowed him to operate in a more independent fashion. In essence, he was able to function almost as an independent contractor while maintaining a loose connection with the corporation. In this way, he could decide his own work goals, though at the cost of a significant reduction in his yearly income. As part of this newly won independence, Perry determined his work schedule and took advantage of this freedom to enjoy his family at home and on frequent trips. The upshot was that he devoted less time to work than he had ever contemplated. With this decisive shift in his priorities, the very fabric of his life was created anew as he blended the mental challenges of his work life with the appreciation of family and rural existence.

Perry was not content to change the balance between work and family. Unwilling to live under exacting expectations even in the more limited work life he now led, Perry applied his new attitude to the challenges of his vocation. He immersed himself in each deal without judging himself against an externally imposed standard. If he felt stimulated by the difficulties any proposed deal presented and the final agreement represented a creative solution, he had a good experience; it was this sense of satisfaction that now became his criterion for success. With the application of this new criterion, Perry created a way of doing business that fit his needs for enjoyment and freedom while relieving his sense of oppression. As Perry made these changes, he realized that this attitude toward business was not just a way to work, but a new way of living. No longer believing that professional challenge and freedom were in conflict, he was beginning to live in accordance with both.

Once his attitude toward business changed and Perry achieved the more independent arrangement with his firm, he felt palpable relief from the onerous burden that had characterized his work life. Of course he was not free from all work expectations, but he was now able to conduct business in a way of his choosing. Creating his own way of managing his professional life completely shifted Perry's experience of business. No longer feeling he was performing for the ever-present judgment of some unseen other, he felt a renewed investment in the day-to-day operations of the company. Seeking new deals and eagerly anticipating the challenge of completing them, Perry found more energy for work than he had in years. Similarly, he was excited about having more time to play with his children at home and take trips with them to the country. The most decisive change, from his viewpoint, was the feeling that he was living his life, experiencing the intensity of all he did, as opposed to his former state of going through the motions. It was as though he had emerged from a walking death.

CONCLUSION: FROM DEPRESSION TO CREATING THE SELF

It must be underscored that Perry's depression lifted completely only after he was able to make these decisive changes in the structure of his life. His emotional existence came alive when he had the freedom to embark on a life that was largely of his own choosing on the basis of what mattered most to him. He then brought to fruition dormant potential to enjoy life and express long-buried values. When this crucially important part of himself came alive, his psychic collapse was reversed as his motivation and enthusiasm for life returned or, we might more accurately say, gained authentic expression for the first time. Although Perry had returned to work early in the therapy, he continued his lifelong feeling of being fated to carry out a course preset for him which had resulted in living with a pervasive sense of emptiness, a life devoid of meaning. Perry's *ennui* changed only after he was able to create a path that satisfied his dual needs for challenge and freedom. Thus, it was not improvement in his depression that allowed Perry to reinvent his life according to his desires but the ability to author his life that resolved his depression.

Perry's therapeutic voyage is illustrative of the therapeutic action of the psychoanalytic therapy of depression. His lack of motivation, energy, and enthusiasm was rooted in the inability to exercise important components of his self and the resultant failure to assume ownership of his life. Consequently, he had a pervasive sense of hopelessness and helplessness. When he used the potential space in the therapeutic relationship to create a therapeutic moment holding both mental stimulation and freedom, however, Perry created a new experience that gave him a future of his own creation and, in this way, diminished his sense of futility. As we saw with Helen in chapter 2, the ability to create a new way of being in the therapeutic space leads eventually to a life in the future-perfect tense. Perry used the potential space of the therapeutic relationship to facilitate his creation of a life constructed from previously buried desires, and living his life on the foundation of these lived authentic affects replaced his depression. This is not to say that all forms and severity of depression can be ameliorated by this model or by any model of psychoanalytic therapy. It is to say that a common source of depression is the failure to develop an authentic self, and for such patients the creation of self is the essence of the therapeutic action.

Another such patient was Helen, whose therapeutic journey was depicted in chapter 2. As you may recall, Helen existed without a future; she moved in her life from moment to moment without anticipating that anything could improve. The lack of hope and complete resignation to an existence outside her control was manifested in her state of depression. The pall of her life was lifted only after she began to use the therapeutic space to elaborate a sense of future, to live her life in the future perfect. Her ability to believe that a future existed was tantamount to overcoming her chronic depression. As with Perry, her diminished psyche was rebuilt only when she was able to use the potential space in the therapeutic relationship to elaborate a new way of being. Helen also transcended her depression by creating a new *modus operandi* based on previously buried authentic desires. Like Perry, Helen did not create a new life structure after her depression was relieved; rather, this creation extinguished her depression. So, when working with depressed patients one sees an especially fitting application of the model of therapeutic action as the creative use of potential space. However well one might understand depression, a patient is unlikely to overcome this painful state until a self is built on genuine affective experience.

This model differs from the self-psychological concept of therapeutic action in depression. From the latter perspective, depression is rooted in a weak self that has not received the phase-appropriate selfobject responses required to formulate realistic ambitions and ideals (Kohut, 1971). The therapeutic action, according to this theory, consists of the provision of selfobject responses, a process that results in the internalization of the analyst and strengthens the enfeebled self (Kohut, 1984). While self psychology overlaps with the present view in finding the roots of depression in a deficiency of the self, self psychological theory puts too much emphasis on the actions of the analyst while casting the patient in a passive, receptive role. The decisive difference is that self psychology emphasizes internalization, and the current theory places the greatest weight on the patient's creation. Self psychology, lacking a concept of potential space, is limited in its ability to conceptualize the patient's creative use of the therapeutic relationship, and, as we have seen, this very process is essential to overcoming depression.

In resolving the depressed conditions of both Perry and Helen I was led to the internal negative "scripts" with which both patients were afflicted. Internalized messages, or "internal objects," were also a major factor in Jenny's somatic symptoms and, in fact, were present in many patients we discussed in Part One, such as Zelda, Leo, and Anna. Because the influence of such bad internal objects seems to be pervasive, we now turn our attention to overcoming these perplexing and stubborn psychological forces.

9

Relinquishing Bad Objects

Danny was plagued by self-attack. Even the most trivial miscue or difficulty unleashed a torrent of self-directed invectives. In an unremitting, unforgiving, harsh internal voice, he would berate himself: "You idiot! You're stupid! What a loser! How could you be so dumb?" Even without committing any apparent peccadillo, he felt a presence hovering, waiting for the opportunity to unleash a string of vitriolic criticisms. Constantly feeling that almost anything he did was flawed, Danny was preoccupied with critical voices inside that seemed to have a life of their own. When he joined a social conversation, he felt he was not as interesting or engaging as the other people. Even more disconcerting, after leaving such a conversation, he inevitably replayed the interactions in an internal monologue in which he found fault with almost everything he said. Regretting his behavior, Danny was usually convinced that he had made a fool of himself and that others had undoubtedly noticed. Even when reassured that his behavior was unobjectionable, Danny remained unconvinced. Over the years, he had become increasingly preoccupied with his internal monologue. He replayed social and vocational interactions in which he lamented his behavior and wished he had the chance to repair the damage he felt he caused to others' image of him.

In psychoanalytic practice we frequently see patients such as Danny, who feel demonized by internal criticisms experienced as though they were visited on the patient without his participation, as though they had a life of their own. These demonic voices are thought of in object relations terms as internalized bad objects. Seemingly unable to register positive experience, the patient seems to possess an internal screen filtering out anything that might feel good but attracting the influence of any negative event. Danny's pattern of oblivious disregard to the praise he frequently received about his work, along with his obsessive rumination on any criticism, however mild, typifies such patients. For example, Danny worked for a sustained period of time on a report, and, when it was finally completed, his boss and other higher level supervisors, some of whom had no direct connection to him, sent him highly complimentary responses, a rare event in his company. Danny noted that there was a mistake for which there might be consequences, and he was certain that he would be fired for the error despite the glowing praise he received. For days and weeks afterward, he was preoccupied with the fear of being fired and sought continual reassurance from me that his trepidation was groundless. Needless to say, he flagellated himself mercilessly for being so "stupid" as to make this error. Whenever I highlighted the compliments directed his way, he expressed fear that he would most certainly be given his walking papers as soon as his mistake was discovered. This self-flagellation maintained a vicelike grip on Danny's psyche, and the analysis faced a formidable challenge in trying reduce its influence.

The elimination of bad objects is one of the most stubborn therapeutic problems encountered by psychotherapists. Clinicians are frequently impressed by the resiliency and intractability of internalized bad objects despite the grief and suffering they cause. Klein (1957) regarded bad objects as so important that she made them the pathogenic factor in all forms of psychopathology. Even after we understand the origin of these bad objects and identify their replication in the transference, they tend to stay adhesively attached to the structure of the patient's psyche. Given the intense level of pain and often dysfunction that results from adherence to bad objects, this stubbornness is perplexing. Furthermore, our interpretive efforts, rather than mitigating the effect of bad objects, are often subsumed by them. With Danny, for example, we identified his assaults on himself as his father's ruthless voice assailing him from within. Despite our insight into their origins, however, these internal assaults persisted. Moreover, Danny, proceeded to berate himself for being held hostage by a figure who had died many years before, thereby folding the interpretive process into his pattern of self-abuse. All such efforts to interpret bad objects, and thereby mitigate their force, quickly became absorbed into Danny's "closed circle of object relationships" (Fairbairn, 1958). The more he understood his adherence to bad object ties, the more he berated himself for his inability to change, a reaction that strengthened their hold on him. Such is the impasse frequently encountered in the psychoanalytic therapy of patients afflicted with tenacious bad objects. The result, at minimum, is a perplexing problem and, at worst, a therapeutic stalemate.

Fairbairn (1943) saw the adhesiveness of bad object ties to be the central therapeutic difficulty in the conduct of psychoanalytic therapy. Consequently, he gave a great deal of attention to the problem of how to loosen the grip of internal negative objects. Therefore, we are well served to consider his work in some detail.

FAIRBAIRN AND THE THEORY OF BAD INTERNAL OBJECTS

Fairbairn (1946) believed the fundamental motive of the psyche is to seek satisfactory object relationships. When this desire is met, the early object relationships become integrated into the ego. But when they are painful and frustrating, the child feels that his love is unacceptable to the caretaking figure. The object then becomes desirable but rejecting, and this bad object is split into the exciting and rejecting objects. According to Fairbairn, the child internalizes the bad object in an effort to master the pain and frustration of the unsatisfying object relationship. The exciting, or libidinal, object continues to seek satisfactory object relationships, but owing to the history of previously frustrating experiences, object seeking evokes anxiety. Therefore the rejecting object represses the longing for object contact to avoid further frustration and the shame of feeling that his love is unacceptable. In Fairbairn's language, the antilibidinal object represses the libidinal object to avoid the pain and shame of object contact.

According to Fairbairn (1944), when an object, whether libidinal or anti-libidinal, is internalized, it is no longer simply an object; it becomes a structure. Fairbairn's reasoning is that the bad object organizes experience, however negatively. It follows that each internalized object has a corresponding ego structure. The exciting object is connected to the libidinal ego, and the rejecting object to the anti-libidinal ego. When an object is internalized, it becomes a structure, a part of the psychic organization. Because the object has a role in the way the psyche is organized, it is but a small step to extend Fairbairn's insight to say that the bad object is a component of the self. For example, Danny's self-flagellation structured his responses to success and error. Accomplishments were diminished, but every misstep was greeted with abuse, an internalization of his father's assaults. In this way, his vitriolic self-castigation structured his contact with the world around success and error. In his interactions with others, Danny was beset with the underlying anxiety of being criticized or judged inadequate. This anxiety issued in a wariness that inhibited his interpersonal relationships. Thus the internalized bad object played a major role in the way Danny's experience was organized, a role that greatly influenced Danny's relationships.

To place Danny's experience in Fairbairn's terms: it is the libidinal ego that moved Danny toward relationships where it encountered the resistant pull of the anxiety-driven anti-libidinal ego. The infant's attraction to an object, for Fairbairn, is not a formless, energetic libidinal impulse but the seeking of an object relationship. Desire includes an organized effort, even if inhibited, to form a relationship with the object of desire. Impulsive, formless, energetic attraction is a pathological phenomenon that results from a "fractionated ego." Such a condition arises from a failure of the early object relationships rather than being a natural condition of their occurrence.

One need not embrace the edifice of Fairbairn's thought to benefit from his insight that internal objects are structures. We saw that Danny had an organized way of responding to positive and negative experiences alike, and this means of psychic organization was his internalized bad object. Because this bad object provided a structure to his experience, he felt it as a part of the self. Thus, Fairbairn's idea that internal objects are structures leads us to conclude that such objects are part of the self, and this conclusion suggests a strategy for the psychoanalytic therapy of bad objects.

BAD OBJECTS AND THE SELF

We may find in Fairbairn's ideas a means for the resolution of the vexing dilemma of patients' adherence to bad objects. If internalized objects are only objects, it is difficult to see why patients cling to them. But, if objects are structures, when an internal object is relinquished, a way of constructing and organizing experience disappears, leaving a gap in the psyche. The stakes in the loss of an internal object are high. The very sense of self is disrupted, and experiences that once fit into known categories become disorienting.

We can see how this process operates by observing Danny's reaction when we focused on the malignant effects of his attachment to his father's voice. He saw that his incessant self-punishment was not only triggered by perceived injuries, but also was a way of interfering with potentially positive experiences. As he began to feel good about a work project, for example, the internal voice denigrated his efforts. Our understanding of this reaction as the internalized image of his father gave him some hope of overcoming this painful self devaluation, but no sooner did this positive feeling begin to appear than a caustic attack reappeared, scornfully accusing himself of doing inferior work. When I noted the virulence with which he castigated himself, Danny spontaneously remarked that the vitriolic criticisms felt so much like his father's verbal abuse that he felt as though his father were present. His self-flagellation, although excruciatingly painful, maintained a connection with his father; indeed hearing the voice was the only way he could hold on to that relationship. His fear of abandonment by his father was so intense that he preferred the pain of self-attack to the risk of losing an illusory connection to the older man.

At this point, our goal was to help Danny give up his imaginary paternal attachment. He began to confront the reality that his connection with his father had never been there, but he had needed this belief to sustain him through a childhood lived without a paternal bond. The process of confronting his father's lack of interest was difficult, but Danny was able to accept that he had never had, and never would have, any relationship with his father.

Unfortunately, Danny's sober recognition that he had been holding on to a forlorn wish did not seem to extinguish the hold of the bad object. Consciously, he wished to erase any vestige of his father's influence, but, whenever he contemplated any type of self assessment, he launched into self-accusation. Fairbairn recognized that a child will hold on to an abusive relationship because the bond to the caretaker is more important than pleasure. However, Danny was not attached to a real relationship but to an illusory connection.

Furthermore, positive affects stimulated the anxiety of being flooded with overwhelming emotional intensity. For example, when Danny felt hopeful about resolving the conflict over his internal image, he felt excited but feared that the intensity of this feeling would cause him to lose control of his behavior. Danny was momentarily elated at the liberating thought of not having to live with continual attacks on his experience, but the relief immediately translated into anxiety that he would "go too far" and have no way to assess his performance. How could he tell if anything he did was of value? Without such a measure, he feared he would accept everything he did uncritically and thereby become "full of himself," be offensively arrogant, and lose any sense of civility. To relinquish his bad objects was to fear an expansiveness that seemed to have no boundary. When I inquired further about this state, Danny said that he felt like a small child who believes he can do anything and that whatever he wishes for will happen. While Danny denigrated this attitude as hopelessly immature, he acknowledged a desire to act on it and said that the sense of unbridled possibilities felt familiar.

We understood this state to be a residue of unresolved childhood grandiosity. Whereas Danny's father was highly critical, his mother was emotionally absent. All his life, Danny felt that, when he looked into his mother's eyes, he saw a vacuum. Never feeling recognized or appreciated by either parent, Danny did not believe that he and his talents were of any importance. As a child, he attempted to compensate for the feeling that he lacked inherent value by impressing people with exaggerated exploits or accomplishments or performing attention-getting acts, such as trying to run farther than other children or spelling words that others did not know. As an adult, Danny regarded those behaviors as pathetic, but he continued to feel a desperate need for approbation from others.

If Danny allowed himself to feel accomplished, he immediately became anxious that he would indulge himself in self-aggrandizement that he would not be able to control. Yet the only alternative to manic, self-indulgent grandiosity that Danny could contemplate was self-punishment: his internalized bad object was an organized way of controlling his tendency toward self-inflation, thus providing him with a structure that relaxed his anxiety of losing control. The price, however, was an inability to realistically judge his own behavior. Rather than assessing how he was doing personally or vocationally, Danny could only self-aggrandize or harshly attack himself, regardless of his actual performance.

In our exploration of his motives for continuing the invectives from internal objects, Danny and I repeatedly saw his unrelenting tendency to greet every smidgen of positive experience with self-accusation. For example, as our understanding of his fear of detaching from bad objects deepened, Danny once again began to feel hopeful of ridding himself of his father's influence. What if he felt successful without his instinctive negative reaction? When I noted that he was beginning to allow himself the feeling of success, he said that hope was naive, but when I countered that this response was an effort to squelch his budding positive feeling, Danny concurred. I suggested that his dilemma was now whether to let himself feel good at the moment or react in his typical way by burying that feeling under a verbal attack. He began to show visible signs of anxiety, tensing his face, tapping his feet, and playing with the tassels on the couch. When I asked him how he felt, he replied, "Anxious, confused, even a little bit eerie."

Our persistent inquiry into Danny's use of the negative voice inside was taking away his habitual response to good news. In the session in question, he became so confused he could not even remember what we had been discussing, and his inability to remember exacerbated his anxiety. At this point, Danny said that he had no idea what was going on and was unable to keep his thoughts clear. He asked me if he was having a panic attack. I said that I thought he became confused when we confronted his refusal to feel good, which deprived him of his long-established pattern of self-abuse. I went on to say that, because he saw no alternative, he was caught in a conundrum that left him paralyzed. He said, "I feel like I lean on that voice. I almost want it back. Not really, but without it, I'm lost. I don't know what else to do." I described his position as an unwillingness to return to the harsh voice of his father and an inability to feel good about himself without feeling selfish, superior, and overly excited. He immediately felt an impulse to assail himself for being so anxious "over nothing," and I commented that he was tempted to avoid the anxiety of losing his sense of self by returning to his default position of berating himself. He tried to sustain the good feeling but could not because, as he said, he had "no place to put it."

This interaction indicated that Danny's motives for his adhesive tie to the bad object were not exhausted by his narcissistic vulnerability and the residual connection to his father. While the anxiety of yielding this tie was an important motive for the tenacity of its bond, it did not capture his lost feeling. Painful as it was, the bad object served to organize his responses to success and failure; it provided him with a self-definition, albeit a painful one. Thus, his stubborn bond to the bad object was not only a way of keeping the connection with his father but also a means for maintaining a self-organization that helped him negotiate the interpersonal world. By regarding himself negatively, Danny knew who he was; losing his father's voice tore a hole in the fabric of his self. Without the bad object, he did not lose only a father, he lost his self.

Understanding the role of the bad object in this way helps the therapist appreciate the patient's need to maintain a powerful tie to the negative voice. The crucial corollary of the principle that the bad object serves a self-organizing function is the threat to the patient's self when the therapeutic process jeopardizes the patient's attachment to it. However, if the therapist sees this endangerment to the existing self structure then the patient's paralysis and disorientation can become a potential space for the creation of alternatives to the bad object. On the other hand, if the therapist does not have a concept of an emergent self-structure that can be created from the ambiguity, the danger exists of the patient returning to the influence of the bad object in order to regain the only sense of self he knows.

THERAPEUTIC ACTION

Given this concept of the function of the bad object, it follows that the first step in letting go of it is to hold the patient's anxiety about losing an important part of the self. Not believing that alternatives to bad object dominance are possible, the patient, who is quickly losing functioning, can see little value in this phase. The analyst's conviction that other possibilities exist holds the situation while the patient suffers the emptiness of existence without the structuring function of the bad object. The purpose of establishing and sustaining the void, despite the intensity of anxiety, is to open potential space.

The patient's experience of disintegration as a necessary prelude to building a different self-organization has been referred to as "regression in the service of the ego" (Kris, 1939) or "regression as progress" (Bettleheim, 1971). While it may be tempting to conceptualize the state of disorientation as regression, it may not be accurate to do so. Danny was not recapturing an earlier point in his life but, rather, was experiencing something new, a letting go of his bearings in the world. One cannot assume that he ever experienced this before; the confusion that so dominated him was a product of a therapeutically induced loss of psychic organization. Although regression does not seem an appropriate term for this state, "regression in the service of the ego" does capture the idea that therapeutically stimulated confusion can be brought into the service of building a new, more authentic self-organization. This concept has been recognized as central to therapeutic progress in the theory of "positive disintegration" (Dabrowski, 1964), according to which mental structure has to disintegrate for forward movement to occur.

The inchoate nature of Danny's current experience and the loss of self to which he was subject left him feeling confused and anxious over losing a primary way of responding to obstacles. To utilize the potential space before us, I insisted that our road map to uncovering new possibilities was his free associational process. Therefore, in response to Danny's "What do I do?" anguish, I asked simply, "What comes up?" In responding this way, I was inviting whatever might surface from the anxiety rather than attempting to relieve it. "I'm an idiot to be suffering like this for nothing," Danny explained. We both recognized this response as a return of the bad object, and Danny was once again frustrated by his inability to shake its tenacious hold on him. I persisted, "What comes up?" Danny hesitated and then said, "This is embarrassing, but the first thing that comes to mind is that I love to solve tough problems that others can't handle. I feel great when I can make something work that others can't fix—what I'm really feeling is how much fun it is to fix something, to find a way. It's not just pride; it's a thing of beauty, like an aesthetic experience. It looks so good! I love it! I hate admitting this, but I love doing it better than others can do it. Now I'm embarrassed." He said that the excitement made him feel immature, like a child who had won a Monopoly game. When I asked him about the embarrassment, he repeated his fear of self-aggrandizement. "Well, it's so petty, I feel like a hot shot, a kid who feels cool and superior because he won a game. It's pathetic."

Danny's incipient positive states had never been articulated, and, now that they were being given expression, he felt chaotic and destabilized. I told him his associations to problem solving had indicated that he often became excited about the intrinsic pleasure of his work, but his distaste for self-inflation showed that he had conflated this excitement with a sense of self-aggrandizement he detested. That comment evoked another concatenation of positive memories, desires, and interests. His associations began with memories of playing with childhood toys—such as his electric train set and model airplanes—that had given him hours of enjoyment. He then went on to his adolescent interest in auto mechanics and his passion for speculating on the financial markets. From his excitement about those activities he associated to sexuality and his desire for a more active, varied sex life with his wife. The thread connecting these diverse topics was his positive feeling about all of them. I underscored the fact that he was expressing interest, excitement, and enjoyment.

My clinical strategy was to refuse to answer his frequent pleas for guidance and instead turn the therapeutic lens on the kernel of potential within each of these emerging positive affective dispositions. For example, I interpreted to Danny that his fears of "doing whatever I want" reflected a fear that he could not control his new-found assertiveness. Wanting to follow the lead of his unfolding affects, Danny feared that his self-expression would spin out of control. I highlighted the difference between his desire for self-affirmation and the fear of unbridled selfishness, an attitude he found abhorrent. In a similar fashion, I interpreted his fear of being smug as his anxiety that his desire for success would become self-aggrandizing and the dramatic explosion as a way of showing us that he longed for intensity of experience and immediate gratification of many types, one of which was sexual.

I encouraged the further elaboration of the pleasurable memories, thoughts, and feelings appearing in the associational train. With an embarrassed grin, Danny admitted to feeling superior when he found a way to solve problems that stymied his bosses. Saying, "This is fun," he then continued to recall memories of other such "victories," small and large, from childhood to adulthood. His recollections ranged from the thrill of doing well in Little League baseball to academic pursuits and his current success in the stock market. But, in each case, he conveyed the fear that his success meant a sense of superiority that implied a devaluation of others and ultimately spoiled the pleasurable moment.

The clinical strategy of welcoming his newly surfacing affective states rather than interpreting them was based on the principle that we were in a potential space in which these unfolding affects represented previously arrested ways of being. Facilitating the articulation of these experiences is the clinical implementation of the decisive difference between conceptualizing these nascent states as unformed potential, on one hand, and repressed contents, on the other. If Danny and I had been uncovering repressed desires, they would have appeared in consciousness as complete entities, and the appropriate clinical posture would have been interpretive. That they appeared in a chaotic, undefined formlessness showed we were touching on incipient psychological states rather than fully defined experiences. These affective dispositions had indeed been suppressed, but they had been occluded before coming to fruition.

So, when Danny said that he was excited by his sexual feelings, my attitude was that he was expressing not only a source of pleasure but also a desire for a more intense, varied sex life. After some consternation about approaching his wife with this desire, he eventually reported a more satisfying sexual relationship. When Danny expressed the satisfaction he derived from achievement, we turned the discussion to areas in which he could feel accomplished. There were many such examples. He decided that he wanted to resurrect his childhood love of construction by engaging in a variety of building projects with his children, and each such completed activity gave him a feeling of mastery. When he bought his son an ice hockey rink for the front yard, he gained immense satisfaction from learning how to build it so that the ice would stay frozen for the longest possible time.

Danny felt that the experience and expression of positive affects in the analytic space marked a decisive turning point in his life. For the first time, he had permitted himself the full expression of self-affirming affective experiences, especially interest, enjoyment, and excitement, without invoking a negative introject. The unfolding of these feelings reflected Danny's bravery in combating the sense of self he had possessed since childhood. He now included positive experiences in his representation of himself, vastly expanding his previously constricted, crippling, wholly negative self-image as a defective being. Danny was excited to have positive experiences available to him, but these feelings were so different from the affective world in which he had been living that he found them alien and guilt-evoking.

Danny continually fought the urge to combat these unfolding states with an attack on himself. During each such occurrence, I highlighted the evolving affect previously dormant under the dominance of the bad object. Danny then typically abandoned the impulse to attack the excitement or enjoyment and allowed the positive affect to flourish. Proceeding in this fashion, Danny and I were able to unearth many sources of pleasure: achievement, sex, mastery of problems, and pursuit of such interests as miniature-train construction. Nonetheless, there remained two sources of delight to which he objected: he felt that his self-aggrandizement and competitiveness were unacceptable efforts to compensate for a feeling of unworthiness.

From this persistent illumination of his nascent affective states, Danny was in a position to create a new structure for his interpersonal life, and that is just what he did. He not only began to express his own desires but also used them as guides for his conduct. When he was excited or angry, surprised or disturbed, he based his behavior on the feeling. His affects no longer suppressed by the bad object, a much wider range of emotional responses became available to him, and he built his interactional patterns on this array of affective dispositions. When he performed well at work, he permitted himself the awareness that his achievement pleased him. But he faced the challenge of sustaining this feeling without the arrogance of smugness; he attempted to achieve this goal by enjoying accomplishment without comparing himself with others. If he began to feel self-important, he decided that such an attitude distorted the pleasure he took in his work and was neither a necessary ingredient of his feeling of success nor a stance he wished to adopt. Danny found his greatest satisfaction in the experience of achievement but, when he did not meet his own expectations, he resisted any fledgling impulse to devalue his effort. By allowing himself to be gratified in the exercise of his talents, he created a new way of being himself, the obverse of which was accepting his drawbacks.

Once the therapeutic process had advanced to the point that Danny could articulate newly appearing affects, he spontaneously used his anger in the evolution of these new experiences. Surprising himself with his willingness to respond aggressively, he began to protest situations to which he objected. One day he felt unfairly criticized for a report he had written and had a brief moment of anger that he would have formerly ignored while concentrating on the sense of injury from the critique. In this instance, he noticed the flash of anger almost pass through his mind but instead of dismissing it he kept it within his awareness. This realization of his anger at the critic eventually led us to the awareness that he possessed a deeper, chronic anger over feeling unappreciated.

To take another example: Danny was pleased with his report and had a fleeting fantasy of receiving special approbation for exceptional work. Historically, he had paid no attention to such momentary psychic events, but in this instance he held the fantasy and realized that he was coveting approval that would never come. Danny immediately felt angry about exerting extraordinary effort for little appreciation from his superiors; this moment connected to an underlying dissatisfaction with his workplace of which he became increasingly aware. In this way, a fleeting moment of anger evolved into a fundamental objection to the way he was treated and his company run. His conflict with the organization then became apparent, and his unhappiness with management ultimately led him to seek employment elsewhere. These reactions were decisively different for Danny; rather than repeating his lifelong pattern of attacking himself for not performing well enough, he sustained awareness of his dissatisfaction with the way he was being treated. He then admitted to himself the extent of his discontent with his employer.

While these examples may seem pedestrian, they represent changes in the way Danny processed and used affects. Historically, he had either ignored such nascent affective dispositions or attacked himself for having them, but now he not only became aware of his subjective life, but also fostered its expansion into new ways of expressing himself. In lieu of the habitually negative attacks, a variety of affective responses were now available to him. Thus the process that had begun with maintaining attention on fleeting affective dispositions evolved into an expanded awareness of Danny's psychic life and the development of these nascent states into patterns of interpersonal relating.

The inclusion of positive experiences into his repertoire of behavioral responses gave Danny a multitude of potential ways to judge his conduct. He now had at his disposal a variety of reactions to his work performance and interpersonal life— excitement, pleasure, interest, disappointment, distress, surprise. This rich and variegated affective life replaced the rigid dichotomy of self-aggrandizement or self-flagellation. Without the dominance of the bad object and with a disposition that now included a multiplicity of affects, Danny was free to judge himself in any arena on the basis of his conduct. Additionally, with the inclusion of positive affects into his ways of relating and self-evaluation, Danny had a new context within which to experience his flaws. Able to feel good about achievement, Danny did not think he had destroyed a project when he saw a mistake; rather, he saw the miscue as a blemish in an otherwise solid performance. In other words, he judged his effectiveness on the basis of the merit of his work rather than on a preconceived need to attack or inflate himself.

Despite the dramatic appearance of new, more positive experiences in Danny's life, the bad object did not die easily. Danny continued to feel an instinctive tendency to rely on it as a default position. Consequently, we oscillated between his ability to judge himself according to his achievements and drawbacks, on one hand, and the regressive pull of the bad object, on the other. This conflict was now also fought outside psychotherapy. In many sessions, Danny indicated that, when experiencing success at work, he caught himself diminishing the accomplishment as trivial and then returned to the feeling of satisfaction. When I asked what success felt like before he extinguished it, he replied that he had begun to feel excited but could not sustain the feeling. I asked him to stick with his feeling of heightened stimulation on these occasions, and, almost as an experiment, he permitted himself the feeling of accomplishment.

A variety of different affective states not directly addressed in therapy emerged and evolved into ways of being and relating. I have found the appearance of new experiences that had never been topical in therapy to be common among patients who are liberating themselves from the influence of bad object experience. The suspension of the bad object allows the awakening of previously dormant affects and desires, many of which were unknown to either patient or therapist prior to their appearance. Therefore, experiences arrested by the bad object can be given voice even if they are not specifically addressed. The therapist does not have to know what experience is hidden from view; he needs only to nurture the patient's unfolding experience and encourage the expression of hidden longings and desires. This creative undertaking does not require the analysis of each individual affect or desire; rather, the process consists of the freeing and further elaboration of previously inhibited affective dispositions.

The explosion of interests and new activities in Danny's life gave impetus to multiple ways of being and relating. His sex life, work performance, and avocations all underwent major changes. As his life now included positive affects, a new psychological structure was emerging. The bad object that had plagued his psychic life gradually faded away and was replaced by a new organization that included interest, excitement, and enjoyment. As can be seen from Danny's case, our direct discussion and understanding of the existence and dominance of the bad object had not markedly reduced its hold on his psyche, but its influence dissipated significantly once alternative ways of being and relating became established.

This sequence of events appears to be a reversal of the expected effects of interpretation. According to the conventional theory of therapeutic action, understanding a pathological phenomenon, such as the bad object, should diminish its power, thus making possible alternative ways of feeling and doing. The therapeutic action with Danny, however, did not work this way, and I have found his therapeutic movement to be typical of patients whose psyches are governed by bad objects. These tenacious forces will not disappear as a result of understanding alone because the prospect of losing the bad object evokes the threat of losing the very structure relied on to engage the world. Understanding the origins and function of the bad object does, however, set in abeyance its influence so that an alternative can be formed. Once Danny and I grasped the meaning of the bad object as his father's voice crushing positive affects, he was motivated to suspend its organizing function. Danny was then able to take advantage of the newly opened space to build positive affects into new ways of being and relating that ultimately replaced the role of the bad object in his psyche. What we have seen, then, is that the therapeutic action in the abandonment of bad objects is not a straightforward connection between understanding and change, but a less obvious process in which interpretation permits the bad object to be suspended so that a new self-organization may be created, thus obviating the bad object.

Undoubtedly, theorists who believe that understanding is not useful for relinquishing bad objects have seen the limited impact of grasping the meaning of these powerful psychological forces. If a therapist expects interpretation to be alterative, he is likely to be disppointed and then doubt the capacity for insight to loosen the hold of these negative influences. But, as we have seen, this conclusion is a product of the assumption of a straightforward connection between understanding and therapeutic action. Once the key role of interpretation in establishing potential space is grasped, its importance in abandoning the hold of the bad object on the psyche becomes clear.

A different form of this anxiety was seen in Lisa, who felt that she was worthless and deserved little from life. Like Danny, Lisa suffered under the grip of a tenacious, negative introject. In her case, the bad object regarded her as incapable of being effective in any endeavor of life. Lisa's mother had had little time for her and regarded her only child as weak, ineffective, and talentless. Despite Lisa's solid academic record, her mother judged her "not college material," and Lisa had always thought of herself as lacking in intellectual capacity. Until she began to alter her self-perception in psychoanalysis, her job history consisted of service employment that required little mental ability. Her long-standing pattern of becoming excessively dependent on men was rooted in the same controlling maternal introject that defined her as helpless, undeserving, and lacking all value. Without being aware of it, Lisa had assumed that she required a man to sustain her in every arena of life because she felt incapable of facing stresses and responsibilities on her own. She enacted these attributions in a variety of ways, the most pronounced being her pattern of submissive relationships with men.

A major focus of the therapeutic process was understanding the origin of her belief that she possessed no intellectual capability or talent of any type. She felt that her existence depended on a strong bond with her mother, and the maternal introject was the only way she could feel a maternal connection. We understood her view of herself as cognitively defective to be a primary symptom of the tenacious hold of the maternal introject. In the process of psychotherapy, Lisa decided that she wanted to put the lifelong conviction of her intellectual deficiency to the test. To find out if she had any degree of academic ability, she timorously took the step of going to college. To her surprise, Lisa found that she could do the work without extraordinary effort. At the cost of considerable sacrifice of time and money, she went on to graduate school and discovered a new world.

As she pursued her graduate studies, Lisa developed a new social group of educated, stimulating, culturally sophisticated, well-informed peers. At that point, however, she began to suffer acute anxiety attacks and gave serious thought to abandoning her plans for higher education and career. We were able to trace the origins of these episodes to her exposure to a new life and an intellectually advanced peer group of which she felt undeserving and had never believed herself to be truly a part. In the intellectually enriching environment in which she now resided, Lisa felt she did not know either who she was or how to form relationships with her peers.

Having sufficiently overcome her lifelong self-perception as deficient to pursue postgraduate education, Lisa now felt as if she were in a foreign land without knowledge of the culture. At this point, she felt she was risking more than she could bear: romantic attachments, her position of being cared for, ties to peers. Absent her subservient position, Lisa believed she would lose her ability to navigate the social world, but her deepest anxiety was that she would lose her dependence on men. Clearly, the bad object had defined Lisa's way of relating to the world, as it had with Danny, and the loss of the bad object was tantamount to the loss of her sense of self and the organization of her interpersonal world.

Understanding her anxiety attacks to be rooted in the advance she had made toward experiencing herself as a capable being, I suggested to Lisa that she felt lost without her self definition as subservient and dependent. Nonetheless, she knew that she could not return to such a view of herself because she had achieved a degree of intellectual success that she prized. Having shown herself to be intellectually capable, I went on to say, she was unable to integrate this realization into her experience of herself. Between two identities she could not embrace, Lisa felt lost, and I proposed to her that in this ambiguous space she had the opportunity to create new aspects of her self. I was thus defining her ambiguity and confusion as necessary components of potential space.

We both knew that she would have to relinquish the need for a maternal object, but to do so required a belief in herself as capable, and the adoption of such a sense of self was impeded by the maternal introject. Caught in a closed circle from which we saw no escape, Lisa and I repeated this cycle many times. As her frustration and confusion intensified, she pleaded with me to bring her out of this conundrum. I responded that she felt her only options were for me to extricate her or for her to be immersed in anxiety. I further commented that this view of her possibilities was rooted in her conviction that she was helpless, incapable of acting on her own, and necessarily dependent on another. Many times I stressed that her feeling of incapability to resolve the therapeutic dilemma reflected the power of the negative maternal image to paralyze her. I held to the stance that the repetition of this cycle and the confusion it embodied provided the opportunity for Lisa to create other possibilities for herself.

When I highlighted the fact that she possessed many significant capabilities, Lisa became anxious and disoriented and denigrated herself for her reaction. She said, "How stupid I am— What a dumb conflict to have and not be able to resolve." I noted that she was withdrawing from the effort to resolve the predicament with me by resorting to her default position of condemning herself as stupid. The thought then occurred to her that she had given the maternal image such power in order to relieve the anxiety caused by freedom and independence. When Lisa said that these feelings were foreign and threatening to her, I noted that she had gained a key insight into her attachment to the negative maternal image. This comment made Lisa anxious because it implied that she had performed an intelligent act. In subsequent sessions, I repeatedly underscored the fact that she had uncovered an underlying motivation for her insistence on her low intelligence, and in each instance she became anxious, frequently insisting that I was wrong because I did not grasp the inadequacy of her intellect.

I interpreted Lisa's anxiety over my remark as the threat she felt in viewing herself as bright, independent, and competent.

She was excited about this feeling but feared that it would stimulate an inflated view of herself that she would not be able to control. I responded that she relieved the anxiety of self-aggrandizement by forming an attachment to her mother that bullied her into submission. Lisa said that she felt excited by the idea that she possessed some intellectual aptitude, but that thought also scared and embarrassed her. When I registered that she seemed to feel either devalued by the bad object or ashamed of an overexcited view of herself, Lisa said that feeling worthless gave her a certain sense of calm and control. I suggested that her fear that she could not feel intelligent without transforming that feeling into a maniacal state of haughty superiority helped explain her difficulty sustaining confidence in her cognitive capabilities. Lisa concurred, saying that when she thought of herself as capable she immediately became excited and feared she "could not put the brakes on" the positive feeling.

Adopting the posture that her confusion, the result of our newly achieved understanding, shifted our relationship away from transference space to potential space, I asked Lisa how she, in fact, felt about her intelligence. She recognized that she had shown herself to possess some degree of cognitive ability, but, as she spoke, she began to feel anxious and feared another panic attack. I both encouraged her to sustain the feeling despite the anxiety and interpreted to her that, whenever she began to recognize her intellectual aptitude, she was in direct conflict with the maternal introject directing her to remain dependent on men. She tried to retain the belief in her mental acumen, but to do so required resisting the temptation to resort to the bad object.

Lisa construed our discussions to mean that she did not know how to view herself as simultaneously capable and limited. I observed that, although her understanding of the relationship between the maternal image and the constraint on her sense of power was an example of her keen insight, she had just described herself as "stupid." I went on to say that expressing both attitudes seemed to reflect her intelligence and the limits on it. Lisa had not noticed that she had conveyed two seemingly contradictory beliefs about herself. At that point, she realized that her self-attribution of "stupid" was the only way she knew to limit positive feelings. It then struck Lisa that her goal in therapy, as in her life, was to learn to appreciate her limitations without needing to attack herself. I commented that the recognition of her insight was stated without the overexcitement of which she was so afraid. At this pivotal point in the process, Lisa saw that the chaos she was then experiencing represented the limitations for which she had so abused herself, and that in the midst of this very confusion she had used her intellect. We both realized that while in the presence of disconcerting anxiety she had exercised her intellectual competence, a fact that showed she could employ her cognitive skills without a state of excitement.

During this process, Lisa exercised her intellect with full recognition of her confusion, a state that restrained her excitement about employing her intelligence. While she remained fully aware of her limitations, she did not abuse herself on account of them. As a result of her ability to deploy her intellect despite its imperfections, Lisa gained confidence in it and her fear of self-inflation abated. Armed with this balanced view of her cognitive aptitude, Lisa became aggressive about problem solving outside the therapeutic setting. When she encountered difficulties at work she was not shy about proposing solutions, even though they did not always work. When I mentioned that she was now relying on her judgment, Lisa seemed surprised, as though she had not noticed this marked change in her behavior. In point of fact, her willingness to tackle work projects proactively won her several promotions, advances she accepted without significant anxiety. The ability to exercise her intellectual judgment without disruptive overexcitement obviated the attachment to the bad object, which faded and gradually disappeared, to be replaced by Lisa's appreciation of her intelligence, talents, and limitations.

We can observe in Lisa's progress that she used potential space to learn to function intellectually and make judgments in the context of her limitations and thus overcome her fear of overexcitement. By using potential space in this way, the bad object became unnecessary to control Lisa's grandiosity. The ability to exercise her intellect, begun in the therapeutic space, then spread to other areas of her life as Lisa gained confidence in her ability to solve problems she had been fearful of confronting.

For both Danny and Lisa, the bad object served a self organizing function. In Danny's case, we saw that he created a means of self-assessment to counter both states. Lisa resolved her problem by using her intellect with a newly achieved awareness of her limitations. For both patients, a new experience became possible as the therapeutic setting contained the chaotic disorganization accompanying the relinquishment of the bad object and then facilitated the expression of the buried self that lay beneath it. Both Danny and Lisa were able to bring forth previously suppressed affects in a newly developed form to provide a structure that supplanted the regulative aspects of the bad object. By giving structure to his desire for intense experience, Danny found a way to have successes and failures, good feelings and bad, without the abuse of the bad object or the chaotic excitement of lifting it. Similarly, Lisa learned how to feel and employ the full force of her intellect without becoming disorganized. In both cases, a new aspect of the self that obviated the need for the bad object was created initially in the therapeutic space and then spread to other areas of life.

GRANDIOSITY AND THE BAD OBJECT

There is a line of psychoanalytic theory beginning with Ferenczi (1911) and culminating with Kohut (1971) that views low self-esteem as a defense against arrested grandiosity. This formulation is valid and useful for many cases of narcissistic vulnerability, and for that reason the tenacity of the bad object, often being a defense against grandiosity, can be easily confused with those cases. It was Kohut's view that, when childhood grandiosity remains vulnerable, it may be split off, leaving the self weakened and lacking in healthy self-regard. This dynamic may appear to apply to Danny insofar as the bad object did protect against the appearance of grandiosity. However, Danny did not have a split-off organized grandiose self waiting for the chance to engage the world. Rather, when Danny tried to relinquish the bad object, he became disorganized at the thought of being able to think, act, and feel as he pleased. His affect soared to a fantasy of self-indulgence in which he had no anchor in the interpersonal world, but this hypomanic excitement was an aspect of a general chaotic disorganization, not a grandiose self.

Patients such as Danny do fear a lapse into a fantasied, self-indulgent state lacking in the normal constraints of reality, but such an attitude is not the self organized around an exaggerated sense of capability depicted by Kohut as the grandiose self. Further, this fear is of what *might* happen without an alternative to the painful affliction of the bad object. With Danny, we did not "find" a split-off grandiose self, but a lack of self, a gap in functioning, to which he reacted with fear of the hyperstimulation of self-indulgence. This difference is important because it shows that the role of the bad object was not so much to protect against the emergence of a grandiose self as to provide a sense of self. Without the feeling of self provided by the bad object, Danny feared loss of all constraints, a state of hyperactivity and even elation.

When the therapeutic process diminished the organizing function of self-attacks, Danny felt like a ship at sea in turbulent waters with no rudder and no steering wheel. If grandiosity were the feared state, Danny would have been shamed, possibly even humiliated, but would not have felt a dizzying loss of psychic equilibrium. While shame is the underside of narcissism, as Morrison (1989) has suggested, disorientation is the underside of the controlling bad object. The difference between patients dominated by the bad object and the narcissistic patients described by Kohut is that, when the bad object's hold on the psyche is loosened, the patient lapses into a chaotic state.

CONCLUSION: RESOLVING THE DILEMMA OF THE BAD OBJECT

The problem of relinquishing the hold of the bad object has been a perplexingly difficult one for psychoanalytic therapists from every theoretical camp. One can find internalized bad objects as major psychopathological components of Freud's earliest published cases (Breuer and Freud, 1895). Freud, subsequent classical analysts, and ego psychologists sought to undo the adhesiveness of the bad object experience by interpreting its roots in early experience. Klein (1952, 1957) moved internalized bad objects into the center of her theory of psychopathology and clinical technique. Although her theoretical innovations shifted the target of analytic investigation to the splitting of the good and bad objects, Klein's clinical technique, like that of classical analysis, was confined to interpretation. However, generations of psychoanalytic therapists have found that all too frequently patients understand the origins of the bad object without being able to undo its influence. This finding has led many theorists and clinicians to search for a clinical strategy embracing more than interpretation to wipe the vestiges of bad object-experience from a patient's psyche.

Fairbairn (1944) has offered an explanation for the frustrating adhesiveness of bad objects with his idea that these malicious voices constitute a component of the self. In this chapter, I have attempted to draw out specific clinical implications from Fairbairn's view of the relationship between the internalized object and the self. In so doing, I have extended Fairbairn's theory to include a detailed clinical strategy not foreseen by the theorist himself. Fairbairn's insight that internalized objects are structures implies that the relinquishment of the bad object requires the collapse of one self organization and its replacement by another. Furthermore, as we have seen, the new self must be created before the old organization can be given up completely. To overcome the malignant effects of bad object dominance, the therapist must take an active role in assisting the patient's creation of a new self structure. This idea extends Fairbairn's thinking to the adoption of a facilitative role for the therapist and aligns his thought with Bollas' (1987) concept that psychoanalytic therapy is not about discrete affects but about the building of a new self organization. At the point at which the function of the bad object is grasped, the therapist shifts roles from interpreter of the patient's experience to facilitator of the new experience.

As we saw with both Danny and Lisa, understanding the origins and function of the bad object was not only insufficient for its abandonment, but also evoked the anxiety of losing a part of the self. The disorganization resulting from the breakup of the old pattern provided an opportunity for the creation of the self from "the inside out" or, as Winnicott (1960) said, "from the kernel, rather than the shell." This shift hinged on my holding the chaos and disorganization that appeared when the grip of the bad object was loosened.

The themes we have been exploring in this book as key elements of therapeutic action come into play as the therapeutic space shifts from interpretation to the creation of the self. The latter requires the therapist to help catalyze the evolution of the patient's sense of possessing a future. Without a sense of futurity, the patient remains enslaved by the bad object rooted in the past. As the bad object tends to stifle forward movement, it has to be held in abeyance for a trajectory to become established. By drawing out arrested interests, passions, and desires, the therapist abets the building of a belief in the future. Once the patient is able to live in the future-perfect tense, the bad object no longer has its former stranglehold on the patient's life, and a new self-organization becomes possible.

For this process to unfold, the therapist must have a vision of the patient's potential beyond the limitations of the bad object and overexcited states. With both Danny and Lisa, I worked on the articulation of affective dispositions into new psychological configurations that became the foundation for a new self. I had a vision of possibilities rooted in the way both patients used the therapeutic process and the capabilities they displayed within it. Consequently, when they became disorganized by the threat posed by the interpretive process, I construed this ambiguous state as a potential ground for the creation of ways of being that could serve as alternatives to the bad object. With both patients, I saw possibilities for the replacement of the bad object in the indices of buried affects that appeared in their associations. When we were able to formulate these undeveloped affects into ways of being and relating, in both cases the bad object was relinquished. The future needed to be created as a component of the psychic organization in order for the patient to have the experience of a self that could replace the bad object. We saw this clinical strategy of building a future so that the past could ultimately be relinquished in our discussion of the treatment of depression. Depressed patients, like persons afflicted with a bad object, cannot overcome the legacy of the past, no matter how well understood, without the alternative of a future. When a new way of being is created that replaces the function once served by the pathological force, the latter will gradually dissipate. The bad object, like the old soldier, does not die—it fades away, often with little recognition from its former prisoner.

We have also seen that this theory of therapeutic action in the treatment of bad objects has clear implications for the amelioration of grandiosity and other narcissistic vulnerabilities. But we have not yet confronted the task of applying this theory to people for whom narcissistic imbalances seem to be the primary difficulty. We now turn to the application of this theory of therapeutic change to the healing of narcissistic wounds.

10

HEALING NARCISSISTIC WOUNDS

Many of the patients discussed in this book suffered from a sense of defectiveness, as though a piece of the self were torn. Anna, for example, had little belief that her own judgment would lead her to a productive life and therefore used the approbation of others as the guide to her behavior. More deeply troubled, Helen had no sense of a subjectivity on which she could rely and was not even able to use others as a compass. Perry, whose depression brought him to psychotherapy, was terrified of failure despite a record of remarkable successes. Danny and Lisa, the subjects of the last chapter, were tormented by self attacks. For each of these patients, the self was damaged and, when exposed to the vagaries of interpersonal life, was vulnerable to further injury. The consulting rooms of clinicians are populated with those who want help with "low self-esteem." This feeling of inadequacy, a state I have previously associated with a defective self (Summers, 1999), is a narcissistic wound. Despite the typicality of this syndrome in clinical practice, the clinical strategy for the healing of such an injury remains unclear. Let us now turn our attention to the application of our model of therapeutic change to the repair of such damage to the self.

THE SELF PSYCHOLOGICAL VIEW

Self psychology, which has made the treatment of narcissistic disturbances its primary focus, is a logical place to begin a discussion of the ameliorations of narcissistic injuries. Kohut (1971) found that patients who suffer from an arrest at an early level of narcissistic development tend to form a transference that fits into one of three broad constellations: (1) the patient may seek the analyst's recognition and approval, a paradigm Kohut called the mirror transference; (2) in the idealizing transference, the patient exaggerates the analyst's positive qualities and seek guidance from this exalted figure; and (3) there may be demands from the patient for the analyst to share his values and feelings in order to be the same, a configuration Kohut called the twinship transference. The therapeutic approach was to mobilize the selfobject transference, in whatever form it appeared, and then respond empathically to its inevitable disappointments until the transference configuration was gradually relinquished. Since Kohut's early work, self psychologists have broadened the categories of transference beyond these three forms (Kohut and Wolf, 1978). Nonetheless, from a classical self-psychological viewpoint, the analyst's strategy, no matter the particular form of the transference, is to empathize with the patient's need without performing any action other than interpretation to gratify it (Kohut, 1971; Segal, 1999). In his last formulation, Kohut (1984) argued that interpretation embodies an "optimal frustration," meaning that the patient's longing is not gratified in the way the patient desires, although the understanding does provide gratification by way of empathy with the need.

Kohut regarded this mixture of gratification and frustration to be the optimal balance required for a patient to internalize the analyst through a process he called "transmuting internalization." That concept refers to a microscopic internalization of the analyst's ministrations in response to disruptions in the selfobject transference. This process differs from the usual type of internalization in that it is so gradual and piecemeal that the internalized object is depersonified. Consequently, this process does not lead to an identifiable object; rather, the analyst is gradually digested and absorbed into the bones of the patient's self. It was this response-by-response interaction between patient and analyst that, for Kohut, led to the laying down of new structure.

Since Bacal's (1985, 1998a, 1998b) reformulation of the gratification–frustration balance as "optimal responsiveness," many self psychologists include responses other than interpretation in addressing the needs of the patient's vulnerable self. This concept shifts the emphasis from frustration to responding to needs, and to the analyst as provider of a variety of functions, not just interpretation. In this expanded view of therapeutic action, the analyst's task is to provide selfobject functions that can be internalized by the patient (Bacal and Newman, 1990). In addition to affective attunement, such functions include validation of affective states, affect containment, soothing and organizing the self, and recognition of uniqueness and creative potential (p. 229). In its most recent formulation, optimal responsiveness means that the analytic task is to identify the selfobject needs of the patient in any specific clinical circumstance and then meet the needs as much as possible (Bacal, 1998a). Empathic attunement is only one possibility. Other responses that may be required in specific circumstances include active containing, such as opposing, limiting, confronting, taking charge; and active reflecting, such as resonating, validating, and informing (Lazar, 1998). This array of analytic responses reflects the trend within self psychology to extend the analyst's responses well beyond interpretation. The analytic stance, from this perspective, is not necessarily to find the right interpretation but to find the optimal response to a particular selfobject need. Nonetheless, some contemporary self psychologists oppose this expansion of the analyst's role. While agreeing that patients' selfobject needs are varied, these more traditional self psychologists believe the appropriate analytic response is to interpret such needs, rather than gratify them (e.g., Segal, 1999).

All these self-psychological formulations of therapeutic action, whether limited to interpretation or extended to other types of response, view the mutative factors of analytic therapy to lie in the patient's absorption of the analyst's interventions. From any self-psychological vantage point, the strengthening of the self comes from the patient's internalization of what the analyst provides, whether in the traditional form of interpretations or a more active responsiveness to need. The debates among self psychologists concern the content of what the analyst offers, but none question the principle of the analyst as a selfobject who must be taken into the patient's psyche. This emphasis in the self-psychological view of therapeutic action raises the question of whether self-esteem is, in fact, enhanced best by a process that relies primarily on the internalization of therapeutic ministrations. One may question whether internalization, in response to either interpretation or the provision of functions, can best heal narcissistic vulnerability. To assess this question we are best served by drawing on what is known regarding the acquisition of positive self-regard.

THE DEVELOPMENT OF SELF-ESTEEM

The available evidence from developmental research suggests that the principal factors that contribute to positive self-esteem in children are the ability to feel competent, trust in one's affective states, and relatedness to others (Demos, 1983, 1988; Sander, 1982, 1985). An infant is born with a variety of affective dispositions and the motivation to increase positive and manage negative affective states (Tomkins, 1978; Sander, 1980; Demos, 1983). Indeed, the child has an inherent motivation to do for herself what has been done for her (Tomkins, 1978). For example, the child sucks initially as a reflex, but then will suck for no biological purpose, as though to demonstrate the ability to do it by herself. The child will play and explore during quiescent states from the first days of life for no purpose other than to employ the capacities to master the environment and gain a sense of effectiveness (White, 1963; Stern, 1985). Both positive and negative affects are inborn and experienced from birth, but the child moves almost immediately to enhance positive affects, such as excitement, enjoyment, and interest. The degree to which she is able to sustain such pleasurable states and gain relief from distress and anger without losing control is the extent to which she will feel she can count on her affects to guide her behavior. It is this fundamental belief that spontaneous affects will direct the individual to the most meaningful and satisfying course of action that I refer to as *trust in affects*. On the other hand, if the child does not have many experiences of sustained positive affects and feels unassuaged distress and anger, she will not find her affective life to be useful in relating to others and attempting to achieve her goals. A child subjected to punishing states she cannot diminish has no reason to believe that her spontaneously occurring affects will constitute a guide to a pleasurable and meaningful existence.

Even more damaging, if the child receives insufficient help enhancing positive states and reducing the intensity of negative affects, she feels helpless to control her own affective life and fails to acquire a sense of agency. A feeling of futility then pervades her interpersonal world. Unmitigated distress and anger become overwhelmingly punishing, and the child is forced to shut down her emotions in order to relieve her pain. Some children do this by crying themselves to sleep; others, by withdrawal. Whatever means the child uses to disengage from her affects, her inability to influence them crystallizes into a feeling of helplessness and ultimately a lack of competence. We call the inability to enhance positive states and transform negative affects the sense of *ineffectiveness*. The child for whom this is a pervasive feeling is missing a crucial ingredient of self-esteem.

The caretaker plays a crucial role in this process because the environmental response to the child's affective expressions is a key determinant in the ultimate meaning the child gives to her spontaneously occurring affects. The developmental evidence strongly indicates that affective matching by the caretaker is necessary for the child to continue to experience and utilize positive states (e.g., Beebe and Lachmann, 1992, 2002). For example, if the child is excited, the parent's excited response promotes the continued use of that affect in subsequent situations. This affective matching need not be exact; it is sufficient for the parent to move her affective state in the same direction as the child's, a process Stern (1985) calls "matching the gradient." If the parent withdraws or ignores the excitement, the child's enthusiasm deflates and becomes associated with negative responses and perhaps even shame. Beebe and Lachmann (2002) have adduced convincing evidence that children who have experienced consistent affective attunement have a significantly greater capacity for relatedness than those who do not. The latter tend to be more isolated and have fewer meaningful interpersonal bonds. These findings show that affective attunement with some degree of imperfection is necessary not only for the continued use of naturally occurring affective states, but also for the capacity for *relatedness*, the third primary component of self-esteem.

Affective attunement does not encompass the totality of the caretaker's role in the evolution of the child's belief in her ability to be an agent in the outcome of her own life. Several developmental research traditions converge in pointing to the importance of both attunement and aloneness in the mother–child dyad. Demos (1992) discovered that agency is best promoted not by the parent who relieves stress, but by the parent who allows the child to experience distress and then helps to relieve it with the child as participant. Bowlby's (1988) studies of attachment found that the most secure babies had mothers who were emotionally available and encouraged autonomy. Similarly, Beebe (1995, 2002) found that the babies with the strongest sense of self were not those to whom the mother was most closely attuned, but those in the midrange of affective and vocal matching. Beebe concluded that there can be too much attunement because the child needs both mutual regulation and the opportunity for self-regulation. In addition to attunement, the infant must be able to experience states of interest, enjoyment, and excitement without connection to the other in what Sander (1980) calls "open spaces." It is essential, then, that the caretaker both becomes attuned to the child's affects and provides opportunity for the child to struggle and cope with her affective states on her own. The sense of relatedness is largely a function of the empathic connection between child and caregiver, but competence and trust in one's affects also require the opportunity to manage affective states without an attuned relationship. Self-esteem, then, is built from both attunement and the opportunity to exercise the capacity to overcome negative states and regulate tension. Demos (1992) concludes that an "optimal zone of affective engagement" allows the child to feel a need and become an active participant in meeting it. By sustaining this experience, the child feels that her affects are to be trusted as guides for her conduct and comes to believe she can influence the environment to relieve her own distress.

All these findings make clear that children are not passive recipients of parenting but interact with parental ministrations to produce a unique outcome. The evidence from a variety of careful child-observational studies depicts babies who can interact with the parents to create new meaning that is neither adopted from the parents nor reducible to what the parents offer. Rather, meaning is created from the parents' offerings in a mutually interactive, dynamic interchange.

Affective attunement without an "open space" leaves the child in a state of narcissistic self-absorption. Such a child does not believe she can manage her affective states and so does not use them to engage the world. The result is often a feeling of being well loved but removed from the interpersonal world and a sense of fraudulence in positive feelings for the self. One sees the results of such parent–child dynamics in adults who feel loved and cared for but who seem passive and ineffective, without a sense of agency. Lacking faith in their experience as a guide for navigating the interpersonal world, such patients tend to be other-directed, continually searching for cues in the behavior of other people. The result tends to be a sense of paralysis, an inability to seize initiative for fear of making an error. This type of patient lacks realistic self-esteem because positive feelings for the self have not been put to the test in the give-and-take of real-world experience. Having internalized the gleam of the mother's eye, such a patient feels loved, but also feels unreal, not quite a part of the world. These patients exemplify Bettleheim's (1982) famous words, "Love is not enough."

For example, one patient, Harry, did not question that his mother adored him; she danced attention on him, and he felt he was the apple of her eye. However, she was so attentive that while he was growing up, he rarely had the opportunity to manage his own tension states. Throughout his grade-school years, Harry's mother rarely allowed him to do anything for himself when she could find a way to intervene. Whenever he encountered difficulty performing a task, rather than helping him, she did it for him. Throughout his adolescence and even into Harry's adulthood, his mother managed his finances and frequently intervened to rescue him from even minor difficulties. Consequently, his adult life was plagued with a sense of helplessness, and Harry was so fearful of testing his capacities that he had great difficulty putting forth effort. When he went away to college, he could not motivate himself and struggled with his schoolwork. Now as an adult, Harry lacked a sense of agency and tended to melt into the background, to eschew visibility. Doubting his ability to perform adequately in almost any area and not trusting his affects, Harry was obsessed with others' opinions and could not make decisions without the approval of a respected other. Although he was ambitious and set high goals for himself, he was fearful of taking initiative and found himself far less successful than he had hoped.

Blatt and Bass (1992) have marshaled an impressive array of evidence demonstrating that there are two fundamental dimensions of human experience: the needs for relatedness and for self-definition. The former is met by an affective connection with early parenting figures, what we have been calling *affective attunement*. The latter, however, is fulfilled by providing the child space in which to explore and master the environment without the ministrations of the caretaker. Furthermore, the researchers argue, these two dimensions are in a dialectical relationship to each other. According to Blatt and Bass, affective attunement promotes relatedness but militates against self-definition. By contrast, self-definition is best achieved by pushing against others, in opposition to a sense of relatedness. Both components are necessary for the child to achieve an adequate sense of self-worth.

Greenberg (1991) has offered a similar conceptualization of human needs. He divides human motivation into the drives for safety and effectance, the latter being the need to have an effect on the environment. The former requires an other to provide a sense of well-being, while the drive for effectance is best met by doing and learning to do. And it is the latter, which results in the ability to have an effect on the environment, that Greenberg believes is most essential for positive self-regard. His way of conceptualizing motivation is remarkably similar to the schemata delineated by Rank (1926) and Bakan (1966), both of whom described a duality in human motivation between the needs for others and for self-realization.

This necessarily selective and brief synopsis of theories of the development of the child's self-esteem is sufficient to show that for the child to achieve a strong, well-regarded sense of self, she must have the following: (1) repeated experiences of affective attunement to develop a sense of relatedness; (2) the opportunity to experience and enhance positive affects; and (3) the experience of participating in the repair of disruptions and negative states. The last requires the experience of distress and the ability to overcome it within a helping relationship that offers aid as well as the opportunity for the child to relieve her pain. All three experiences are necessary if the child is to develop a belief in the value of her own experience and the sense of efficacy. If the child is afforded these experiences continually, she will attain the three essential ingredients of self-esteem: *effectiveness, trust in affects,* and *relatedness.*

Conversely, if the child does not have these experiences on a consistent basis, she will not trust her affective states, fail to develop a feeling of competence, and will tend to gravitate toward isolation. Such a child will possess not only the fundamental pathognomonic deficits that result in narcissistic damage but also the need to protect her exposure with a panoply of narcissistic defenses. Beneath the defenses of a narcissistically disturbed patient lie feelings of helplessness that lead to longings to depend on others without the ability to do so. As Fairbairn (1943) and later Guntrip (1969) have argued convincingly, an exposed feeling of inadequacy leads to a sense of shame. For this reason, as noted in the last chapter, shame has been called the underside of narcissism (Morrison, 1989). The threat of exposing vulnerability tends to be protected by resilient, intractable defenses. Such protective strategies may take many forms, but whatever the particulars of an individual case, the defenses protect against exposing the feeling of defectiveness; it is the discovery and repair of this injury that becomes the target of the therapeutic process. We may now apply this understanding of the requirements for healthy narcissism and the effects of its absence to the healing of narcissistic wounds.

THERAPEUTIC ACTION AND
NARCISSISTIC VULNERABILITY

Given our understanding of narcissistic vulnerability as the inability to have an impact on the environment owing to a lack of trust in one's affects, it follows that trusting affects and believing in one's own ability to influence events in life are central to overcoming this deficit. The capacity to impact the environment is best promoted by providing opportunities for the patient to have an effect on the therapeutic relationship. The resolution of narcissistic deficit, then, requires that the therapeutic relationship afford the patient the chance to influence the relationship and gain trust in her affects. Given the importance of competence and the mastery of distress in the development of positive self-esteem, the therapeutic action of narcissistic injury requires an active role for the patient. Therefore, it is crucial to the patient's overcoming of her sense of defectiveness that she give her own meaning to the analyst's offerings. For that reason, the capacity for effectance is unlikely to emerge from internalization alone, no matter how empathic the responses of the analyst may be. The internalization process, while an important component of any psychodynamic psychotherapy, has to do with absorption, with taking in the analyst's offerings, and therefore does little to foster the sense of agency.

This created relationship must not only be new but also more fundamentally true to the patient's experience than the formerly dominant protective strategies were. For the development of these emerging states into well-formulated affective configurations and, ultimately, new ways of being and relating, there must be a potential space between patient and therapist. As discussed in chapter 4, it is within this space, this ambiguity of meaning between the analytic pair, that new meaning can be created by the patient. To be sure, it is the analyst's ministrations that provide the material from which the patient creates new meaning, but the outcome of these interventions depends on the use the patient makes of them. In creating a new relationship, the patient gains both trust in her affects and a newfound belief in her own effectiveness, a conviction that she can influence the environment in accordance with these states.

As noted in chapter 4, Phillips (1998) has referred to analytic patients as failed artists of their own lives. Such a concept finds a cogent application in work with patients who suffer from narcissistic wounds, for such patients are blocked by childhood anxieties from fashioning a life of their own creation. The concept of therapeutic action based on the metaphor of creating a work of art is different from the self-psychological notion of transmuting internalization. In the latter process, the therapist's ministrations are digested and lose their identity as they become absorbed into the patient's self. By way of contrast, in making use of potential space, the outcome of the process is newly created meaning. Whereas in transmuting internalization the object becomes depersonified, in using potential space, a new object is created. Therein lies the difference between the self-psychological emphasis on the patient's absorption of the analyst's interventions and a view that stresses what the patient creates from therapeutic offerings. This dissimilarity is important because the use of incipient affective states in an act of creation is critical to the development of affective trust and competence.

While the concept of transmuting internalization is problematic for the mastery of narcissistic vulnerability, the same does not hold for the idea of affective attunement. The latter is essential for the development of relatedness, a major component of healthy self-regard and trust in affects. The therapists's ability to resonate with the patient's affects not only forms and strengthens the necessary affective bond but also confirms the analysand's emotional states, thus facilitating the patient's ability to believe in her own affective responses. Affective attunement as stressed by self psychology is an important component of the therapeutic process that leads to overcoming narcissistic vulnerability.

The view of therapeutic action proffered here suggests that "optimal responsiveness" for a narcissistically damaged patient is an intervention out of which the patient can create new meaning. The analyst's role being to offer something the patient can forge into a useful creation, this conceptualization changes the locus from the analyst's provisions to the use the patient makes of them. The optimal responsiveness criterion as currently conceptualized measures the effective analytic response by the degree to which the analyst meets a particular selfobject need (e.g., Bacal, 1985, 1998a). By contrast, the optimal analytic response proposed here puts the focus on what the patient does with the analyst's offering. The application of this principle requires a different clinical sensibility, a sensitivity to the importance of an open space between patient and therapist for the patient to "play" with newly won analytic understanding.

It follows that the analytic process with narcissistically disturbed patients requires an optimal zone of affective engagement analogous to the parent–child relationship (Demos, 1992). Whereas optimal responsiveness typically refers to the therapist's actions, an optimal zone of therapeutic engagement designates a balance between the contributions of both members of the therapeutic dyad. The therapist's provisions include both empathic attunement and the opportunity for the patient to create from it an authentic relationship. Because the patient plays an active, creative role in the establishment of the new relationship, its construction promotes the patient's belief in her ability to influence the events of her life.

The patient's trust in her affects, sense of competence, and capacity for relatedness all rely on the patient's ability to use affects for the creation of meaning. As the patient deploys these new ways of being and relating in the analytic process, she finds that she can build a relationship on the foundation of her own experience rather than resorting to entrenched protective strategies. The "doing and learning to do" that Greenberg (1991) noted as one of the two fundamental human needs becomes integrated into the patient's developing self, replacing the former feeling of helplessness and the narcissistic defenses against it. This acquisition of new interpersonal patterns follows the model of procedural learning in which behavior is learned by doing (Evans, 1999; Reiser, 1990). As the patient operates more authentically and effectively in the relationship with the analyst, she is acquiring competence in a manner more akin to the development of bicycle riding skills than to declarative-semantic learning.

The emphasis on the active role of the patient is best encompassed within self psychology by the concept of the selfobject need for efficacy (Wolf, 1988; Hartman and Milch, 2000). According to proponents of this concept, some patients lack a sense of agency that can be provided in the therapeutic process. To the degree that this concept sees the patient's contribution as part of the mutative experience, it represents a significant step toward the inclusion of an active role for the patient in the self psychological view of therapeutic action. However, because self psychology has not delineated a process by which such a need is met, the development of efficacy remains an ambiguous aspect of the self psychological theory of therapeutic action. It is difficult to imagine how transmuting internalization, a concept that emphasizes the patient's passive absorption, could meet the need for efficacy. As we have seen, to become effective the patient must have a space in which to have an effect on the other, and this opportunity is provided by potential space. Whereas the inclusion of a need for efficacy in the group of selfobject functions is a welcome addition to self psychological theory, potential space is necessary for the need to be met within the therapeutic process.

It may well be that in many self psychological analyses the patient does indeed use the analyst's ministrations to create new meaning, but the importance of self creation is not conceptualized in the theory. The self psychological emphasis on the analyst's responsiveness orients the analyst to relatedness but runs the

risk of not sufficiently attending to the development of
competence and the patient's ability to utilize her own affects. A
clinical theory that appreciates the importance of faith in one's
own affects as reliable beacons for conduct will attempt to find
buried affective potential and help the patient articulate it. The
greater the opportunity for the patient to create new ways of
being and relating out of her own incipient affective states, the
more likely she will be to trust the value of her own reactions. It
is this trust in one's affects that ultimately engenders a positive
view of the self.

ANNA, AGAIN

To show how potential space can be used to heal narcissistic
wounds, let us revisit the therapeutic journey of Anna, whose
case we considered in chapter 5. Recall that she had a history of
subjugating her subjectivity to the interests of others and, in the
process, disavowed any potential responses that did not fit
with the expressed opinions or implicit expectations of other
people. Although Anna never questioned her compliance, she
was unhappy with both her friendships and her romantic
relationships. Realizing that she spent a great deal of time and
effort trying to please other people, she gradually became aware
that others did not necessarily feel an obligation to reciprocate.
An organizer of plans within her social group, Anna put excessive
amounts of time into making sure all her friends were pleased
with whatever they were intending to do. Nonetheless, her friends
frequently complained that their desires were not sufficiently
recognized, and Anna would become anxious at the thought and
intensify her efforts to make sure everyone was happy. Similarly,
with the men she dated, Anna invariably felt that the burden of
forming and continuing the relationship was hers.

As we probed her growing dissatisfaction with her pattern
of accommodation, it became apparent that Anna had complex
and often ambivalent feelings that conflicted with her overt
behavior. For example, she regarded some of her friends as self-
centered, many as superficial, and still others as intellectually

limited. Not seeing the relevance of these fledgling, unarticulated states, Anna dismissed them without their gaining full consciousness. After I encouraged the articulation of the nascent feelings, Anna realized that she had dismissed a series of intense affects and values that in fact reflected deeply held convictions. Anna believed that the expression of these negative feelings would jeopardize any relationship, no matter how close and enduring it had been. To secure the bond, she disavowed her negative impressions of anyone with whom she had even a minimal relationship.

Anna's motive was not limited to fear of abandonment. She also avoided conflict because she feared she was "wrong." What if she objected to a friend's behavior, or disagreed with her, only to find out later that her friend's conduct or opinion was better than hers? She imagined the potential injury from such an event to be so shameful that she could not imagine taking such a risk. Thus, a fear of being shamed by exposing an inadequate opinion also led to the suppression of any feeling or thought that might be vulnerable to criticism. Anna believed she was safer following the lead of others than taking action based on her own beliefs, but she was not aware of the connection between this denial of her experience and her chronic dissatisfaction. She felt that her life was at the whim of others whom she was continually trying to please, resulting in a chronic sense of emptiness and helplessness. She questioned her self-subjugation only after I linked it with the malaise in her life.

When asked why she did not base her conduct on the affects and beliefs we were beginning to identify beneath her surface behavior, Anna replied that she "lacked confidence" in them. She gave more credence to the views of others, so she sought approbation before she could even consider using her own experience; if approval was not forthcoming, her own point of view was cast aside. She feared that if she let her feelings direct her behavior, she would make "mistakes" visible to others. The only meaning Anna could give to "mistake" was a behavior that somehow drew criticism. Anna was convinced that something at the core of her self was defective. Any negative response she might receive would provide external confirmation of her inadequacy and hurt her deeply. To protect her "defect" from public view, Anna hid behind accommodation to others' opinions. Her "low self-esteem" was the primary derivative of the belief that she was deeply wounded at the core.

This way of understanding Anna's poor self-regard reverses the usual understanding of the connection between negative self-attitude and the inability to trust one's subjective experiences. Typically patients feel they cannot believe in their own judgment because they suffer from a poor self-image. Moreover, clinical theory tends to view the causal arrow in this direction. For example, Kohut (1971, 1984) claimed that pathological narcissism was rooted in the failure of the early self–selfobject relationships to provide needed functions, leaving the self weak and with little capacity for vital, energetic self-expression. From this viewpoint, the patient's inability to believe in the value of her affective states is a symptom of this defective self. Our understanding of Anna looks at this connection in the other direction: it was her inability to see her affects as reliable beacons of conduct that made her feel defective, resulting in a low opinion of herself. From this viewpoint, failures in early relationships lead the child to doubt the importance and value of her affective states, resulting in a feeling of defectiveness.

Anna gained clarity about her sense of inadequacy when we linked it to the abandonment anxiety she felt from her mother and the resulting lack of trust in her subjective experience. However, she was unable to use this insight to change the pattern. Although Anna understood that by submerging her desires and opinions she hoped to secure relationships and avoid the risk of error, she was unable to break her habitual pattern of telling others what they wanted to hear. No matter how often we understood her anxiety and the defensive need to comply with others, Anna could not come to believe in her experience enough to use it as a guide for behavior. Her feeling of inadequacy seemed intractable, and she felt driven by a force outside her control to accommodate herself instinctively to what pleased others.

The inability to believe in her affective responses also permeated her romantic relationships. Since early childhood,

Anna had felt an intense desire to be married and a foreboding threat that it might never happen. Marriage being the goal of her life, Anna assessed every man she dated as a potential husband. When she was not dating someone, she would invariably panic, filled with the catastrophic fear that she might never marry. When a man entered the picture whom she felt might be a suitable partner "on paper," she pushed the relationship to a conclusion and, predictably, scared off many men in the process. In some instances, the man did not seem invested in pursuing a serious relationship, but Anna doggedly pushed the pace and insisted on frequent contact. Attempting to create more of a relationship than was there, Anna was frequently disappointed when the man did not respond as she hoped.

She had never reflected on her assumption that life without marriage would be a failure until I asked her what made marriage seem so essential to her. As Anna struggled with this question, it became clear that being married meant that she had secured a relationship in which her partner would not leave her, but it also implied that she "fit in." Having a husband felt as though her ticket to life was being validated. In her mind there was a community of peers to which she would be guaranteed admittance only with a marriage license, and entrance into this imagined society would extinguish forever her lifelong abandonment anxiety.

Anna's lack of belief in her own subjectivity began to change when her anger finally erupted in the therapeutic dyad (as we discussed in chapter 5), but this aggressive explosion was only the first step in a long and difficult process of coming to use her affects. First, she had to confront the challenge of using her aggression and desire for self-expression in conjunction with her respect for others. As we have seen, Anna's ability to meet both these needs was a major step in her self-development. She risked trusting her experience by confronting conflict with me, but this new-found behavior did not easily transfer to other situations. While Anna appreciated my acceptance of her aggressiveness, she doubted that others would be so generous with her. But bringing some authentic affects into our relationship nonetheless profoundly affected her. Having tasted the joy and freedom of self-expression by engaging me in conflict, she began to make fully conscious and articulate a variety of affects and opinions. For example, she acknowledged not only angry, but bitingly hostile feelings toward many of the people in her life. Cutting in her assessment of others' character flaws, Anna felt that many of her friends lacked depth; they were seemingly content to "sit on the couch and eat bonbons." I connected her hostility to the obligation she had felt to accommodate and to pursue relationships based on her lifelong conviction that any connection was better than none at all. I added that her newly expressed vitriolic attacks on these people suggested that she did not covet these friendships but felt impelled to secure the bonds to relieve her anxiety, much as she believed marriage would allay forever her fear of abandonment.

In this context, Anna began to assess her relationships from the viewpoint of her capacity for authentic self-expression within each dyad. Acknowledging to herself that she had been taken advantage of with disturbing frequency, she concluded that some of her friends were selfish, and she was troubled by her pattern of capitulating to self-centered men who showed little interest in her. Concluding that she could no longer pursue relationships that inhibited her self-expression and obliged her to assume a subservient position, Anna made a conscious choice to voice her desires and opinions and weigh them equally to the wishes of others. Some of her friends were shocked at her forthrightness and stubborn refusal to comply with their desires; they felt that Anna was damaging a formerly good friendship. Others made the effort to understand Anna's viewpoint and were willing to continue the relationship on a more equal footing. The upshot was the loss of some friendships but an immeasurable improvement in her self-regard.

It was a step forward for Anna to end friendships with those who gave her little, but a far greater challenge was presented by direct self-expression. With considerable trepidation, she became direct in her communications with her mother. When the older woman reacted anxiously to a difficulty in her life, Anna told her mother that such reactions hurt her. Well aware of her mother's fragility, Anna feared that she would feel crushed by this expression of aggressivity. She was relieved to find that her mother survived these encounters and saw the validity of her daughter's point.

A major turning point resulted from Anna's growing dissatisfaction with her best friend, Gayle. She came to realize that Gayle expected her to adapt to her wishes without any obligation to reciprocate. Their phone conversations were consumed with Gayle's life, and their plans always reflected Gayle's needs. When Anna began to express even minimal desires of her own, such as injecting information about herself into a phone chat, Gayle ignored her. As Anna became angry about this pattern, she began to voice dissatisfaction and asked Gayle to listen to her. Gayle was offended, and eventually Anna's worst fear was realized: Gayle ended the friendship. Anna was initially distressed, but she realized that Gayle's investment in her had been completely self-centered. Once Anna asked to be recognized as a person, the bond ruptured, not because of conflict in a friendship, but because a pattern of exploitation had been interrupted. As she put it, "It was a loss for Gayle: she lost a servant. As the servant, I lost nothing." Anna saw that what had ended was only the illusion of a friendship, an illusion that helped allay her abandonment anxiety.

The end of her friendship with Gayle marked a decisive shift in Anna's application of the therapeutic process to her life outside the consulting room. Recognizing that she felt better about herself without Gayle than being in a relationship of submission, Anna shifted her value system: Self-respect was more important than the tie to the object. At long last she relinquished the principle that it was most important to sustain a relationship at any cost. This transformation in her self-organization altered her way of relating to virtually everyone in her life. Anna now made a conscious choice in each relationship with respect to what she was willing to sacrifice and what she needed for herself. Mutuality became the paramount principle on which she based all relationships, and she was willing to let go of any attachment that did not meet this criterion. In this way, her friendships took on the character of the self-expression she had begun in the therapeutic relationship.

Although Anna's new attitude began with the articulation of her aggressivity, it was but one step in the development of her capacity for self-expression. I must emphasize this point because it would be easy to conclude that Anna's outpouring of aggression indicated that the crux of her difficulties lay in the repression of anger. In fact, the ability to articulate her anger, while an important step in the loosening of her inhibitions, was only one element in the formation of her newly created self. The decisive change in her relationship with Gayle occurred when Anna began to express her desires. Anna's anger at Gayle's response was secondary to her assertion of interests and viewpoints. The ability to bring her desires into any relationship and the willingness to bear the consequences of so doing constituted the essence of a fundamental change in who Anna was, and the communication of aggression was but one aspect of this new psychic organization.

Anna was discovering that as she built her life on previously aborted affective states, she was gaining self-respect, a perspective on herself that was replacing her "low self-esteem." This attitudinal transformation eventually permeated that most problematic arena of her relationships: romance. The insight that her urgency to be married was rooted in the need to "belong" made her desperation understandable, but it did not completely relieve the feeling that a single life would be a catastrophe. This understanding was now coupled with the importance she placed on self-expression. On dates, Anna was forthright about her affects, values, and opinions, and, if they met with a negative response, she was willing to risk the possibility of relinquishing future contact. Dating shifted from an effort to win the man's favor to a meeting of minds. If there was not a meaningful emotional exchange, she did not feel an urgency to repair the gap but accepted the fact that she and the man might not be a good match. Living as authentically as possible was at the top of her value system, rather than gaining the man's favor. Even when a relationship broke off, Anna felt good about herself as long as the termination of contact occurred within the context of her self expression.

It would be difficult to underestimate the enormity of this attitude change. The focus of her life since adolescence had been on finding a man and marrying him. For Anna to place authenticity above marriage represented a decisive change in the very meaning of her life. She had transformed her purpose in life from "fitting in" by finding the right man to articulating her self in the world. Instead of looking for meaning in the building of a family unit at any cost, she now gained purpose from expressing her affects, ideas, values, and opinions and exchanging them with others. If she could find the right man to interact with, marriage would be meaningful. In this way, recasting her attitude to include romantic relationships fortified an emerging movement to live according to her subjectivity.

Liberated from the burdensome belief that being connected to a man was necessary to be a part of the human community, Anna felt a new freedom to use her affects as guides in every area of life. For example, although she had always been highly successful in her job, Anna had never been gratified by her success. She attributed the lack of meaning in her work to the fact that it had a low priority in her life. As a result of her determination to live according to what felt meaningful to her, Anna was no longer satisfied to spend all day in activities she found empty, so she quit her job and went back to school to embark on a career in the social services. This significant change in her life was never discussed in psychotherapy until after she made the decision. Anna simply decided that she wanted to do something that felt meaningful to her, and she pursued the change without any need to discuss it with me.

CONCLUSION

The therapeutic process leading to this transformation of Anna's life is a direct application of understanding low self-esteem as the result of a lack of trust in affects, rather than the reverse. Enhanced self-regard did not lead Anna to believe in her subjective experiences; rather, her self-respect grew out of her willingness to rely on her affective states and subjective experiences. When she was able to risk bringing her affects into the analytic relationship, Anna began to develop and value the capacity to utilize formerly buried, nascent states. As she did so, she found that this experience issued in self-respect and enriched her life to the point that she began to prefer it to the subjugating bonds that had formerly eroded her view of herself. It was the new-found ability to live her life on the basis of her affect, values, and beliefs that provided the foundation of her esteem, not the other way around.

Anna was able to use the therapeutic dyad in this way because a potential space had been established in which she could create a new experience. This aspect of Anna's liberation from her anxiety-filled childhood demonstrates the healing of a narcissistic wound by the use of potential space to create new experience. Anna felt defective as long as she could not believe in the value of her affects, even after the historical roots of her conviction and its repetition in the transference were understood. Her intractably low self-regard was relieved only after she came to believe in the value of her affective states, and this change began when Anna was able to use the therapeutic space to create ways of being out of her aggressive responses to the analytic process. On the basis of this use of the therapeutic space, Anna began to build her life on her authentic experience. Even if the result of her self-expression was not what she wished, she continued, undeterred in her determination to live from the "inside out." The transformation of her friendships and romantic relationships based on self-expression and mutual respect, rather than maintaining the object tie at any cost, further enhanced her growing self-esteem.

This discussion of Anna's therapeutic journey demonstrates a shift in analytic posture from "need responsiveness" to the opening of a space for the patient to learn to articulate and utilize her affects and develop a sense of competence. While interpretations and optimal responsiveness are both necessary for the mutative shift leading to positive self-esteem, such interventions will help the patient only if the analyst provides the potential space in which the patient can unearth buried affects, learn to rely on them, and use them for the creation of a new relationship. Out of these experiences emerges the foundation for solid self-esteem and the healing of narcissistic wounds.

11

CONCLUSION

I have attempted to address the problem of how change can be promoted when even the most intense affective response to an interpretation is not alterative. Much contemporary psychoanalytic clinical discussion has centered on what in addition to interpretation is needed to produce therapeutic change. The emphasis in this discourse has been on what the analyst can offer that the patient can absorb. This type of clinical thinking, wittingly or not, has kept the patient in a passive position. Such a model does not fit the contemporary analytic goals of authentic and meaningful living. The present work has been an attempt to shift our clinical model to include a major role for the analyst as an assistant to the patient's self creation. In this way, I hope to have reduced the gap between analytic thinking about change and contemporary clinical objectives.

By offering a clinical model directed to changing the structure of the self, I have proposed an alternative to the time-honored concept of working through. As we have seen, the attribution of the connection between understanding and change to working through has been inadequate both clinically and theoretically as this concept does not offer a clinical strategy beyond continued interpretation. This problem has been recognized by a growing number of analytic theorists who have proffered a variety of techniques for overcoming the stagnancy of a patient's patterns, including even the introduction of cognitive-behavioral interventions to the analytic process (e.g., Wachtel, 1982). The model of therapeutic change offered here departs from most of these techniques in its emphasis on the patient's creation of new patterns and the therapeutic stance conducive to this process. Building on Winnicott's (1971) concept of potential space, this clinical strategy proposes a new approach to the recalcitrance of pathological patterns. Rather than working through the understanding of pathological configurations, I have suggested that the therapist needs to help the patient create alternatives from dormant potential.

I have tried to show that the restructuring of the therapeutic relationship from a modality of understanding to a field for the creation of new psychological configurations provides the best opportunity to translate insights into meaningful personality change. To paraphrase Karl Marx, psychoanalytic theories have sought to understand people; the point, however, is to help them change. The model of therapeutic change first proposed in *Transcending the Self* (Summers, 1999) and continued here can be employed from the standpoint of various psychoanalytic theories. I have approached the therapeutic action of psychoanalytic therapy from the point at which an understanding has been won that the patient accepts and finds relieving but still cannot use to make concrete life changes. I have suggested that, by shifting the therapeutic field to potential space, we can promote the use of insight by helping the analysand create new ways of being and relating.

The question naturally arises: If the shift to transitional space is necessary for a mutative process to take place, how has it been possible for change to occur in therapies conducted without this clinical strategy? Must I contend that either such changes have not occurred as claimed or my contention is invalid? I do not believe I have to draw either of these conclusions. Undoubtedly, analytic therapy conducted without an explicit sensitivity to potential space benefits many people who submit to it, and for some it has been life transforming. But the fact that the therapist does not conceptualize a shift to potential space does not mean that such a transformation is not a component of the change process. Many analytic therapists, without conscious design, provide a space for the patient to create. Often patients will use the therapeutic space to experiment with ways of being and relating before they risk new behavior in less protected environments. They, too, may not be aware that they are trying out new behaviors even as they do so. This is to say, potential space is often a part of the therapeutic action, although its use is intuitive. We cannot be satisfied to leave the critical factor of self-creation to an implicit clinical strategy. Because potential space may offer the best chance for the translation of insight into concrete change, it should be established by conscious design whenever a dynamic insight is grasped but does not effect the sought-for change. The purpose of this book, then, has been to show how analytic therapy works when it is most effective and therefore to do by conscious clinical strategy what is too often left to the clinician's intuition or the patient's initiative.

The shift from transference space to potential space and back again can occur many times in the course of a single psychotherapy. The decision of the therapist to alter his stance from one type of analytic field to the other is a judgment call made on the basis of his convictions about the level of understanding achieved. If the therapist believes the patient is absorbing insight at an intellectual level, he will continue to work on making conscious the walled-off affect. If, however, the insight contains the accompanying affect and still has no significant impact, the time may be at hand for a shift in the psycho-therapeutic dyad. Once the sought-for change is made, a new issue or symptom may call for understanding of a new dynamic, thus shifting the psychological field back to transference space.

The therapist, then, must decide which stance he is adopting at any given moment. Since his task is not complete when a dynamic is understood, this decision is a major event in the therapeutic action. The determination to attempt further understanding or move the insight into action is decisive for the evolution of the therapeutic process. Thus, the responsibility falls on the therapist to make a conscious choice of therapeutic attitude at key junctures, a psychological activity that is missing if a single stance is taken to be the only therapeutic posture. It is the therapist's responsibility not only to be aware as possible of the stance he is assuming, but also to be as conscious as possible of its effect at each moment. In this sense, the therapist bears the burden of continually adjusting his therapeutic approach. Nonetheless, the pivotal feature of the therapeutic action is not the therapist's behavior, but what the patient creates from the therapeutic intervention. In potential space, the therapist must be willing to yield a great deal of responsibility and control to the patient.

I hope I have demonstrated in these pages the clinical usefulness of thinking in terms of fostering the patient's creation of new ways of being. We have seen several fundamental aspects of this therapeutic posture. The therapist using this model looks to the future, rather than only to the present and the past, and to the patient's creation of a future. Not limited to understanding what is, the therapist has a vision of who the patient can be that is continually tested and reformulated throughout the course of the work. Most important, the key ingredient in therapeutic action is what the patient creates from the therapist's vision and invitation. We have seen that the therapist has an active role in this process: first, he has to decide which posture to adopt at each phase; and, second, in the facilitative role, he abets the patient's creativity with his vision, sense of futurity, promotion of potential space, and focus on new possibilities.

In Phillips's (1998) beautifully worded phrase, the patient is a failed artist of her life, he captures the dilemma described in this book. Nonetheless, analytic theory has lacked a clinical strategy designed to aid the patient in becoming a successful artist. I hope I have contributed to filling that gap by delineating a clinical strategy that provides the means by which the patient can create his life. If the patient is the struggling artist, the therapist is the mentor whose job is to foster the creative work. As we have seen in each of the cases discussed, the failure in the patient's art is not simply a lack of creativity but a restriction of imagination. The patient often cannot even contemplate a different life, a life with a future or a life built on genuine affects. One of the new therapeutic tasks embedded in this model is the stimulation of the imagination, the creation of new possibilities. While the patient has to see new possibilities before he can forge a different way of living, the therapist has to have a vision of those possibilities before the patient is able to imagine alternatives to the life he has always known and expects to continue.

Historically, psychoanalytic therapy has not theorized about how to stimulate a patient's imagination, to reach and evoke the latent part of the self that contains the potential for new ways of living. Only in recent years have an increasing number of analytic thinkers attended to the therapist's role in helping the patient create new psychological configurations. Benjamin (1995), Strenger (1998), Modell (1991), and Sanville (1991), among others, have each suggested different ways for the therapist to move out of the interpretive role to aid the patient's creative use of the process. Although none of these theorists has been explicit about the shift in clinical theory to a different form of therapeutic space, such a decisive change is implied in their theoretical innovations. This growing trend moves the clinician's work toward the goal of promoting the creation of self. I hope to have shown that a clinical strategy designed specifically around self creation can help us meet this objective by codifying theoretically trends that are emerging from both clinical work and theoretical discourse. Others will no doubt extend this discussion in other ways. If I have contributed to a new dialogue on the analyst's role in helping the patient create a life of his own, then this work has served its purpose.

References

Ainsworth, M., Blehar, M., Waters, E. & Walls, S. (1978), *Patterns of Attachment: Assessed in the Strange Situation and at Home*. Hillsdale, NJ: Lawrence Erlbaum Associates.

Akhtar, S. (1996), "Someday . . ." and "If only . . ." fantasies: Pathological optimism and inordinate nostalgia as related forms of idealization. *J. Amer. Psychoanal. Assn.*, 44:723–753.

Alexander, F. (1943), *Fundamentals of Psychoanalysis*. New York: Norton, 1963.

Aron, L. (1996), *A Meeting of Minds: Mutuality in Psychoanalysis*. Hillsdale, NJ: The Analytic Press.

Austin, J. H. (1962), *How to Do Things with Words*. Oxford: Clarendon Press.

Bacal, H. (1985), Optimal responsiveness and the therapeutic process. In: *Progress in Self Psychology*, Vol. 1. ed. A. Goldberg. Hillsdale, NJ: The Analytic Press, pp. 202–226.

———— (1998a), Optimal responsiveness and the specificity of selfobject experience. In: *Optimal Responsiveness: How Therapists Heal Their Patients*, ed. H. Bacal. Northvale, NJ: Aronson, pp. 141–176.

———— (1998b), Is empathic attunement the only optimal response? In: *Optimal Responsiveness: How Therapists Heal Their Patients*, ed. H. Bacal. Northvale, NJ: Aronson, pp. 289–302.

———— & Newman, K. (1990), *Theories of Object Relations: Bridges to Self Psychology*. New York: Columbia University Press.

Bakan, D. (1966), *The Duality of Human Existence*. Chicago: Rand McNally.

Balint, M. (1968), *The Basic Fault*. London: Tavistock.

Beebe, B., Jaffe, J. & Lachmann, F. (1992), The contribution of the mother–infant influence to the origins of self- and object-representations. In: *Relational Perspectives in Psychoanalysis*, eds. N. Skolnick & S. Warshaw. Hillsdale, NJ: The Analytic Press, pp. 83–118.

———— & Lachmann, F. (1998), Co-constructing inner and relational processes: Self and mutual regulation in infant research and adult treatment. *Psychoanal. Psychol.*, 15:1–37.

———— ———— (2002), *Infant Research and Adult Treatment: Co-Constructing Interactions*. Hillsdale, NJ: The Analytic Press.

Benjamin, J. (1995), *Like Subjects, Love Objects*. New Haven, CT: Yale University Press.

———— (1997), *The Shadow of the Other*. London: Routledge.

Bergson, H. (1910), *Time and Free Will*. New York: Harper & Row, 1960.

Berliner, B. (1947), The psychodynamics of masochism. *Psychoanal. Quart.*, 16:459–471.

———— (1958), The role of object relations in moral masochism. *Psychoanal. Quart.*, 27:38–56.

Bettleheim, B. (1971). Regression as progress. In: *Tactics and Techniques in Psychoanalytic Therapy*, ed. P. Giovacchini. New York: Science House.

———— (1982), *Love Is Not Enough: The Treatment of Emotionally Disturbed Children*. New York: Free Press.

Blatt, S. & Blass, R. (1992), Relatedness and self-definition: Two primary dimensions in personality development, psychopathology, and psychotherapy. In: *Interface of Psychoanalysis and Psychology*, ed. J. Barron, M. Eagle & D. Wolitsky. Washington, DC: American Psychological Association, pp. 399–428.

Bollas, C. (1987), *The Shadow of the Object*. London: Free Associations.

———— (1989), *Forces of Destiny*. London: Free Associations.

———— (1993), *Being a Character*. New York: Hill and Wang.

Bowlby, J. (1969), *Attachment and Loss: Vol. 1, Attachment*. New York: Basic Books.

———— (1988), *A Secure Base*. New York: Basic Books.

Brenner, C. (1987), Working Through: 1914–1984. *Psychoanal. Quart.*, 56:88–108.

Breuer, J. & Freud, S. (1895), Studies on hysteria. *Standard Edition*, 2:1–313. London: Hogarth Press, 1966.

Bruner, J. (1986), *Actual Minds, Possible Worlds*. Cambridge, MA: Harvard University Press.

Burland, J. (1997), The role of working through in bringing about psychoanalytic change. *Internat. J. Psycho-Anal.*, 78: 469–484.

Buhler, C. (1951). Maturation and motivation. *Personality*, 1:184–211.

Busch, F. (1995), *The Ego at the Center of Psychoanalytic Technique*. Northvale, NJ: Aronson.

Chodorow, N. (1999), *The Power of Feelings*. New Haven, CT: Yale University Press.

Cooper, S. (2000), *Objects of Hope*. Hillsdale, NJ: The Analytic Press.

Csikszentmihalyi, M. (1996), *Creativity*. New York: Harper.

Dabrowski, K. (1964), *Positive Disintegration*. London: Little, Brown.

Damasio, A. (1989), Time-locked multiregional retroactivation: A systems level proposal for the neurosubstrates of recall and recognition. In: *Neurobiology of Cognition*, ed. P. Eimas & A. Galaburda. Cambridge, MA: The MIT Press, pp. 25–62.

DeCasper A. & Carstens, A. (1981), Contingencies of stimulation: Effects on learning and emotion in neonates. *Infant Behav. & Develop.*, 4:19–35.

Demos, V. (1983), A perspective from infant research on affect and self-esteem. In: *The Development and Sustaining of Self-Esteem in Childhood*, ed. T. Mack & S. Ablon. New York: International Universities Press.

———(1988), Affect and the development of the self: A new frontier. In: *Frontiers in Self Psychology: Progress in Self Psychology, Vol. 3*, ed. A. Goldberg. Hillsdale, NJ: The Analytic Press, pp. 27–53.

———(1992), The early organization of the psyche. In: *Interface of Psychoanalysis and Psychology*, ed. J. Barron, M. Eagle & D. Wolitzky. Washington, DC: American Psychological Association, pp. 200–233.

Dewald, P. (1964), *Psychotherapy: A Dynamic Approach*. New York: Basic Books.

Edelman, G. & Tononi, G. (2000), *A Universe of Consciousness*. New York: Basic Books.

Ekstein, R. (1966), Psychoanalytic concepts and structural theory. *Internat. J. Psycho-Anal.*, 47:581–583.

Erikson, E. (1963), *Childhood and Society*. New York: Norton.

Evans, H. (1998), Nonverbal communication, learning, and memory in the analytic process. Unpublished manuscript.

Fairbairn, W. R. D. (1943), The repression and the return of bad objects (with special reference to the 'war neuroses'). In: *Psychoanalytic Studies of the Personality*. London: Tavistock, 1952, pp. 59–81.

———(1944), Endopsychic structure considered in terms of object-relationships. In: *Psychoanalytic Studies of the Personality*. London: Tavistock, 1952, pp. 82–136.

———(1946), Object-relationships and dynamic structure. In: *Psychoanalytic Studies of the Personality*. London: Tavistock, 1952, pp. 137–151.

———(1958), On the nature and aims of psycho-analytical treatment. *Internat. J. Psycho-Anal.*, 39:374–385.

Fenichel, O. (1938), *Problems of Psychoanalytic Technique*. New York: *Psychoanal. Quart.*, 1969.

———(1945), *The Psychoanalytic Theory of Neurosis*. New York: Norton.

Ferenczi, S. (1911), Stages in the development of the sense of reality. In: *First Contributions to Psycho-analysis*, ed. S. Ferenczi. New York: Brunner/Mazel, 1952.

Frank, K. (1993), Action, insight, and working through. *Psychoanal. Dial.*, 3:535–577.

Frankl, V. (1984), *Man's Search for Meaning*. Boston: Beacon Press.

Frenkel-Brunswick, E. (1963), Adjustments and reorientation in the course of the life span. In: *Psychological Studies of Human Development*, ed. R. Kuhlen & G. Thompson. New York: Appleton-Century-Crofts, pp. 161–171.

Freud, A. (1936), *The Ego and the Mechanisms of Defense*. New York: International Universities Press.

Freud, S. (1895), Psychotherapy of Hysteria. In: Breuer & Freud, Studies on hysteria. *Standard Edition*, 2:255–305. London: Hogarth Press, 1966.

——— (1905), Fragment of an analysis of a case of hysteria. *Standard Edition*, 7:7–124. London: Hogarth Press, 1953.

——— (1909), Notes upon a case of obsessional neurosis. *Standard Edition*, 10:153–318. London: Hogarth Press, 1955.

——— (1911), Formulations on the two principles of mental functioning. *Standard Edition*, 12:213–226. London: Hogarth Press, 1955.

——— (1912), The dynamics of transference. *Standard Edition*, 12:97–108. London: Hogarth Press, 1958.

——— (1914a), Remembering, repeating, and working through (further recommendations on the technique of psychoanalysis). *Standard Edition*, 12:145–156. London: Hogarth Press, 1958.

——— (1914b), On narcissism. *Standard Edition*, 14:73–104. London: Hogarth Press, 1957.

——— (1915a), Instincts and their vicissitudes. *Standard Edition*, 14:109–140. London: Hogarth Press, 1957.

——— (1915b), The unconscious. *Standard Edition*, 14:161–216. London: Hogarth Press, 1957.

——— (1917), Mourning and melancholia. *Standard Edition*, 14:239–260. London: Hogarth Press, 1957.

——— (1920), Beyond the pleasure principle. *Standard Edition*, 18:3–66. London: Hogarth Press, 1955.

——— (1923), The Ego and the Id. *Standard Edition*, 19:3–68. London: Hogarth Press, 1961.

——— (1937), Analysis terminable and interminable. *Standard Edition*, 23:211–254. London: Hogarth Press, 1964.

Gadamer, H. (1976), *Philosophical Hermeneutics*, trans. & ed. D. E. Linge. Berkeley, CA: University of California Press.

Gedo, J. & Goldberg, A. (1973), *Models of the Mind*. Chicago: University of Chicago Press.

——— (1979), *Beyond Interpretation: Toward a Revised Theory of Psychoanalysis*. New York: International Universities Press.

Gill, M. (1981), *Analysis of the Transference, Vol. I: Theory and Technique*. New York: International Universities Press.

——— (1994), *Psychoanalysis in Transition*. Hillsdale, NJ: The Analytic Press.

Glenn, J. (1984), Practice and precept in psychoanalytic technique. Selected papers of Rudolph Lowenstein. *Psychoanal. Quart.*, 53:315–322.

Gray, P. (1990), The nature of therapeutic action in psychoanalysis. *J. Amer. Psychoanal. Assn.*, 38:1083–1097.

Greenberg, J. (1991), *Oedipus and Beyond*. Cambridge, MA: Harvard University Press.

Greenson, R. R. (1965), *The Technique and Practice of Psychoanalysis*. New York: International Universities Press.

Grinker, R. (1940), Reminiscences of a personal contact with Freud. *Amer. J. Orthopsychiat.*, 10:850–854.

Grossman, W. & Stewart, W. (1976), Penis envy: From childhood wish to developmental metaphor. *J. Amer. Psychoanal. Assn.*, 24 (suppl.): 193–212.

Gunsberg, L. & Tylim, I. (1998), The body-mind: psychopathology of its ownership. In: *Relational Perspectives on the Body*, ed. L. Aron & F. Sommer Anderson. Hillsdale, NJ: The Analytic Press, pp. 117–135.

Guntrip, H. (1969), *Schizoid Phenomena, Object Relations, and the Self.* New York: International Universities Press.

Hartmann, H. (1939), *Ego Psychology and the Problem of Adaptation*. New York: International Universities Press.

Hartmann, H. & Milch, W. (2000), The need for efficacy in the treatment of suicidal patients: transference and countertransference issues. In: *Progress in Self Psychology*, ed. A. Goldberg. Hillsdale, NJ: The Analytic Press, Vol. 16, pp. 87–102.

Heidegger, M. (1936), *What Is a Thing?* Chicago, IL: Henry Regnery, 1964.

———— (1926), *Being and Time*. New York: Harper & Row, 1962.

Hendrick, I. (1942), Instinct and the ego during infancy. *Psychoanal. Quart.*, 11:33–58.

Hirschmuller, A. (1989), *The Life and Work of Josef Breuer*. New York: New York University Press.

Hoffman, I. (1998), *Ritual and Spontaneity in the Psychoanalytic Process*. Hillsdale, NJ: The Analytic Press.

Hopkins, L. (1998), D. W. Winnicott's analysis of Masud Khan: A preliminary study of the failures of object usage. *Contemp. Psychoanal.*, 34:5–47.

Husserl, E. (1904), *The Phenomenology of Internal Time Consciousness*. Bloomington, IN: Indiana University Press, 1964.

———— (1913), *Ideas: General Introduction to Pure Phenomenology*, trans. W. Gibson. New York: Collier Books, 1982.

Kardiner, A. (1977), *My Analysis with Freud: Reminiscences*. New York: Norton.

Kernberg, O. (1976), *Object Relations Theory and Clinical Psychoanalysis*. New York: Aronson.

———— (1988), Object relations theory in clinical practice. *Psychoanal. Quart.*, 57:481–504.

Khan, M. (1971), The role of illusion in the analytic space and process. In: *The Privacy of the Self*. New York: International Universities Press, 1974, pp. 251–269.

———— (1974), *The Privacy of the Self*. New York: International Universities Press.

Klein, M. (1952), The origins of transference. In: *Envy and Gratitude, 1946-1963*. New York: Dell, 1975, pp. 48–56.

———— (1957), Envy and gratitude. In: *Envy and Gratitude*. New York: Dell, 1975, pp. 176–235.

Kohut, H. (1971), *The Analysis of the Self*. Monograph Series of the Psychoanalytic Study of the Child, No. 4. New York: International Universities Press.

———— (1977), *The Restoration of the Self*. New York: International Universities Press.

———— (1982), Introspection, empathy, and the semi-circle of mental health. *Internat. J. Psycho-Anal.*, 63:395–407.

———— (1984), *How Does Analysis Cure?* Chicago: The University of Chicago Press.

———— & Wolf, E. (1978), The disorders of the self and their treatment: An outline. *Internat. J. Psycho-Anal.*, 59:413–425.

Kris, E. (1939), On inspiration. *Internat. J. Psycho-Anal.*, 20:377–389.

———— (1956), On some vicissitudes of insight in psychoanalysis. *Internat. J. Psycho-Anal.*, 37:445–455.

Kuhlen, R. (1964). Developmental changes in motivation during the adult years. In: *Relations of Development and Aging*, ed. J. Birren. Springfield, IL: Charles Thomas, pp. 209–246.

Lacan, J. (1949), The mirror stage as formative of the function of the I as revealed in psychoanalytic experience. In: *Les Ecrits: A Selection*. New York: Norton, 1966, pp. 1–7.

———— (1953), The function and field of speech and language in psychoanalysis. In: *Les Ecrits: A Selection*. New York: Norton.

Lazar, S. (1998), Optimal responsiveness and enactments. In: *Optimal Responsiveness: How Therapists Heal Their Patients*, ed. H. Bacal. Northvale, NJ: Aronson, pp. 213–234.

Lear, J. (1998), *Open-Minded: Working Out the Logic of the Soul*. Cambridge, MA: Harvard University Press.

Levenson, E. (1982), Language and healing. In: *Curative Factors in Dynamic Psychotherapy*, ed. S. Slipp. New York: McGraw Hill, pp. 91–103.

———— (1991), *The Purloined Self*. New York: William Alanson White Institute.

Levin, F. (1991), *Mapping the Mind: The Intersection of Psychoanalysis and Neuroscience*. Hillsdale, NJ: The Analytic Press.

Lichtenberg, J. (1983), *Psychoanalysis and Infant Research*. Hillsdale, NJ: The Analytic Press.

Loewald, H. (1960), The therapeutic action of psychoanalysis. In: *Papers on Psychoanalysis*. New Haven, CT: Yale University Press, pp. 221–257.

———— (1962), Superego and time. In: *Papers on Psychoanalysis*. New Haven, CT: Yale University Press, pp. 43–53.

———— (1972), The experience of time. In: *Papers on Psychoanalysis*. New Haven, CT: Yale University Press, pp. 138–148.

McDougall, J. (1985), *Theatres of the Mind: Illusion and Truth on the Psychoanalytic Stage*. New York: Basic Books.

Meninger, K. & Holzman, P. (1958), *Theory of Psychoanalytic Technique*. New York: Basic Books.

Mitchell, S. (1988), *Relational Concepts in Psychoanalysis*. Cambridge, MA: Harvard University Press.

———— (1997), *Influence and Autonomy in Psychoanalysis*. Hillsdale, NJ: The Analytic Press.

Modell, A. (1991), *Other Times, Other Realities.* Cambridge, MA: Harvard University Press.

Morrison, A. (1989), *Shame: The Underside of Narcissism.* Hillsdale, NJ: The Analytic Press.

Neugarten, B. (1968), The awareness of middle age. In: *Middle Age and Aging,* ed. B. Neugarten. Chicago, IL: The University of Chicago Press, pp. 93–99.

Novey, S. (1962), The principle of working through in psychoanalysis. *Journal Amer. Psychoanal. Assn.,* 10:658–676.

Parens, H. (1979), *The Development of Aggression in Early Childhood.* New York: Aronson.

Peck, R. (1968), Psychological developments in the second half of life. In: *Middle Age and Aging,* ed. B. Neugarten. Chicago, IL: The University of Chicago Press, pp. 88–93.

Phillips, A. (1998), *Beasts in the Nursery.* New York: Vintage.

Pizer, S. (1998), Negotiating potential space: illusion, play, metaphor, and the subjunctive. *Psychoanal. Dia.,* 6:689–712.

Plato (n.d.), The Meno. In: *The Collected Dialogues of Plato,* ed. Hamilton & Cairns. New York: Pantheon Books, 1961, pp. 353–383.

Racker, H. (1960), *Transference and Countertransference.* New York: International Universities Press.

Rank, O. (1926), *The Technique of Psychoanalysis.* Leipzig: Deuticke.

Rapaport, D. (1951), The theory of ego autonomy. In: *The Collected Papers of David Rapaport,* ed. M. Gill. New York: Basic Books, 1967, pp. 357–367.

———— (1953), Some metapsychological considerations concerning activity and passivity of the ego. In: *The Collected Papers of David Rapaport,* ed. M. Gill. New York: Basic Books, 1967, pp. 530–568.

———— (1957), The theory of ego autonomy: A generalization. In: *The Collected Papers of David Rapaport,* ed. M. Gill. New York: Basic Books, 1967, pp. 722–744.

Reiser, M. (1990), *Memory in Mind and Brain.* New York: Basic Books.

Sander, L. (1980), "Reflections on Self Psychology." Paper presented to the Boston Psychoanalytic Society and Institute, Boston, MA.

———— (1982), Toward a logic of organization in psychobiologic development. Paper presented at the 13th Margaret S. Mahler Symposium, Philadelphia, PA.

———— (1985), Toward a logic of organization in psychobiological development. *APA Monograph,* January.

Sanville, J. (1991), *The Playground of Psychoanalytic Therapy.* Hillsdale, NJ: The Analytic Press.

Schafer, R. (1976), *A New Language for Psychoanalysis.* New Haven, CT: Yale University Press.

———— (1983), *The Analytic Attitude.* New York: Basic Books.

———— (1992), *Retelling a Life.* New York: Basic Books.

Schutz, A. (1932), *The Phenomenology of the Social World*. Evanston, IL: Northwestern University Press, 1967.

Searle, J. (1983), *Intentionality: An Essay in the Philosophy of Mind*. Cambridge, UK: Cambridge University Press.

Sedler, M. J. (1983), Freud's concept of working through. *Psychoanal. Quart.*, 52:73–98.

Segal, A. (1999), The optimal conversation: A concern about current trends within self psychology. In: *Pluralism in Self Psychology: Progress in Self Psychology, Vol. 15*, ed. A. Goldberg. Hillsdale, NJ: The Analytic Press, pp. 51–82.

Segal, H. (1981), *The Work of Hannah Segal*. New York: Aronson.

Shane, M., Shane, E. & Gales, M. (1997), *Intimate attachments: Toward a new self psychology*. New York: Guilford.

Slavin, M. & Kriegman, D. (1998), Why the analyst needs to change: toward a theory of conflict negotiation and mutual influence in the therapeutic process. *Psychoanal. Psychol.*, 8:247–284.

Slochower, J. (1996), *Holding and Psychoanalysis*. Hillsdale, NJ: The Analytic Press.

Spence, D. (1982), *Narrative Truth and Historical Truth*. New York: Norton.

Spezzano, C. (1993), *Affect in Psychoanalysis*. Hillsdale, NJ: The Analytic Press.

Stern, D. (1985), *The Interpersonal World of the Infant*. New York: Basic Books.

——— Sander, L., Nahum, J., Harrison, A., Lyons-Ruth, K., Morgan, A., Bruschweiler-Stern, N. & Tronick, E. (1998), Non-interpretive mechanisms in psychoanalytic therapy: the 'something more' than interpretation. *Internat. J. Psycho-Anal.*, 79:903–921.

Stern, D. B. (1997), *Unformulated Experience: From Dissociation to Imagination in Psychoanalysis*. Hillsdale, NJ: The Analytic Press.

Stern, S. (1994), Needed and repeated relationships. *Psychoanal. Dial.*, 4:317–346.

Stewart, H. (1973), Tactics and techniques in psychoanalytic therapy. *Internat. J. Psycho-Anal.*, 54:359–363.

Stewart, W. (1963), An inquiry into the concept of working through. *J. Amer. Psychoanal. Assn.*, 11:474–499.

Stolorow, R., Brandchaft, B. & Atwood, R. (1987), *Psychoanalytic Treatment: An Intersubjective Approach*. Hillsdale, NJ: The Analytic Press.

——— & Atwood, R. (1992), *Contexts of Being*. Hillsdale, NJ: The Analytic Press.

Strachey, J. (1934), The nature of the therapeutic action of psychoanalysis. *Internat. J. Psycho-Anal.*, 15:127–159.

Strenger, C. (1998), *Individuality, the Impossible Project: Psychoanalysis and Self Creation*. Madison, CT: International Universities Press.

Summers, F. (1993), Implications of object relations theories for the psychoanalytic process. *The Annual of Psychoanalysis*, 21:225–242.

——— (1994), *Object Relations Theories and Psychopathology*. Hillsdale, NJ: The Analytic Press.

——— (1996), Self psychology and its relationship to contemporary psychoanalytic theories. *The Annual Review of Psychoanalysis*, 24:157–171.

———— (1997), Transcending the self: an object relations model of the therapeutic action of psychoanalysis. *Contemp. Psychoanal.*, 33:411–428.

———— (1999), *Transcending the Self.* Hillsdale, NJ: The Analytic Press.

———— (2000), The analyst's vision of the patient and therapeutic action. *Psychoanal. Psychol.*, 17:547–564.

———— (2001), What I do with what you give me: therapeutic action as the creation of meaning. *Psychoanal. Psychol.*, 18:635–655.

Tolpin, M. (1993), The unmirrored self, compensatory structure, and cure: The exemplary case of Anna O. *The Annual of Psychoanal.*, 21:157–178.

Tomkins, S. (1962), *Affect, Imagery, and Consciousness: The Positive Affects.* New York: Springer.

———— (1963), *Affect, Imagery, and Consciousness: The Negative Affects.* New York: Springer.

———— (1978), Script theory: Differential magnification of affects. *Nebraska Symposium on Motivation*, 26:201–263.

Valenstein, A. (1983), Working through and resistance to change: insight and the action system. *J. Amer. Psychoanal. Assn.*, 31:353–373.

Wachtel, P. (1982), Vicious circles: 1—the self and the rhetoric of emerging and unfolding. *Contemp. Psychoanal.*, 18:259–273.

———— (1986), From neutrality to personal revelation: patterns of influence in the analytic relationship (a symposium)—on the limits of therapeutic neutrality. *Contemp. Psychoanal.*, 22:60–70.

———— (1993), Active intervention, psychic structure, and the analysis of transference: commentary on Frank's "action, insight, and working through." *Psychoanal. Dial.*, 3:589–603.

White, R. (1963), *Ego and Reality in Psychoanalytic Theory.* New York: International Universities Press.

Winnicott, D. W. (1951), Transitional objects and transitional phenomena. In: *Through Pediatrics to Psychoanalysis.* New York: Basic Books, 1975, pp. 229–242.

———— (1954), Withdrawal and regression. In: *Through Paediatrics to Psychoanalysis.* New York: Basic Books, 1975, pp. 255–261.

———— (1956), Primary maternal preoccupation. In: *Through Paediatrics to Psychoanalysis.* New York: Basic Books, 1975, pp. 300–305.

———— (1960), The theory of the parent–infant relationship. In: *Maturational Processes and the Facilitating Environment.* New York: International Universities Press, 1965, pp. 37–55.

———— (1965), *Maturational Processes and the Facilitating Environment.* New York: International Universities Press.

———— (1971), *Playing and Reality.* London: Routledge.

Wolf, E. (1988), *Treating the Self.* New York: Guilford Press.

Zola-Morgan, S. & Squire, L. (1990), Neuropsychology of memory: Parallel findings in human and nonhuman primates. New York Academy of Science, 608:434–456.

Index

Abandonment anxiety, 99, 111, 133, 184, 195, 219, 257, 258, 259

Adhesiveness of bad objects, 216–217, 219–220, 227, 233, 239–240

Adult development, 13–14

Affect, theory of, 119–125

Affective attunement, 248–250, 251, 254

Affective matching, 247–248, 249

Affects, caretaker role in, 247; disengagement from, 247; inborn, 246; trust in, 246, 248–249, 253, 254, 256, 258

Agency, psychoanalytic concept of, 248, 252

Aggressive drive, 117, 122

Aggression in children, 123

Ainsworth, M., 161

Akhtar, S., 131

Alexander, F., 170

Analytic alliance, 58

Anna O (Bertha Pappenheim), 61–65, 172–174

Antilibidinal ego, 218

Antinomies in the psychotherapeutic process, 56, 67, 68, 106–108, 171

Anxiety, symptoms of, 170, 233; of losing self, 222–223, 233, 240

Aron, L., 8, 9

Artist, patient as an, 270

Attachment theory, 12, 161, 248

Attendant, therapist as an, 103, 105

Austin, J., 29–30

Authenticity of affect expression, 163–164, 193–195, 211, 262–263

Authorship of the self, 73, 171–172, 211

Bacal, H., 8, 244–245, 254

Bakan, D., 251

Balint, M., 8

Beebe, B., 11, 12, 31, 161, 247, 248

Benjamin, J., 21, 23, 55–56, 68, 71, 95, 107, 108, 113, 162–163, 171, 271

Bergson, H., 29

Berliner, B., 170

Bettleheim, B., 223, 249

Blass, S., 250

Blatt, S., 250